D0400589

THE
ILLUSION
OF CHOICE

DISCARD

SUNY SERIES IN ENVIRONMENTAL PUBLIC POLICY
LESTER MILBRATH, EDITOR

DISCARD

THE ILLUSION OF CHOICE

How the Market Economy Shapes Our Destiny

ANDREW BARD SCHMOOKLER

STATE UNIVERSITY OF NEW YORK PRESS

Published by
State University of New York Press, Albany

© 1993 State University of New York

All rights reserved

Printed in the United States of America

No part of this book may be used or reproduced
in any manner whatsoever without written permission
except in the case of brief quotations embodied in
critical articles and reviews.

For information, address State University of New York
Press, State University Plaza, Albany, N.Y., 12246

Production by E. Moore
Marketing by Dana E. Yanulavich

Library of Congress Cataloging-in-Publication Data

Schmookler, Andrew Bard.
    The illusion of choice : how the market economy shapes our destiny
  / Andrew Bard Schmookler.
        p.   cm. — (SUNY series in environmental public policy)
    Includes bibliographical references and index.
    ISBN 0-7914-1265-2 (CH : acid-free). — ISBN 0-7914-1266-0 (PB :
    acid-free)
        1. Social change.   2. United States—Social conditions—1980–
    3. United States—Economic conditions—1981–   4. Consumers—United
    States.   5. Consumption (Economics)—United States.   6. Social
    values.   I. Title.   II. Series.
    HM101.S325 1992
    330.12′2—dc20   91-43874
                                                                          CIP

10 9 8 7 6 5 4 3

To Reuel Young
for more than a quarter century
my companion
in walking the earth

Contents

vii

Acknowledgments

I would like to thank, first, those friends and colleagues who gave me the benefit of their counsel on this project. Especially important were my friend, David Landau, and my brother, Edward Schmookler. David served as my principal reader, as an encouraging stand-in for a not-always-encouraging world. On countless occasions, and on a great variety of matters, I had the good fortune to be able to turn to him for his wise counsel. Ed served, as he often has, to help me keep in touch with my spiritual values. His ability to stay with what is real, regardless of the pain or effort it takes, is an inspiration.

Also helpful and generous with their time were Ken Mayers, Gene Leach, Lester Milbrath, and my mother, Pauline Schmookler.

Several colleagues shared their work and their knowledge with me, such as Roland Marchand and Floyd Rudmin. It is to Russell Belk of the University of Utah that I am especially indebted. As I ventured into areas new to me but familiar to him, he was generous with his advice when I asked for it, and he gave bibliographic guidance that was extremely useful.

I wish also to thank those whose financial support kept me in oatmeal even while engaged in so impractical an undertaking as this critique of the market. At a particularly dire moment, substantial help came from the Damien Foundation. Over the past three years, additional support has come from the M's, who wish to remain anonymous, from my life-long friends, Reuel Young and Marvin Fabyanske, from Paul and Ann Sperry, from Lloyd Wells and Joseph Havens, and, again, from my mother. Both the funds and the votes of confidence are deeply appreciated.

My gratitude also to John Steiner who has striven to find benefactors so that this work could continue.

I would like to thank also John Marks and Bonnie Pearlman of Search for Common Ground, in Washington, D.C., for their adoption of my project.

Finally, and perhaps most of all, I want to thank my wife, April Moore, who never complains about her husband's attending to other voices than those of the market.

CHOICES:
AN INTRODUCTION

How are we to create a more humane and viable civilization? For much of the past two decades, asking myself that question, I have focused on the problem of war. Now, as the superpowers extricate themselves from the perilous dynamic of the cold war, my attention is drawn to the other main engine of our destructiveness: the insatiable materialism of our civilization.

This problem of our materialism is both like and unlike the problem of war.

Like war, our materialism endangers this beautiful, living planet. And like war, our materialism is a symptom of something amiss in both our systems and our spiritual condition.

But about our materialism, unlike our proclivity to make war, we are complacent.

Now that the threat of nuclear holocaust is fortunately receding, it is becoming more visible that what we are doing on this planet even in the state we call "peace" is killing the earth. But the idea that we might have to make fundamental changes in the ways we live is one that most of us still do not seriously entertain.

It was clear to us that the spiraling arms race revealed something terribly wrong about our civilization. But we look with equanimity at our ceaselessly escalating race for material wealth.

Some of the reasons for this difference of attitude are easy to see.

Though there have been some who love war, for most people the sight of mangled bodies and crying orphans and smoking rubble is proof enough that peace is better than war. Even the hawks say that peace is better. Even Achilles, in the *Iliad*, displays on his shield idyllic visions of life in a peaceful world.

But our drive for wealth creates a kind of comfort. Our bodies are not bleeding; they are sleek and well fed. Our children are not orphaned, for our wealth buys most of us more than the proverbial threescore and ten. If we are doing damage to ourselves with our lust for wealth, it is far more subtle.

In the case of war, we have a direct experience of a better alternative. War is a problem that has been not continuous but recurrent. From living both at war and at peace, everyone knows that building a world at peace is a worthy goal.

But we have no alternative experience to living in our materialistic society, to finding our way through the structures laid out by our economic system. Most of us—even if we complain about the excesses and the sterility of much of the "good life" as conceived by our society—remain basically attached to the world as it is. At a deep level, we have "bought into" the materialistic worldview of our civilization.

If we are to create a civilization that is viable and fulfilling to the human spirit, it is imperative that we work our way through this complacency so that we can tackle the problem of our excessive materialism.

It is our insatiability that is the clearest sign that something is amiss. It seems that our market society is predicated on the idea that there can be no such thing as enough. The mainstream vision of a better future is simply of *more*. Having so much, we remain hungry. In our insatiable appetite, we are devouring the earth.

What is it that makes us so driven to amass and consume wealth without limit, even at the cost of many other important values? This is the question that I will be exploring in a series

4

of books of which this is the first—seeking to uncover the roots of our society's voracious drive for wealth.

Part of the answer lies in our systems. And part of the answer lies in the state of our souls.

It will be important to examine the ways our own spiritual condition drives us to seek happiness through riches, even though humankind's greatest teachers have told us that this is not the true path to fulfillment, and even though we inwardly sense from our own experience that they are right. Such an exploration will be the task of a subsequent book, *Filling a Sieve*.

The place to begin looking for an answer is in the dynamics of our economic system. The market system, I will show here, has great powers that are scarcely visible to us. It has powers even to shape the spiritual condition of the people who live in the market society. *The Illusion of Choice* will show how a market system, if insufficiently controlled—as ours presently is—drives a society into the very excesses that characterize our world today.

The market, of course, is our servant, attending well to many of our needs. This helps to lull us into a comfortable state in which we do not bother to see how the system is also our master. So long as we buy into the illusion that our systems are allowing us to choose our destiny, we will be trapped in our complacency. The first step in our liberation is to recognize our bondage. We will gain the power really to choose our future only when we understand the ways in which what the market system gives us is the illusion of choice.

Stranger in a
Familiar Land

OF TWO MINDS

To live in this prosperous market society of America feels to me both a blessing and a curse.

What a blessing it is to live in America. My ancestors, not so many generations back, lived in fear of starvation. But as I sit here at my word processor, I know that at any moment I can satisfy my hunger. I can get up and go to the kitchen, get a bowl and fill it halfway with water that is reasonably pure and safe to drink. Into the water I can sprinkle the correct quantity of quick oats. Then I put the water and bowl into the microwave, to heat for just ninety seconds—at the end of which I have a bowl of oatmeal. To the oatmeal I can add nuts, dried fruit, sesame paste, maple syrup. Filling, nutritious, comforting.

In America, even a struggling writer can afford this snack. A bowl's worth of oatmeal costs only a few pennies, since I can buy it in bulk at a mere fifty cents per pound at a nearby discount supermarket. The toppings may add at most a nickel to the cost, when I am generous with them. The microwave, bought through a discount store for $120, has already been used for probably five thousand cooking jobs and shows no signs of wearing out. If it died today, the cost would have been just over two cents per job. The total cost of my snack cannot be more than a dime.

In America, a wage of $6 an hour is not a great deal of money. If I suppose that my labors with the pen ultimately yield me such a wage, I must conclude that to earn the right in this society to have my quick, nourishing and tasty snack, I need to ply my trade for just one minute.

How fortunate we are to enjoy the benefits of a market society such as we have in America. For it is our economic organization that makes all this possible. Without the division of labor the market fosters, how else could I hope to get a big handful of oats into my bowl in exchange for less than twenty seconds of my labor? Without the incentives that the market provides, how else would we develop the stream of innovations that now enables us to cook our oatmeal without even the bother of a pot? Without the immense network of exchange that the market creates, how could complex goods be produced and distributed so inexpensively that even people of relatively modest incomes can afford conveniences that previous generations could not imagine?

The market system works miracles. This is what members of my generation—baby boomers growing up in a prosperous postwar America—were taught by the society around us. And I recognize that it is true. What a blessing to live in America.

What a curse it is to seek the "good life" in America. The young couple in my neighborhood adore their beautiful baby, but every day they leave him for nine hours in a deadening day-care situation to be attended by someone who does not love him. Every day the light that was born in his eyes gets a little dimmer. The parents' careers seem to come before establishing a sound foundation for the child's life. Their behavior suggests that money may be more important to them than their child's heart. Or maybe they have been taught that the best way to care for a child is to make sure that they can provide it with all the good things—buying the child nice clothes and the right lessons, eventually sending it off to expensive schools.

Our ancestors, for all their privations, enjoyed a greater sense of rootedness in a human community than most of us can find in America today. Even if I had stayed in my hometown, my friends and other members of my family would have moved off in their pursuit of new lives. My "community" would have left me anyway.

But—on the other side of the same coin—what a privilege it is to enjoy the freedoms that we enjoy. In our society, a person with initiative, a person with a vision, is free to work to make his vision a reality. There are no laws that compel us to follow in the footsteps of our parents. In a free-enterprise society, the state does not dictate what path each of us is to follow. If one can invent a better mousetrap, it is the world that will beat a path to us.

This liberty has meant a lot to me. Twenty years ago I had a vision that I felt I must develop and communicate. (Eventually it was published as *The Parable of the Tribes*.) Had I not lived in a society where I could be free to pursue that work and to seek a way to communicate it to my fellow human beings, it would have been a terrible burden.

Yet the vision I have felt compelled to share includes a good deal of pain at witnessing what the dynamo of our market economy does to the sacred things within its grasp.

What pain it is to see the American landscape being molded by the bulldozers. At the beginning of 1983, I visited some friends whose little house looked back over an exquisite little canyon in San Diego, where the cholla glistened silver in the sunlight, while beyond the cactus and shrubs the cottonwoods made a border along the stream and at night sometimes the coyotes sang. By the time I saw their place again in late 1984, the bulldozers had flattened the canyon so that a few hundred new condos could be built.

Around the same time, I watched in pain as a lovely little hollow across from a grand eighteenth-century mansion near where I lived in Maryland was turned into an ugly shopping center.

Wherever you are in America, you know you'll not have to look far to find a plethora of goods of good quality at reasonable prices. Wherever you are in America, you know you will not be able to escape the transformation of the spaces we travel into unsightly commercial strips.

IS THIS THE WORLD WE WANT?

Many of the blessings of life in America are the fruits of our market economy. But many of these afflictions and burdens are also products of the market system.

The ideology of the market economy is quite willing to take credit for the abundance the system produces. But the idea that the market system creates evils is, for the most part, emphatically denied.

According to the dominant way of thinking in our society, what the market produces is the result of people freely making choices. This leads to an outcome that is close to optimal, though by the nature of things it cannot be perfect. Even wise choices involve trade-offs, and part of the consequence of liberty is that people are allowed to make unwise choices.

Thus it may be unfortunate from the point of view of my friends that their communion with the San Diego canyon was terminated, but the "invisible hand" of the market system, according to our dominant ideology, has found a more optimal way of utilizing that space. My friends lose their view, but many other people gain a place to live.

Who said there could be progress without costs? Commercial strips may not be as aesthetically pleasing as national parks, but they are there because they perform a valuable service for people—people who need to be able to get food and clothing for their families, gas for their cars, and jobs to keep the whole productive miracle happening.

And as for supposedly "unwise" choices that people make, say the ideologues of the market, that is their right. Leaving young children in day care so that the family can have two incomes may or may not be a good choice. But the choice made by the young couple across the street was theirs to make. No one forced them to do it, and we are better off to have the freedom to make unwise choices than we would be if we established some power that could prohibit them.

Besides, such an argument would continue, who are we to judge what is best for another person? The liberty of the market enables each person to be the arbiter of his or her own moral hierarchy. In any event, the market takes people's preferences or values as a given and simply helps to satisfy them whatever they are.

Thus, according to this argument, the world as it is rendered by market forces is the world we want—given the constraints imposed by reality. Of course it is not perfect, but it is the world that we, acting together by expressing our individual preferences through the market, have chosen.

This understanding of the market contains much that is valid. This book will show that it is also wrong in fundamental ways.

The market is, indeed, a marvelous mechanism for channeling human choices. The market economy gives its participants an enormous range of choice, and it is driven by the choices they make. But to conclude from these obvious facts that the market allows people to choose their destiny is a widespread and enormously influential fallacy.

Imagine a restaurant menu. The menu can be as long as a telephone book, but if all it offers are meat dishes, a vegetarian will not find anything desirable among all those choices. No matter how diverse the options, if one can get nothing to drink with one's food, the meal will be less than fully satisfying.

The market society, this work will show, is in many ways like such a restaurant. It is the nature of the market that it is simultaneously exquisitely sensitive to some categories of our needs and wants and is virtually blind and deaf to others. As a result of the inherent dynamic of the system, the market gives us a menu rich in some kinds of options and impoverished in others. Our choices are thus skewed by the nature of the system within which we make them.

The analysis of the market's selective inattention and its incapacity therefore fully to reflect the range of human values is developed in part 1, "Tunnel Vision: A Radical Critique of the Market."

We are free to pursue our private dreams. But we are not free to live in a community where human activity and the systems of living nature are in healthy balance. We are free to furnish our own homes according to our own aesthetic, utilizing a staggering variety of available goods. But we are compelled to endure the ugliness and spiritual vacuity of a landscape contorted by the narrow and uncompromising demands of producing, buying, and selling.

Not only does the market system take some vital options off the menu, even while it is offering an extraordinary range of options of wholly different kinds, but it shapes our choices in another less visible way: over time, the market system shapes the values that govern the choices we make.

Over the generations, the culture of values that emerges in a market society bears the imprint of the market's distortions. In a superficial perspective, the young parents who choose careers and money over care of their young infant are simply making their own free choice. But in a deeper perspective, the minds and hearts that make such choices have been molded by a society that has itself been shaped by the forces of the market.

Were the market a perfect lens for providing an image of human wants, needs, and values, this warping of our choices would not occur. The market would be the magical channel that its ideologues describe it as being. But the market's selective attention, and the skewed image of human choice that results, will in the course of time distort the very needs and values the system is supposed to satisfy.

The power of the market to form us goes far beyond what the many critics of advertising describe. A social-evolutionary perspective captures a more complete and profound picture, for whatever shapes our society will thereby mold us as well. Acting subtly over the generations, the market will shape a society and its members in directions that are predictable from the nature of the system and independent of human choice.

This social evolutionary way of revealing how the market can itself choose the course of a society's development is developed here in part 2, "We Are Driven: The Market as the Engine of Change in America."

After market forces have been unleashed in America for a couple of centuries, it is no wonder that we are a people who attend more to the dimensions of the "good life" provided by the market than to those good things that cannot be bought and sold. It is no wonder that a great many parents in our country sacrifice family values for greater riches, even in families that are already living like royalty—in material terms— by the standards of human history. It is no wonder that men in America typically channel the best of their energies into the pursuit of professional advancement and choose to allocate little time for friendship. It is no wonder that shopping centers, not parks or sacred groves, become centers of our communities.

How much is a friend worth? What is the value of a loving bond with one's children? And what is the worth of an unspoiled sylvan landscape? To these questions, the market's answer is: Does not compute. And we, as children of the market society, learn to ignore what our system ignores.

Every society tends to cast its members in a mold that corresponds with what it demands, what it offers, what it rewards. The market society is no exception.

The market is no neutral tool of human agency. The market is a tool for our purposes, but we are also tools for its purposes. It is our servant, but it is also our master. It has given us choices, but—by a sleight of the invisible hand—it has also created the illusion of choice.

The exploration of the illusion of choice, therefore, will show that the world we have created with the dynamic activity of our economic system cannot be regarded as one we have chosen to create. But the question nonetheless arises whether the world the market creates is the one we would opt for if we were free to choose and if we were wise.

STRANGER IN A FAMILIAR LAND

Evaluating the market and the life it gives us requires us to ask two questions. How much do the benefits of the market system weigh in relation to their costs? Is anything better possible than the system as it is now organized?

Weighing the blessings and curses of the market is not easy. Man does not live by bread alone, but neither does he live without bread. That bowl of oatmeal should not be taken for granted.

The ideology of our market system is bolstered greatly by the fact that it makes us the envy of much of the rest of the world. And rightly so. Surely it is evidence that our market society is giving us something of real value, when hundreds of millions of people would enter this country if they could, even to live off the crumbs from our tables.

In addition, the transformations of the Communist world are proof that the Marxist critique has proved incapable of generating a social order the equal of, let alone superior to, that of liberal capitalism. The combination of inefficiency and injustice previously displayed in the communist nations of Eastern Europe also buttressed the sense in our society that we are on the right track.

If a social order superior to ours is possible, where is it to be found? The absence of a clear answer to that question must make the critic of the market system hesitate. Is it merely "utopian," in the perjorative sense, to look for something better than this? Is one who focuses on the shortcomings of the market system merely an ungrateful child who snaps at the invisible hand that feeds him?

Possibly. But there are several reasons why we should presume that our system warrants more, not less, critical examination from us—reasons why our view of the market is likely to exaggerate its virtues and underestimate its defects.

First, the "goods" of the market—the abundant and diverse options it offers—are quite clearly visible, while the ways the market warps our society and distorts our approach to life are much harder for us to see. It is clear how the market gives me my quick and inexpensive bowl of oatmeal. But it requires far more subtlety to see the market's role, over long stretches of time, in molding people so that many of the young fathers I know find it difficult to get home from work much before their babies' bedtimes. It's easy for me to grasp my debt to the system that gives me a good quality VCR and TV to record my daily news shows and watch them at my convenience in the comfort of my own home. But less apparent is how the market has helped make so many of our neighborhoods places where people are compelled to find private pleasures to compensate for the absence of meaningful connections among a community of families.

It is obvious how abundant are the goods on our supermarket shelves. But we must use our imagination to notice what we can't buy, especially those things we cannot obtain even by other means. In the very nature of things, therefore, it is easier for us to be aware of what *is* than of what *not* on the menu we are given. Just as it took a Sherlock Holmes, in the famous story "Purple Blaze," to hear the crucial clue—that the dog did not bark—so do we need to be detectives to discover what are the silent costs of our abundance.

A second factor is that our socialization teaches us to see the benefits of the system we live in and to be blind to its defects. Every social order imparts propaganda to strengthen the allegiance of its members, or subjects. The market society teaches us in a thousand ways—least subtly in the tidal wave of commercial messages that flood our consciousness everyday—that goods are what is good. The material standard of living becomes virtually identified as the standard for judging our lives. When we speak of what someone is "worth"— "This guy is worth $2 million"—we typically speak in the market's language.

By implication, entire universes of discourse about value are moved into the shadows of our awareness, or perhaps disappear altogether. To understand the importance of what we may have lost—in interpersonal relationships or intrapersonal integrity, in community and in a reverent and harmonious relationship with our natural surroundings—requires a breakthrough of consciousness, an awakening, to achieve.

But then there is the pain. One should never underestimate the influence on our consciousness of the desire to avoid pain. Whatever the goods and evils of the world as it is, we have a strong motive to believe the world is as it should be.

Part of the pain of seeing clearly the sicknesses of our society is the pain of alienation. It hurts to put ourselves at odds with the world we live in. There is the temptation to remain in harmony with our own society rather than to be out of joint even with a world that itself is out of joint. Who wants to feel like a stranger in one's own country?

When I was a child, I had a football-game mentality that put me in good stead for succeeding, and for being comfortable, in the world around me. More was always better than less; the score was everything. We lived in a small town in Michigan then, and I took great pride in such things as the proportion of the world's automobile production that took place in my home state, not to mention the impressive tonnage that was shipped through the port of Sault Ste. Marie, also in my state. Numbers on scoreboards accounted for much in the game of life.

Whatever was impressive and dramatic and powerful was good, as far as I was concerned. When my family and I traveled to the big city of Philadelphia to visit relatives, I thought it grand that Philadelphia was surrounded by these enormous and complex refineries. The flames shooting up from some of their vents were fantastic; even the sulphurous smell I regarded as positive, it being an indication of the wondrous processes taking place within this network of tubes and tanks.

I now see these things differently, and there is a cost to the difference. I do miss being able to see the sprawling industrial apparatus of our economy with the same sense of awe and appreciation that I could then. In a way that is no longer true, I felt I truly belonged to my world then.

But I must recognize that there was much that my childish eyes did not understand in what they saw. Back then, when we drove in the streets of Philadephia, there was something else I enjoyed seeing that I didn't see at home. I thought it was "neat" to see the drunks wandering the city streets. It is embarrassing to remember, and to report, my insensitivity to the human tragedy each one of these derelicts embodied. To me, each drunk represented an exciting drama. I took satisfaction in counting how many I saw.

In time, I put away my childish eyes and began to see the world in other ways. Sometimes, now, I feel like a stranger in a familiar land. There is pain in that.

It hurts in another way, too. The more we see the agony of the world around us, the more suffering we ourselves must endure.

In my own life, I have found the most fundamental and fateful choice to be: to see or not to see. My own awareness vacillates between two different modes. In one, my usual one, I more or less accept the world as it is and feel comfortable in it. In the other, I feel an acute awareness of how out of joint the world is, how much of sacred value is being destroyed. At those times, I feel a profound and painful feeling of loss.

But the difference in terms of pain versus comfort is not the only difference between these two states of consciousness. The one that hurts also feels more alive and real. When my eyes are clear, when my heart is most open, then I am most likely to see the distress of the world. And the fullness of the experience always seems to me a validation of the perception.

Reality hurts. But, ultimately, it is reality that we live in and that we have to deal with. You don't have to know about the toxic waste dump in your backyard to get cancer from it. We don't have to feel the pain in our children's lives to reap the harvest of what we sow in them.

We in America have much to be thankful for. The market system has served many of our needs well. But the market also creates a world askew, more out of joint than most of us, most of the time, wish to see. It behooves us, therefore, to look carefully into the market system, to evaluate critically the destiny the market is shaping for us. And, perhaps, to reshape the system in order to fashion a better destiny for ourselves and for those who come after us.

Perestroika in America

CITY UPON A HILL

It has always been a central part of Americans' sense of themselves that we are something special. In thinking ourselves special, we are not, of course, any different from most of the other peoples of the world.

But as a nation formed of immigrants, deliberately defining ourselves in relation to a rejected Old Country, we have been somewhat more than usually self-conscious in our sense of mission and superiority. Even before the boat landed in the New World, John Winthrop called upon the group of Puritans he was leading here to make the society they were about to establish "a city upon a hill"—a visible manifestation of a superior way of being, inviting admiration and emulation from all who saw it.

The accomplishments of the American society the Puritans did so much to institute have been rather different from what Winthrop had in mind. Nonetheless, the sense of being a city upon a hill has remained. My generation, born in the decade after World War II, grew up with a very strong sense that all the world wanted what American society provided. It is a motif in our imaginative works: the outsider standing in rapt amazement at the abundance of the American marketplace. One form of it can be seen in the classic fictional image of the scruffy child from the backwoods staring wideeyed at the fine city merchandise, then getting bathed and prettied up by the townswoman who introduces the child to the good life. More often, it is a foreigner awstruck by the cornucopia of our supermarkets—sometimes it is in films, sometimes on the network news, as some new immigrant (perhaps a Soviet) discovers the wonder of American abundance.* The newcomers look as though they had died and gone to heaven, and we are deeply gratified by the implication that we have created a heaven on earth.

Over time, the vision of America changed into "the American dream." The city on a hill became a supermarket. Productive miracles were the proof that God had shed his grace on the American market system.

THE MARXIST CHALLENGE

As the twentieth century approaches its end, our sense of the rightness of the American system has been buttressed by the collapse of the system that most directly challenged capitalism. Communism stands discredited and, by the zero-sum way of thinking that characterized the whole worldview of the cold war, the downfall of our rival's system is taken as vindication of ours. Their being wrong implies our being right.

Our side feels itself finally to have gained a full triumph in the famous "kitchen debate" of 1959, at which Richard Nixon stood toe-to-toe with Nikita Khrushchev admidst an exhibition

---

*In an article about the pent-up frustration of Soviet consumers in "their Marxist-run-down society," John Hughes quotes a Soviet author, Zinovii Yuriev, describing his experience of shopping at a Boston supermarket: "Never in my wildest dreams did I imagine such variety and abundance of food. Not on any planet, and certainly not in the shops of my country. I stood at the meat, fish, and fresh produce counters and thought I was hallucinating. It simply could not be true . . . [O]nly a heroic effort prevented me from falling into the cart I was pushing." ("Moscow's Consumer Revolution," *Christian Science Monitor*, September 15, 1989.)

in Moscow of the latest American consumer technology—a combative version of the foreigner confronting American abundance. The Soviets did not "bury" us, as Khrushchev once predicted. Rather, it is the Soviet system that is being consigned, in the words of another of our cold warriors, Ronald Reagan, to the ash-heap of history.

Competition is ever central to our view of life and our sense of ourselves. The world is divided into winners and losers. The identity of a winner, in such a worldview, is defined by the contrast with losers. Missionary zeal is also part of the core of our culture. The world is divided into the righteous faithful and the ungodly unbelievers. The defeat of our competitors, their conversion to doctrine more like ours, helps us push down whatever nagging doubts we may have about whether we are on the right path.*

In late 1989, as the collapse of Marxism-Leninism gathered momentum, the most celebrated idea in some elite circles in Washington, D.C. was the notion that our system represented "the end of history." In an article of that name, Francis Fukuyama argues that the question of history—how should human society be organized—has at last been resolved. The economic and political systems of the West, he suggests, appear to represent the final form of human institutions.[1] To think that the way we have organized society embodies the last word, that it represents the promised land, seems to me to bespeak an appalling poverty of imagination.

This self-congratulatory response to our apparent victory in the cold war may be quite natural. But it is a mistake.

The world is not cloven between the right and the wrong. We are all human beings groping to find our way in a terra incognita as civilization develops. None of our economic systems begins to approach the viability and efficiency of the economy of exchange in ecological systems, of what Wendell Berry calls "the Economy of God." None of our ideologies is God's Truth itself. The error of our rivals in no way abnegates the serious imperfections in our own social order.

---

*When Americans, in the gloom of the recession of 1991, tell pollsters that they fear the nation's "heading in the wrong direction," they reflect only a momentary concern about the efficacy of our current game plan. The game itself, and the way score is kept, are not in question. When the numbers on the score board improve, so, too, will the numbers in the polls.

The apparent decline of Marxist ideology can be an important point in the history of our understanding of our own economic system—not in vindicating our system but in opening the way for a different, more useful critique of liberal economics.

ON BEYOND MARX

The rise of capitalism produced great dislocations in nineteenth-century Europe, and out of the suffering of that world there arose voices to decry what the economic machine was doing to the body of society. Karl Marx's was the most powerful of those voices, and his analysis of capitalism has stood for a century and a half as *the* critique of the market system. It is as if there were a niche to be occupied in the ecology of our thought about political economy, and the Marxist theory occupied that niche. When people have tried seriously to approach the shortcomings of the market, it has almost always been along the path that had been opened by Marx.

The problem with the predominance of the Marxist perspective in the niche of radical theory is that Marx, for all his brilliance and frequently penetrating insights, opened the wrong path.

In the capitalist societies studied by Marx a century and a half ago, the most visible evil was the squalor in which the working class was forced to live. Consequently, in the radical critique that Marx developed, the essential problem was seen in terms of class conflict and the unjust distribution, among classes, of the fruits of production. It has often been observed that Marx's predictions concerning the evolution of capitalist society—the increasing degradation of the proletariat until, with a growing class consciousness, they rose up in revolution to overthrow the capitalist order—have failed to come true. What is important to note, however, is that the predictions failed because the economic analysis at the foundation of the Marxist critique was likewise flawed.

Fundamental to Marx's condemnation of capitalism is the assertion that the worker does not get what he deserves. How else could one reconcile the production of so much wealth with the persistence of so much poverty among those who produced it? To explain this presumed injustice, Marx utilized the concepts of the labor theory of value and of surplus value.

Marx did not originate the labor theory of value, which indeed arose in the tradition of classical liberal thought (with John Locke). But Marx did find it useful for his own purpose, which was to establish that the market system exploits workers. What the labor theory of value says is that all the value of economic production comes from the labor that goes into it. ("As values, all commodities are only definite masses of congealed labour-time."[2]) Yet, Marx said—and in this, too, he was drawing upon the mainstream, classical tradition (in this case, Malthus)—the capitalist pays the worker only what it takes to keep him alive. ("The average price of wage labor," Marx and Engels wrote in The Communist Manifesto, "is the minimum wage, i.e. that quantum of the means of subsistence which is absolutely requisite to keep the laborer in bare existence as a laborer."[3]) Since the workers receive in wages only a part of what their product sells for, they are not getting paid according to the value of their contribution. The difference between workers' wages and the exchange value of their products—a difference that the capitalists pocket in the form of profits, rents, and interest—Marx called "surplus value."

The problem with this economic analysis is that it is simply wrong. Elsewhere,[4] I have explored in some depth the Marxist claim about worker exploitation. For the present discussion, it may suffice simply to point out the historical record. Contrary to Marx, it is demonstrably not true that it is the nature of the market to pay workers only a subsistence wage. Nowhere in the history of the world have the average laboring people risen to a level of such affluence as in the market societies of the West. Essentially the same economic system that relegated industrial workers of nineteenth-century Liverpool to life in cramped and dreary circumstances now allows the factory worker in South Bend to drive his family in their camper to vacation in Yellowstone. There has been no revolution because the economy of the market system has given workers substantially more to lose than their chains.

Exploitation and injustices among social classes have plagued human societies since the very beginning of civilization. And market societies are no exceptions. But the injustices of market societies do not, for the most part, ensue from the operation of the market itself. The original distribution of property may have been due to theft and violence, so that some of the rich capitalists of Europe are the descendants of aristocratic families whose wealth originated in some ancient conquest.

And in some (largely) capitalist societies—for example, South Korea of recent decades—the coercive arm of the state may be used to confer advantages, not gained in free-market transactions, upon the politically powerful owners of industry at the expense of their largely disenfranchised workers. (This is true to a meaningful degree even in those societies we call "democratic," including our own.) But the recent revelations, in East Germany and Czechoslovakia, of the great luxury set aside by Communist Party rulers for themselves, while the masses were compelled to live in great austerity, show that exploitation is a likely consequence of any system where political power is unequally distributed. And so powerful is the engine of the market system in creating wealth, and so pronounced is the tendency of the market—contra Marx—to pay workers according to the value of their contribution, that even the historical injustices of European societies and the undemocratic politics of Asian capitalist societies (such as South Korea) have not prevented the standard of living of workers in those nations from rising spectacularly.

History shows, therefore, that liberal economics—the standard kind of economics taught in Econ 101 in universities all over America—explains the fate of wages far better than does the economics of the Marxist left. The price of labor, as of other commodities, is set by supply and demand. The demand for labor at a given wage is determined by the value to the employer of adding extra workers. If I can make more money from hiring new workers than it costs me to take them on, I will hire them. If I can't get any more workers unless I raise wages, I will do that, so long as it increases my own profits.

Under such a system, wages will rise over time so long as two conditions obtain. First, the economy becomes more productive, which it will do if there are improvements in the quality of labor and of the technology with which they work. Second, it is necessary that Thomas Malthus not be right, that is, that workers do not simply reproduce more quickly whenever wages rise above the subsistence level, with extra mouths consuming whatever extra wealth the working class might obtain, thus preventing the material standard of living of the working class from ever rising.

Both these conditions have obtained in the past century and a half. Education has raised the quality of the work force, and technological innovation has further greatly magnified labor's productive power. And Malthus has been thoroughly refuted by the reproductive record of the advanced industrial societies; indeed, affluence has led to a reduction rather than an increase in the birthrate. As a result, workers are now rich by any historical standard.

With the passage of the generations, therefore, the proportion of people who see themselves as having a stake in the capitalist economic system has only increased. It is complacency, rather than the predicted desperation, that has grown.

Yet the predominant critique of the market economy has continued to hammer at alleged class exploitation. It is true that the market produces inequalities of wealth, but the fact of inequality does not prove exploitation or injustice. Problems of injustice and inequality do exist and should be addressed—for example, the way some agribusinesses have abused migrant farm workers, the callous indifference over many years of the asbestos industry about the health of its workers, the plight of the homeless on American streets—but these do not point to the fundamental flaw in the market system and its ideology.

There is a basic problem with the market. But it is not visible through the prism of the class struggle.

TOWARD A NEW CRITIQUE

A new critique is possible that is not only sounder at the level of analysis but also more promising at the level of strategy. It is not surprising that the dominant middle and capitalist classes in America are not galvanized by calls for them to relinquish their allegedly ill-gotten gains in favor of the poor and oppressed. But what if it could be shown that the system, while giving benefits, prevents *all* (even the most fortunate) from choosing their own future? Instead of having to rely upon guilt or altruism to move people, such a critique might allow one to enlist an enlarged understanding of self-interest. The ideologist of the market should surely be able to appreciate the strategic advantages of such a change in motivational leverage.

Surprisingly, the key to this new critique can be found in the traditional economic analysis. Even such neoclassical ideologues as Milton Friedman acknowledge what I will show to be vital defects in the system. What is not generally recognized is how grave are the implications of these imperfections.

Even a Milton Friedman will admit that the price of burning coal in Ohio does not include the costs of compensating the fisherman in New York State who finds that trout have been eradicated from his favorite stream by acid rain created by the coal's combustion. But the market is so close to correct, the economists have customarily supposed, that the slight error can safely be disregarded. This work will demonstrate how dangerously erroneous is that supposition.

The crucial element missing from traditional economic analysis is *a long-term, social-evolutionary perspective.*

It may indeed be true that, in the static perspective that characterizes most economics, the market is almost right on the money, missing the ideal only slightly. But if one looks at the development of a society over time, even a small error—if it is systematic and constant—will lead to profound, potentially catastrophic distortion.

The market is like a car slightly out of alignment. Unless there is someone at the steering wheel to lean continually against the tug, in time the car will swerve far off the intended course. The static perspective cannot reveal the cumulative implications of a chronic error in steering. The still picture of the market society provided by classical analysis has permitted the market's ideologues, from Adam Smith's *The Wealth of Nations* onward, to focus on the overall correctness of the vehicle's orientation and thus to argue that we should keep our hands off the steering wheel. In other words, government—collectively determined social policy—should not interfere with the market's functioning.

As we will see, a social evolutionary perspective—replacing the still picture with a time-lapse movie—reveals the real problem with the market system: over time *the system,* because of its biases and distortions, *carries us to a destination chosen by that system and not by us.* The discovery that, ultimately, the market system gives us only *the illusion of choice* in determining our collective destiny should mobilize all of us to find more effective ways of controlling the market by collective political decisions.

HOW DEAD IS THIS HORSE?

The critique offered here will propose a substantial increase in certain dimensions of political intervention in the market mechanism.

But, it may be objected, the days of laissez faire, when there were no hands on the wheel, are long gone in America. The government is very deeply—many would say too deeply—involved in our economic affairs. The ideology of the market, according to this argument, retains no power, so why beat a dead horse?

That "dead horse," I would maintain, is still a major driving force behind our society's evolution.

On the one hand, there is a problem not only with the (insufficient) extent of present government involvement but also with the nature of it. For a variety of reasons,* a good many of the regulatory interventions by the political system compound the vices of the market, while others impair the market's virtues. (One thinks of the justified objections of the business community to a regulatory system that is unnecessarily cumbersome and arbitrary.) A more illuminating crtique of the market can help target government regulation toward the real deficiencies of the market and its ideology—which are those germane to the problem of real choice.

Presently, the efforts of the political system to correct the important deficiencies of the economic system have been far too tentative and erratic to get the vehicle of the market pointed straight on the road to a destination of our choosing. And a predominant reason for this inadequacy is the persisting vigor, especially in the United States, of that "dead horse," the market ideology.†

Thus, although there is now widespread recognition of the legitimacy of environmental protection legislation, there is continually a strong pull from the ideology of the free market that calls into question the legitimacy of any interference with the "proper workings" of the market. Thus in the 1970s, the president of the United States (Ford) could veto a law to require

---

*On this, see Chapter 4. "Reining In the Market."
†While American society is the principal focus of this work, the essential points of its diagnosis and prescription can be applied also to other liberal societies, even to the most social-democratic societies of Western Europe. Although the market ideology enjoys less hegemony in those nations, the main thrust of the European efforts to correct the problems created by the market have been geared toward ameliorating the traditional (generally legitimate) left-wing concerns about income redistribution. The creation of the welfare state still leaves the market largely free to structure the productive process according to its skewed calculus of costs and benefits.

the restoration of strip-mined land, saying that the country could not "afford" such a law—and many people would concur with the implicit free-market assumption that the law imposes rather than simply recognizes a cost. Thus in the 1990s, a president (Bush) can dally about limiting the nation's contribution to the greenhouse effect, and the country will concur with the free-market calculus that sees any reduction of GNP as a loss of wealth and well-being.

In our political culture, that which derives from the market wears a halo of legitimacy, while that which comes from government falls under a cloud of suspicion. (Galbraith's vivid formulation still rings true: "Alcohol, comic books and mouthwash all bask under the superior reputation of the market. Schools, judges and municipal swimming pools lie under the evil reputation of bad kings.[5]) Our ingrained distrust of government power has probably helped us preserve our liberty for more than two centuries. But we remain too much under the enchantment of the market, not sufficiently alarmed at its power, if unchecked, to distort our world. And the only tool available to us that has sufficient power to divert the market's intrinsic momentum is the instrumentality of government.

In the search for the proper balance of power between the atomistic market and the collective decisions of our politics, we continue to err in the direction of leaving too much power in the economic system. From the laissez faire point of view of many conservative politicians and businessmen, the diffident measures enacted to protect the environment seem like a massive intrusions, an infringement on liberty, and a menace to the free-enterprise system. But I would suggest that our perspective on the balance between political and market forces is itself quite imbalanced: as an alcoholic might find it "extreme" to go without a drink for six hours, so also do our present efforts to rein in the excesses of the market system seem extreme only to a consciousness that is itself in the grip of the very forces that need to be controlled.

A treatise to raise our alarm about the dangers of the market, to erode the hold of the market's ideology on our worldview, does not have the same revelatory and heretical quality it might have a century ago, or even half a century ago. But the power of the market and its ideology remain enormous. With the recent political trends in the West and the fall of communism in the East, that power may indeed be growing.

Moreover, even if a horse is dead, it can block one's path. Ideas, history shows, often persist as obstacles long after they have lost the spirit that once truly animated them. The market is still molding our world. A good critique of the system's flaws is essential—whether it be to rein in the runaway horse of an ideology that is not taking us where we want to go, or to carve up the carcass of the dead beast that obstructs our way.

THE CHALLENGE FACING US

Marx was right that the market system does stand in need of a radical restructuring, but what is needed is not the revolution of collectivization that Marx envisaged. The critique to be developed here will appear a good deal less radical than that of the traditional left. It does not depend, for example, on a different economics, antagonistic to mainstream economic thought; it accepts Adam Smith's fundamental insight, but explores how the gaps in that liberal framework must place the whole market edifice in a new light. Nor will I call for the disbanding of the market system, which is indeed a phenomenal tool for many purposes. In these ways, it may seem a tame vision. But what it calls for is, nonetheless, a radical transformation in our political economy and in our consciousness.

What is needed is a radical change in the balance between the pieces and the whole. To become truly the masters of our destiny, we need to effect a fundamental realignment in the relationship between the capitalist economic system, in which private actors take separate actions to pursue their own purposes, and the democratic political system, in which the entire community makes collective decisions to promote the welfare of society as a whole.

The challenge facing us, this implies, is twofold. One challenge is to utilize the political system to correct the flaws of the market system. But in order successfully to meet that challenge, we must also meet another: to transform our polity into one that corresponds much more fully with our own democratic ideals.

Now is a good time to confront these challenges. In one frame of mind, the fall of our long-time Communist rivals seems an occasion for self-congratulation; but in another, more enlightened state of consciousness this development constitutes an opportunity for more open self-examination. Extricating ourselves from the constriction of a defensive posture, we can become more open to looking at our own shortcomings. Freed of some of the burden of external threat from the cold war, we can direct our energies toward internal renewal. If a closed, reactionary society like the Soviet Union can confront its weaknesses and work to recast itself in a more viable form, surely a free and vibrant society like America can do so as well.

It is a good time for perestroika in America. Meeting this challenge can make our city worthy of the place on the hill that we so often claim for it.

PART I
TUNNEL VISION

A RADICAL CRITIQUE
OF THE MARKET

A vital clue about the nature of the problem of our materialism I didn't even recognize as a clue until my brother pointed it out. The clue was that plunging into the literature on the subject of our economy gave me a somewhat flat, empty, dead feeling.

The study of war was not like that (except perhaps the works of military game theorists). To enter the realm of war is to enter a field where passions are at play—the rage, the desperation, the pain. I always felt close to the core of the human condition.

When I turned to the economic dimension of modern life, I felt like some spark went out of me. I complained to my brother, Ed, that my thinking felt mechanical. I was having trouble getting to the living, palpitating heart of the matter.

The problem, my brother's intuition told him, was itself the clue. What was happening was not that I was failing to get into the matter but that having entered it, I was picking up on the spiritual condition that is at the heart of it. My further work has persuaded me that my brother was right: here was a clue to the nature of the sickness of our materialism.

There is an aroma of deadness in the subject of our materialism. Our economy, with its focus on the material and the mechanical, embodies an approach to human life with the spirit drained out of it. Our material becomes dead stuff.

Our war system inflicts wounds on us and possesses us with its fiery spirit. Our materialism takes the life out of our lives, leaving us without spirit. (Recall the famous passage of outrage in Max Weber, where he speaks of "nullities without spirit" who "imagine they have created a level of civilization never before attained.")

The cost of worshipping Mammon is evidently high, for like Midas's touch it turns our living treasures into dead material.* Contact with the dead stuff of our economic system tends to be deadening.

That was the clue my brother read. And so I have become aware of the special challenge we face as we try to see the nature of our predicament in our struggle to create a world ruled by life-affirming values while living in a market society. All cultures have their spiritual traps and their corresponding spiritual challenges. For us, the challenge is to keep human life and its meaning alive in our hearts.

This is an especially demanding challenge with the assignment at hand here, with *The Illusion of Choice*. For there is a job to do, having to do with moving our beliefs, that requires us to enter a realm of abstraction and logical structure—attributes that underlie both some of the important virtues and the deadly deficiencies of the modern economy.

Market society understands itself—through the ideology of the market—as a self-regulated machine. Human affairs are reduced to terms of mechanism, comprehensible in terms of number and calculation. It is like the Newtonian clockwork universe that epitomized the worldview of the era in which the market arose and developed its power and rationale.

To free ourselves from the machine, it will be necessary to understand better the nature of the machine. But as we de-

---

*One of the very few exceptions to the generalization that I found readings about our materialism to lack a full-bodied life-energy was Jacques Ellul's book *Money and Power*, probably because Ellul was committed to seeing the problem of our materialism through the perspective of a spiritual worldview—a Christian theology in which God and Mammon are rivals—that was alive in him.

scend into this mechanical worldview, with its contagious life-lessness, I hope it will be possible for us to keep contact with the flesh-and-blood, spiritually important realities that are at stake in the struggle between ways of understanding the dynamism of the market machine.

1

The Mythology
of the Market

There is an Eden that human beings can create on earth. It is the free market. In this garden, people enjoy both liberty and abundance. So we are taught by the mythology of the market.

The economist Carl Kaysen writes:

> [P]eople have preferences in respect to what kinds of goods they buy; where they live and work, what kinds of occupations they pursue . . . what kinds of mortgages, automobile loans, bank loans they owe. The working of the market, provided that it is competitive, makes the best possible reconciliation of these preferences with the technical possibilities of production, which in combination with these preferences . . . determine what jobs, goods, services are available.[1]

The market, in other words, gives us the best of all possible worlds. It is the optimal marriage of human choices ("preferences") and hard reality ("technical possibilities of production").

The word *myth* has fallen on hard times. Whereas once myths were the stories peoples used to make sense of their world, nowadays people use the word to mean "erroneous belief." When I speak here of the mythology of the market, I mean it in the older sense—though the question of the validity of our "stories" remains, as we will see, an important one.

In our scientific age, we imagine ourselves to be above and beyond the use of stories and imagery to comprehend our world, and to guide us through it. But we are not so different from our ancestors as we think. Our society, like traditional societies of earlier times, buttresses itself by the creation of myths. Liberal economic theory is part of our mythology.

THE MYTH OF EFFICIENCY

As befits our age, the deity of the market is represented as a great machine, harnessing and transmitting the natural energy of human self-interest, its wonders to perform. As befits our age, the myths of the market economy have been told in scientific, even mathematical language to show that the myth does indeed capture the nature of reality.

The market can be seen as an intricate information-processing mechanism that, according to the mythology of liberal theory, effects the best possible combination of what is desired and what is possible. The science of economics has produced a great many graphs and formulae that demonstrate how the market creates a system of prices that truly reflects both the costs (on the producers' side) and the benefits (on the consumer's side) of an infinite variety of goods and services. With its unerring translation of values into prices, the market machine allocates resources to maximize both productivity and utility. This maximization constitutes one of the market's great achievements: efficiency.

The market achieves its efficiency simply by allowing buyers and sellers to come together to make whatever transactions they freely choose to make. One of the wonders of the market is that the same system that grants each such social atom the freedom to pursue its own interest also can knit together the entire world in an integrated productive arrangement of great efficiency.

The magical mechanism of the market can reach across the whole planet, bringing together natural resources and human ingenuity to create an almost infinite variety of goods and to make them available to us at a tiny cost. Adam Smith told the famous story of the manufacture of pins to show how the division of labor in a large market magnifies the productive efficiency of human labor. Milton Friedman, a latter-day apostle of the laissez faire creed, tells the story of what goes into making a pencil.[2]

Friedman tells how the wood comes from a cedar log from California or Oregon, how loggers and complicated machines process the wood that will surround the pencil's "lead," which in turn starts out as graphite mined in Sri Lanka (then Ceylon). Friedman goes on to describe the metal, which is brass, that comes into being from the efforts of miners of zinc and copper, and of others who make the sheets of brass; into the metal ferrule will go the eraser plug, which is made partly from rubber and partly from rapeseed oil from Indonesia. Thousands of people and resources from all over the world combine to create the "simple" pencil.

And we can go to a store near our homes and buy this marvelous device for ten cents.

The efficiency of the market derives not only from how resources are *allocated* but also from how human energies are *unleashed*. In one sense, labor is just one more natural resource to be allocated. The market has the virtue of directing human efforts along the optimal channels, rewarding people according to how much what they do helps other people get what they want. But it is not as though human effort is fixed in quantity or in quality. Labor can be inspired and creative or begrudging and dull; different situations can elicit from people efforts of widely differing value. As James Fallows says in *More Like Us*, his recent book celebrating the dynamism of the American market system, people give their best when they think they have a fair chance to better their condition. The market, by giving a better reward for a better effort, has the further virtue that it unleashes the best of human energies.

Pertinent to this point is the story Milton Friedman tells about two waves of Chinese immigrants fleeing Communist China for Hong Kong. Those who came immediately after the Chinese seized power, Friedman writes, "gained a deserved reputation for initiative, enterprise, thrift, and hard work." But a later group, who had been formed by thirty years under a Communist system, "show little initiative and want to be told precisely what to do. They are indolent and uncooperative."[3]

The market, by using the natural desire of people to improve their lot, will solve this problem. Of the indolence of those refugees from communism, Friedman concludes, "No doubt a few years in Hong Kong's free market will change all that."

The Assumption of Competition

The efficiency of the market is predicated on the system's competitive nature. There are presumed to be so many buyers and sellers in the marketplace that no single actor can affect the price of exchange. If you are charging more than the market rate, I will buy from someone else. If you are offering less than the market rate, I will sell to someone else. The market is a demanding taskmaster, telling any who cannot measure up to the competition, in the efficiency and/or quality of their products, to shape up or ship out.

If markets stop being competitive, their virtues can vanish. If, by whatever means, a single producer or a group of producers acting in collusion can gain control over the supply side of the market for some important commodity, the price will cease to represent that optimal balance between costs and benefits that economists celebrate. What one gets then is the worst aspects of the public and private spheres combined: instead of the impersonal forces of the market, decisions are imposed, but these are the decisions of a private, wholly self-interested party. One illustration is the infamous company store in some turn-of-the-century coal town of Pennsylvania or West Virginia where the sellers could enrich themselves by gouging their captive buyers. Without competition, moreover, producers are not compelled by market forces to strain continually to improve their product and their methods of production. So, for example, the oligopoly that existed in the American automobile industry contributed to a deterioration of quality in American-made cars. Eventually, this opened the door to the penetration of the American market by foreign manufacturers, making the market competitive once again.

As the example of the American automobile market demonstrates, the market system does tend to erode positions of market dominance. Another example is the collusion of the Organization of Petroleum Exporting Countries (OPEC) in the early 1970s. Oil being a commodity of enormous importance to industrial economies, the ability of many major producers to act in concert gave them the power to quadruple their prices virtually overnight. Economies dependent on petroleum were hostage to their own addiction and were compelled either to pay the price set by the producers or to watch their economies break down. But with the passage of time, market forces seeped in to corrode the iron grip of this oligopoly. The high price of oil stimulated the search for additional oil reserves around the world, and in time supplies from non-OPEC countries increased. Time also allowed wasteful consumers of oil, like the United States, to introduce energy conservation measures for which the high OPEC price provided the incentive. And the same high cost of oil spurred the search for alternative fuels. In all these ways, the market showed its inherent antagonism to the artifice of monopolistic domination, and within a decade the domination of the cartel was washed away as an oil glut flooded the world market.

At the same time, however, the market has a natural tendency to undermine the very competitiveness on which its virtues of efficient allocation depend. Competition produces winners and losers, and the losers tend to disappear. Competition goads all the actors to strive continuously for improvements in how and what they produce. Those who innovate successfully are rewarded with profits and with the privilege of continuing to have a place in the market. Those who fall behind, fall out. The Big Three automakers in the U.S. are those that survived an extremely competitive process of elimination that occurred during the industry's early decades. More recently, we have witnessed the beginnings of a similar shakedown to narrow the field in the burgeoning and comparatively new industry of personal computers.

The market system, therefore, does not automatically maintain its competitive nature. This has been recognized in the United States for more than a century, and it has long been recognized as one of the legitimate roles of government in a market system to prevent the accumulation of market power in the hands of any actors. In recent years, particularly under the Reagan administration, the commitment to maintain market competition has been quite feeble. Industry after industry has become more concentrated, as the ostensible champions of the market system have shown themselves more truly the partisans of big wealth.

But long before Reagan, many in America have said of the free market: *what free market?* In the 1950s, critics of laissez faire economics—people like John Kenneth Galbraith—decried the oligopolistic nature of an increasing part of the American economy. Many would say that what we have in America today is not the free-market system of economics texts. Too much of our economy, they would say, functions very differently from thousands of wheat farmers producing grain for sale on the board of exchange.

The question of competitiveness is an important one—but henceforth it will be disregarded here. It is important to make a judgment as to how much or how little the concentrations of market share in various American industries may distort the market's proper functioning, and it is important also to determine whether or not our political system is sufficiently vigilant in protecting the competitive integrity of our markets. However, the discussion here will waive any such reservations about the market economy.

Our inquiry will assume the open and competitive markets beloved of laissez faire ideologues. Our concern will be with the question: how optimally are resources allocated *even in a perfectly functioning free market?*

THE CASE FOR LIBERTY

If efficiency is one aspect of the market's virtue, liberty is the other.

To many of the devotees of the market, it would not be enough for the market to be a splendid machine of production if each of us felt like just a piece of mechanism. Human freedom is of essential importance. The machine of the market is not our master, but our slave. Each of us is at liberty in the market to seek our own destiny according to our own vision of the meaning of life. (Society as a whole, according to the ideologist of the market society Friedrich von Hayek, has no purpose beyond facilitating the various ends of its participants.[4])

As producers, that is, as economic actors working to earn our livelihood, we are free to choose our own path. A complex economy offers a plethora of available roles, and in the free market the intrepid and the creative are at liberty to carve out their own niche in the economic environment. The liberty of the market allows us to channel our energies according to our own sense of our calling and, says this mythology of the market, the system will reward us according to the value of our contribution.

The market, with its invisible hand, achieves wholeness and coordination without employing coercion. Friedman ends his paean to the manufacture of the pencil by remarking how "astounding [it is] that the pencil was ever produced. No one sitting in a central office gave orders to these thousands of people. No military police enforced the orders that were not given. These people live in many lands, speak different languages, practice different religions, may even hate one another—yet none of these differences prevented them from cooperating to produce a pencil."[5]

If productive miracles can be accomplished by people acting freely, the market's ideologues argue, what good reason can there be for the intrusion of government? Government, they point out, effects its will ultimately through coercion, the power of force that stands behind its law. So, they tell us, let's get the government off our backs.

Friedman entitles his book in praise of the market system *Free to Choose*. As actors in the market, we are "free to choose" not only in our role as producers but also as consumers.

Whether we enter the market as buyers or sellers, we are always free to make the deals we want to and to refuse transactions that we don't like. It is the *voluntary* nature of market exchanges that, in the market's mythology, is proof of the market's goodness. If a buyer and a seller each choose to make a deal, it can safely be inferred that each regarded the exchange as serving his interests. A deal that makes both parties better off is a good thing. And since the market comprises a multiplicity of such beneficial exhanges, the market itself is good.

The market thus surveys the world of its creation and declares that it is good. Liberty assures the beneficial nature of its results. Efficiency assures the goodness is the maximal possible.

Much is valid in this mythology of the market. All its essential points contain a large measure of truth. If it were altogether valid, this world of abundance the market has created might indeed be the best of all possible worlds. But there are a couple of holes in its logic, and through these holes some serious ills can and do enter this presumed utopia to despoil it.

2

Questions of Power
and Justice

THE CLAIM OF ECONOMIC DEMOCRACY

Power to the people! This is a central part of the mythology of the market. Where once the soverign made all beneath him subject to his will, the market is governed by the principle of consumer sovereignty.

Here is how another famous ideologist of the market, Ludwig von Mises, describes how the market, in contrast with the repressive regimes of the past, empowers people:

> Those underlings who in all the preceding ages of history had formed the herds of slaves and serfs, of paupers and beggars, became the buying public, for whose favor the businessmen canvass. They are the customers who are "always right" . . .
>
> In a daily plebiscite in which every penny gives a right to vote the consumers determine who should own and run the plants, shops and farms. The control of the material means of production is a social function,

subject to the confirmation or revocation by the soverign consumers.[1]

The market is often likened to a democracy, in which we all vote with our money.[2] Each time we spend, it is as though we have put our vote into the ballot box of this economic democracy.

The image of the market as a democracy, in which von Mises's liberated serfs are free to vote and thereby to rule the material forces of production, is deceptive.

Despite the parallelism asserted between consumer sovereignty in the market and the sovereignty of the people in a democracy, the market is quite undemocratic in a fundamental way. Whereas a democracy operates on the principle "One person, one vote" the market operates on the principle "One dollar, one vote." To the extent that different people command unequal numbers of dollars, they will exert as consumers correspondingly unequal amounts of power to govern the economic organization of the world around them. And, of course, it is in the nature of the market to foster considerable inequalitites of wealth and thus a very undemocratic allocation of voting in this "economic democracy."

The defenders of the market will concede all this. But they will say that with the regime of consumer sovereignty the real question is not equality but justice. The distribution of wealth in the market system, though unequal, is not unjust, they will argue, because the market justly gives unequal rewards in correspondence with the unequal contribution of different people to the well-being of their fellows. Thus von Mises applauds the justice of what he calls the "law of the economic democracy of the market": "Those who satisfy the wants of a smaller number of people only collect fewer votes—dollars—than those who satisfy the wants of more people."[3] This, says von Mises, shows that there is justice to the great sums paid to people like professional athletes, whom many want to watch, compared to the paltry incomes of poets, whose work interests few.

Thus, according to this argument, the inequalities are a fitting part of a system that is based on the satisfaction of human needs and that justly rewards people according to how well their efforts serve the cause of human welfare.

But there is a problem of circularity in this reasoning. If the votes (dollars) we cast as consumers are a measure of how many votes (again in the form of dollars) we have received for our contribution as producers, it is hardly established that greater wealth goes to "those who satisfy the wants of more *people.*" This balloting is so weighted that all we can say is that wealth goes to those who satisfy the wants of wealth.

The development of medicines in the pharmaceutical industry demonstrates this quite clearly. Billions of dollars have been made in this market, as researchers create drugs to use against a vast array of diseases. But some medical problems have received significantly more attention than others. The maladies that afflict the members of affluent societies have been researched in depth, and drugs for their treatment have been invented in abundance. But there are crippling and debilitating diseases that plague tens or even hundreds of millions of impoverished people in the tropics that have largely been ignored. You can't make money selling goods needed only by people who have no money, even if they need them desperately. The "economic democracy" of the market is deaf to the voices of those without the dollars with which to express their needs. So, the system that is governed by dollars voted will produce dozens of varieties of tranquilizers for unhappy middle-class housewives but will not bother to look for a cure for diseases that afflict only the financially disenfranchised.

And if a group of altruistic scientists were to find cures for these tropical diseases of the poor, though they would have satisfied the wants of more people than their brethren at the big drug companies, they would be rewarded with fewer "votes" to "control the material means of production." They are not the people to whom the market gives disproportionate power to determine who will own the plants and shops and what will be produced and sold.

This example of the pharmaceuticals demonstrates that, ultimately, it is not satisfying more people's needs that leads to wealth but satisfying the needs of those with money.

A GLIMPSE AT THE REAL
PROBLEM OF POWER

The traditional concern regarding the problems of power and justice focuses on inequalities of power between one group of people and another. Is it fair that the market provides some people with luxuries while others go without necessities? Is it right that the scientists who cure the ills of the penniless are rewarded less than those who attend to the discomforts of the wealthy? Such questions of justice we will look at in a moment.

However, a less visible, though ultimately more important, issue concerns the question of power between human beings, on the one hand, and the economic system, on the other. The clue to this problem lies in that circularity we saw in the reasoning of von Mises's argument that the market creates economic democracy. If the people who rule the system as consumers are those who make the most money as producers, and those who make the most money as producers are those who best satisfy the wants of those who are rewarded best by the system, then ultimately in considerable measure *it is the system that rules itself.* Put another way, if the system can decide who will decide, then it is the system that decides.

Just as it has been said that a hen is an egg's way of producing another egg, so also might it be said that a rich person is a dollar's way of producing another dollar. Or a successful business is the market's way of furthering the dynamics of the market.

The market thus has the attributes of what I call a "power system," that is, a system that unfolds according to a dynamic of its own, uncontrolled by human choice. Of course, the question of whether it is the market or human beings that governs how the economic system evolves is not an all-or-nothing matter. It is both. To the extent that it is our system that governs, we have a problem. As the argument of this work unfolds, I hope to demonstrate that the market has quite considerable power to usurp much of our freedom to choose our destiny.

A LESSER, LIBERTARIAN
CLAIM TO JUSTICE

The "economic democracy" celebrated by many free marketeers does not, upon inspection, look very democratic. The market may take power out of the hands of central authorities, as von Mises says, but we cannot conclude that it creates economic equivalent of democracy.

Yet "undemocratic" does not prove "unjust." It depends on one's understanding of justice.

If we assume axiomatically that an economic system should be equally responsive to all people's needs, we will lament the market's deafness to those without money. This is the familiar criticism from the left. Seeing the society in more collectivist terms, these critics regard everyone in society as entitled to make certain claims on the society as a whole. A reasonable case can be made for the point of view that any system that ignores the fundamental needs of some people is inherently unjust.

But the critique offered here will not be predicated on this collectivist view of justice. I shall not endorse the idea that everyone is *entitled* to a level of well-being, which the society is obliged to provide. In this, we will be joining the free marketeers in their more individualistic concept of society.

Von Mises, we saw, put forward one argument for the justice of the market's allocation of wealth, that greater wealth goes to those who satisfy the wants of more people. This argument proved fallacious, but I don't think it constitutes the core of the free marketeers' argument. Indeed, I suspect that the argument is sometimes put forward somewhat disingenuously, as a means to persude the people that the system is set up to serve people, that the system gives power to the people. But the free-market ideology is not about democratic equality but about human liberty. Not the greatest good for the greatest number—which is a collectivist form of justification—but about individualistic justice.

Justice means that we each have the precious right to pursue our own way. That does not preclude the possibility that some may lose their way. Justice means that each person—in his or her dealings with others—gets what is owed to him or her. Injustice is when one party takes what rightfully belongs to another party without that party's consent. Inequalities of wealth can therefore be just if they ensue from dealings that are just by that definition.

In this essentially libertarian view, we have two basic rights. We have the right to be left alone. And we have the right to be assured that people will honor the agreements they make with us. The state has two concomitant responsibilities. The state should protect its citizens from being coerced by others, for our right to be left alone is violated when others force us to deal with them. And the state should be available to enforce valid contracts.

Justice should not be understood as an all-encompassing virtue, mandating everything that is good. It is, rather, specifically the antidote to the misuse of power.[4] According to the libertarian view of the market, power is not a factor in free-market transactions. And if the power of the state is used neutrally—to make sure that all transactions are mutually agreed upon, not compelled, and all agreements kept—power has been neutralized and justice assured.

We are each responsible for ourselves. According to this libertarian, free-market view of society, we make contact with another person when we think that other person may be of use to us. The marketplace is the contact point for people to meet for mutually useful exchanges.

This individualistic view of the nature of society and its members is at the core of an ideology that arose with capitalism and that facilitated its development. The philospher C. B. Macpherson explores this ideology in his study called *The Political Theory of Possessive Individualism*. The individual, according to this political philosophy that emerged in seventeenth-century England, is "essentially the proprietor of his own person or capacities, owing nothing to society for them."[5] Society, meanwhile, is simply "a lot of free equal individuals related to each other as proprietors of their own capacities, and of what they have acquired by their exercise. Society consists of relations of exchange between proprietors."[6] (Recall the image from Hayek—a *twentieth*-century thinker—of society having no purpose beyond facilitating the various ends of its participants.)

All we are obliged to do is mind our own business. We are not our brother's keeper—owing each other nothing but to keep our part of our bargains.

Justice does not require that I, who have much, remedy the plight of you, who have little. If you have nothing to offer of value to me, I do not *owe* it to you to give you what I have that is of value to you. Justice, therefore, does not require that anyone in the marketplace invest capital or labor to cure the ills of people in the tropics who have nothing to give in exchange.

The market, according to this view, does not—cannot—inflict wrongs on people. The system may not right the wrongs that have been inflicted by other forces, but—given the distribution of property the market finds—it inflicts no new injustices.

Thus the market's disregard of impoverished peoples of the tropics is not unjust. These people are poor not because of the market but for other historical and cultural reasons. Western imperialism may have contributed some to their woes; but, if so, it was because of very nonlibertarian, coercive measures, not as a result of free exchanges in the marketplace. Those free exchanges, because they are voluntary, are always just. If any party fails to benefit from a market transaction, it is the party's own responsibility for having made an error of judgment. If smart and hardworking poor people are given good access to a free market, they can, in time, make themselves richer (as have the recently poor inhabitants of newly industrialized countries of Asia, such as Taiwan, Korea, and Singapore).

The world has been so long filled with injustice that the special virtue of allowing free exchange to define the relationships among people should not be underestimated. The libertarian order of the free market may not—on its own—clothe the penniless or feed the orphan. But how great an improvement is the injustice of free exchange in a world where the mighty have so often simply taken the clothes off the backs of the lowly and the food off their tables?

Where differences in wealth are the result of free—and therefore just—exchange, the market ideology continues, the rich do not *owe* the poor anything. The rich may choose, outside of market transactions, to give to the poor. This charity goes beyond what is required for justice. But justice does not embody *all* the virtues; charity or philanthropy can help do good things that the market, which gives only justice, cannot do by itself. Rich individuals, for example, might fund research into tropical diseases (e.g., through the Rockefeller Foundation or the Ford Foundation), helping to fill the gap in the market's attentions.

Such charity or philanthropy is good, being given freely by the donors and received gladly by the beneficiaries. But, in the strictly libertarian view that is the essence of the market ideology, the state has no business filling that gap. For the recipients are not *entitled* to charity, and the donors are not obliged to give it. Taxes are not voluntary, but coerced. Therefore, when the state takes from one party what is rightfully his and uses it for a purpose—not required by justice—to which that party has not freely consented, then the state itself inflicts an injustice.

The fact that the market is blind to the sufferings of the penniless may make it difficult for the system's partisans to argue that the market by itself creates the best of all possible worlds. For ideally, the suffering millions would not be abandoned to their tropical diseases. But this suffering still leaves room for the important claim that the system of free exchange is the best way to assure justice.*

We are all entitled to justice. So let us use the market for our transactions and keep the government "off the backs of the American people" (quoth President Reagan). Let us leave "good works" to the free choice of free people, to "a thousand points of light" (quoth President Bush).

This is the essence of the libertarian/free-market ideology. The individualistic view of society on which it is based can be challenged on a variety of grounds. There are anthropological grounds: Is this universe of social atoms true to the realities of human nature? Does it offer the kind of community that people find most fulfilling? There are historical grounds: Does this take sufficient account of how social relations actually have developed? How are we to factor in the legacy of past injustices—slavery injuring American blacks, corrupt U.S. laws enriching the railroad tycoons—in deciding what will foster justice in the present? And there are moral grounds: Is this the most desirable way to organize a human society? Is the justice of free exchange an adequate virtue for defining the nature of our social obligations?

These are all important questions. But—for purely strategic reasons—I am going to waive all those potential challenges. Because they tend to take the discussion off the maps of the free market ideologues, they are limited in their power to loosen the grip of the ideological vision. My strategy, rather, will be to mount my challenge, as it were, on the free marketeer's home field.

We all have a right and a responsiblity to mind our own business, they say. Free exchanges assure justice. But I will

---

*And beyond that, free marketeers would argue that attempts to use government to create "the best of all possible worlds" is dangerous. So great are the dangers of governmental tyranny and corruption, as they see it, that a government authorized to create the best *conceivable* will lead to something far worse than the best *possible*. These questions of "What is possible?" and of how much we should fear or hope for from government will be explored in Chapter 4.

show that free exchanges regularly mete out injustice because they do not allow people to mind their business.

MINDING OUR BUSINESS

Voluntary exchange is presumed to be good because the parties would not consent to the transaction if they didn't think it would benefit them. But what of the people who are *not* party to the transaction? They don't matter because, presumably, it is none of their business.

But the reality is that the transactions that other people make have an impact on us in countless ways. And if our well-being is affected by something, it *is* our business.

This is the key to a fundamental fallacy at the root of the free-market ideology. It is the notion that the interests of the buyer and the seller are the only interests at stake in their exchange. A system of myriad exchanges between people who know what is good for them is assumed, on the basis of that supposition, to be inevitably beneficial.

But bystanders have interests too. If the farm next to mine is turned into a steel factory, or into a housing development, that will change my world, not necessarily for the better. But my interests are not taken into account in the market transactions in which the fate of the property is determined.

In our world of social atoms, each one of us is free to move to Los Angeles if we calculate that such a move will better our own condition. But, as the steady deterioration of life in L.A. in recent decades demonstrates, that calculation by each immigrant need not take account of the effect of the new arrivals on the welfare of those who are already there.

The idea that what we do with ourselves and our property is "our own business" is merely a fiction. It is a useful fiction, in some ways. For this idea of 'liberty' has indeed helped to get the government off people's backs and allowed them to live according to their own vision. No one who values human freedom can help but appreciate an ideology that has helped protect individual lives from the historically ubiquitous iron hand of oppressive governments.

I myself was long an unambivalent devotee of "On Liberty," in which John Stuart Mill argued the right of every individual to live as he (or she) sees fit, so long as that individual does no harm to others. I remain a fairly radical advocate of civil liberties, believing in almost absolute rights of free thought and speech, of assembly and association, and in the separation of church and state. In general, I favor repealing laws against what are called victimless crimes, such as laws forbidding sexual practices among consenting adults. And in the current debate over whether the current "prohibition" against various drugs should be repealed, while I am of more than one mind, my sympathies lie with legalization's advocates (who include, incidentally, Milton Friedman), and largely on grounds of libertarian arguments like Mills's.

Yet I have come to see that even in the most sacrosanct areas of liberty, our business is not wholly our own. The practices we civil libertarians like to call "victimless" do have an effect on the fabric of society. I oppose laws banning obscene material. But I have to recognize that the commerce in pornography does change the world in ways that make it a notably less pleasant place for those who are offended by such material. I agreed with the ACLU that those American Nazis should have the right to march in Skokie, Illinois. But who can deny the pain they caused the residents of that city who had survived the Nazi holocaust? I even have to acknowledge that my freedom to write helps make the world a place that other people find less congenial. The way Salman Rushdie's exercise of his liberty disturbed the Ayatollah Khomeini was remarkable only in the global nature of its repercussions.

So when Mill writes of the parts of one's conduct "which merely concern himself,"[7] he is simplifying considerably. We do not live each of us on a separate planet. We are neighbors, fellow citizens, partners in making history, housemates in the same ecosystem, breathing the same atmosphere and subject to the same climatic system. Very little we do "merely" concerns ourselves alone.

What does this imply about our liberty? A thoroughgoing exploration of the costs and benefits, the rights and wrongs, of different dimensions of liberty would require too much of a digression for our present discussion. But I would say that the complex web of interconnections among us particularly undermines those libertarian claims that undergrid the market economy.

Liberty of thought and expression, though not so *absolutely* defensible as Mill would suggest, warrant special protection. Though Michael Novak, another contemporary market ideologue, likens government intrusion into the market to censorship in the realm of ideas,[8] the analogy does not hold up. Thought and expression, I would maintain, are more fundamental to our very humanity than economic enterprise, but I doubt that all free marketeers would concur with this. So, once again, let us make the case in terms congenial to the liberal philosophy. Freedoms of thought and speech should be treated more as absolutes because they are more central to political legitimacy. If it is agreed that government is legitimate only if it rules with the consent of the governed, then the freedoms that make truly free consent possible cannot be abridged. No free consent is possible unless it is given on the bais of thoughts freely conceived and freely exchanged. Thus any use of the state to restrain the free expression of belief must lead over time to the erosion of the legitimacy of that state.

Even in the absence of the idea of a zone over which the individual is absolutely sovereign, therefore, the intrusion of government into the realm of thought and expression quickly calls into question the justice of the government itself.

However, with the free market, the issue of liberty cuts very differently. In the light of our interconnectedness, we will now see, what is called into question is the very legitimacy of the market.

BRINGING THE EXTERNALITIES IN

There is nothing revolutionary about the idea that people not party to a transaction may be affected by it. Economists call these incidental effects on bystanders "externalities." A typical externality is pollution. If I am downwind of some factory that belches smoke into the atmosphere, the productive activity of that factory imposes a cost on me to which I have not consented and for which the free market provides no compensation. There are beneficial kinds of externalities as well, ways that the economic activities of others help us and for which the market does not require us to pay. My neighbor's growing an orchard will help my honey business, for example, without any deal being made between us.

It can be assumed that the great preponderance of externalities are costs, not benefits.

Even Milton Friedman readily recognizes the existence of externalities or, as he calls them, "third party effects." "[T]hird party effects of private actions do occur that are sufficiently important to justify government action."[9] One such government action that he recommends is the imposition of a tax per unit of polluting effluent discharged, say, into a lake or a river.[10] Friedman prefers such a solution to one in which the government specifies exactly what kind of waste treatment plant firms should use, or in which the government sets a required level of water quality in the effluent. The tax has the advantage, he says, of allowing the market to do what it does well: process information and provide incentives. Easily remedied problems of pollution would disappear quickly in response to even a relatively small tax. And products that engender a lot of pollution in their manufacture would go up steeply in price, leading to a change in demand away from polluting and toward nonpolluting products.

I substantially agree. If the tax is sufficient to bring the price of goods up to the *true cost* of their production (and use), the market should be able to effect a kind of optimal level of production and consumption. Assuring that prices reflect "true costs" is a big "if," but given that stipulation, I agree the market can be trusted.

So, with all this agreement, how can the problem of externalities function as a wedge to open up a radical critique of the market?

It is because these externalities are everywhere. They are like what physicists these days call the "dark matter," stuff in the universe that is invisible to us but nonetheless is believed to make up most of the mass of the universe. How much dark matter there is may spell the difference between our universe being one that expands forever and one that has sufficient gravity to stop the expansion and bring the universe collapsing back on itself. Likewise, the net magnitude of the impacts of "private" transactions on third parties, who are invisible to the market's calculations, may determine whether the market can be trusted to expand the universe of human satisfactions, or whether the gravity of the problem is sufficient to bring the free market ideology, or the society that has entrusted its fate to market forces, collapsing on itself.

Third parties are all over the place. For every transaction to which we are party, there are a great many transactions to which we are third parties and which nonetheless affect us.

Where I live, there are leaves to clear in the fall. The quickest and easiest way to do the job is with a power blower. Most of the men in the neighborhood, each acting on his individual liberty, get the job done quickly and easily. The result is that during autumn weekends, when one would like to enjoy the fine weather outside, the oppressively loud roar of machinery spoils the beautiful days. It is possible that for each of us, the disadvantages of third-party costs when our neighbors are blowing the leaves outweigh the first-party advantages for ourselves in using the noisy machines. But we each mind our own business.

In the winter, there is the problem of ice. Rock salt is quite effective in keeping both private driveways and public highways from icing up. In a highly informative communication to the *Washington Post* in 1988, David Morris clarified the problem with rock salt. The runoff of the salt, he explained, causes damage to underground cables, car bodies, bridges, and groundwater. The cost of these damages is twenty to forty times the price of the salt to the person or organization buying and using it. (When the Romans wanted to be sure that Carthage never rose again they salted the Carthaginian earth. We are slowly doing that to ourselves.)

There is an alternative product to rock salt that produces no such damage from runoff. It is called CMA, and it costs a good deal more than the salt. It costs less, however, than the damages the salt inflicts. Yet, as Morris writes, "No highway department, homeowner or business would purchase large quantities of CMA today even if it were widely available, because the individual doesn't care about cost, only price."[11] Like Friedman on the effluent problem, Morris suggests imposing taxes to bring price in line with costs.*

---

*An example of how "bringing the externalities in" can transform economic behavior concerns the use and disposal of chemicals by the Massachusetts Institute of Technology (MIT). It used to dispose of 125,000 pounds of filled or partially filled containers of chemicals each year, reports Robert C. Cowen, science reporter for the *Christian Science Monitor*. Many of the junked containers were ordered but never opened, because scientists thought it might be good to have them on hand, and the chemicals did not cost all that much. Now, however, the costs of disposal have increased to reflect the rights of the rest of the world to have a livable environment, so that "It now costs more to get rid of used chemicals and unused but unwanted supplies than it cost to buy them." When it costs thirty-two dollars to dispose of a gallon of benzene that cost seventeen dollars to purchase, it becomes

How is rock salt different from a million other things we use and countless things we do except, perhaps, in degree? The cost of rock salt is many times higher than its price. But are not the costs of most things we consume in our economy higher than their prices?

Everything that in production or use involves the consumption of carbon-based fuels is contributing to the greenhouse effect, which, according to present scientific consensus, threatens disruption of the global climate and possible worldwide famine within a human lifetime. (There is talk, now, among experts on energy and environment, of a "carbon tax.") Every time we start our cars in the summer, we increase the burden of those whose heart and respiratory problems are exacerbated by the presence of ozone. Whoever turns on a light in Cleveland, Ohio, or buys something made of Pennsylvania steel, is helping to kill off the northern lakes and forests where the acid rain falls. Not to mention those atrocious burgers, atrocious not in their taste but in their contribution to the atrocity of stripping the tropical forests so that beef could be grazed there for a few years.

The list could, of course, go on and on.

In all these cases, the market is giving out false information about the costs and benefits of each of our transactions. The market does not tell me, when I go into Burger King, that the purchase of this meat encourages the destruction of one of the earth's treasures. The American landscape is now dotted with thousands of toxic waste sites, filled with the poisonous chemical by-products of manufacturing the goods we have been using all our lives. The market was not equipped to notice this cost, and it told us nothing to induce either us or those who sold us their goods to respect the true costs our lifestyle entailed.

Those of the Milton Friedman school just don't seem to realize that these externalities are so pervasive that, like so much rock salt sprinkled liberally across the landscape, they rust out the iron-clad logic of the market ideology. As a result, many of their ideological assumptions become questionable.

"cheaper to buy chemicals for particular purposes in small quantities," the director of MIT's" Safety Office is quoted as saying, "to minimize—or eliminate waste." (Robert C. Cowen, "Pollution Prevention Gets a Powerful Prod," *Christian Science Monitor*, October 17, 1989.)

(1) If important costs and benefits are disregarded in market transactions, how meaningful are the values that the market assigns to the goods exchanged, and what happens to the market's claim of efficiency? (2) If nontransactors must suffer damages to which they have not consented, what happens to the claim that the market metes out justice? And, finally, (3) if each of us is the unwilling victim of countless transactions in which we have no say, how well does the market protect the liberty of any of us to choose our destiny?

3

Missing Our Connections

SMALL CHANGE?

Is the problem of externalities, of third party effects, really so important? The free marketeers, while acknowledging a problem, clearly do not think it is of much gravity. Milton Friedman was quoted above suggesting that there are some third-party effects "sufficiently important" to justify state action. The implication was that if there are a great many such effects, most of them can safely be disregarded. Can they?

Perhaps an argument could be made that most of these effects are "small change," involving values so trivial that there is no harm in ignoring them, like telling the clerk to keep the change when you pay $8.00 for an item costing $7.98. Why quibble over a few pennies?

Or perhaps someone like Friedman thinks that it is a matter in which everything gets evened up in the end. On some occasions, according to this argument, I am a bystander to transactions and pay an uncompensated cost. And sometimes it is I who am a buyer or a seller and am consequently the beneficiary of the system's failure to impose all costs. These events cancel each other out, this argument would assert. We need worry about it no more than friends who take turns taking each other out to lunch.

Unfortunately, it isn't like that. The benefits we get from the market's blindness do not cancel out the costs we pay. The reason is: *the costs and the benefits are different in nature.*

Earlier, I asserted that it can be assumed that the preponderance of the market's externalities can be assumed to be costs, not benefits. But if the costs and benefits are different in nature, the market creates a problem for us whether this is true or not.

The chief external benefit of economic activities is that they foster more economic activities. In what economists call the "multiplier effect," every additional dollar put into the system stimulates still more economic activity when its recipient spends a good proportion of it, and those who receive that money also spend some more, and so on. Every new factory in our midst, therefore, means more jobs in the area, more revenues for local stores, and so forth.

The market does indeed help us to get rich in income. And even its third-party effects contribute to that benefit. But there is another economic concept that should enter into our calculus: that of "diminishing marginal returns." From abject poverty to reasonable comfort is an important step. But when a dollar increment of the same size takes us from real wealth, by any historical standard, to still more wealth, is the benefit so significant?

Meanwhile, the same system that is giving us more and more of the same benefits is also imposing more and more of the same costs. And since these costs are in a different realm of our values than the benefits, but not necessarily any less important, their progressive depletion in our lives will result in the opposite of diminishing marginal returns. The more depleted is that realm, the more vital is each additional loss. For Midas, the marginal utility of gold decreased quickly while, with every hour, his inability to eat or drink, since the food and beverage turned to gold in his mouth, became increasingly important.

The image of Midas of a hyperbole of the impact of third-party effects in a market economy as it evolves over time. Even if at the outset the costs were less than the benefits, the two curves—one falling, the other rising—would soon cross, until the skewed world the system created was failing to serve our needs well.

A WHOLE LESS THAN THE SUM
OF ITS PARTS

The market is exquisitely sensitive to the needs we have as "social atoms," and it disregards the needs we have as a social community.

Any of us can choose among hundreds of nearby stores, at which we can purchase countless goods for our private use. In making these purchases, we do not have to pay many of the true costs of the goods' production and use. But meanwhile, we all endure together the destructive effects on our common surroundings of this economy of free exchange. For all the products and services so lavishly available to us, there is no place you and I can go to buy a clean environment, a coherent landscape, an intact social community.

The market system creates prices that are consistently skewed in a particular direction. It favors those values that concern us as separate actors, and it hampers us in fulfilling those needs we have as an interconnected community of people. We make dozens of decisions daily that are warped by this effective market *subsidization* of our social atomism: should I drive or walk to the drug store a mile away? (Don't worry about the pollution, the market says, or our contribution to traffic congestion.) Should I use washable dishes in my fast-food restaurant or disposable paper and styrofoam. (Don't worry about the solid waste problem or the disappearing ozone layer over the earth.)

In the market society, the dynamics of the system work to make fact fit theory. Theory says we are autonomous entities, separate except at those points at which we choose to come together for exchange. The system makes it hard for us to be anything else.

Some neighbors of mine convened a group of their friends to discuss how they could make a community together. They felt the lack, in their lives, of a sense of interconnectedness, of mutual caring, with an extended group of people. Growing up in America, "making a life" for themselves in the ways the market teaches, they had not experienced the kind of mutual support and bonding of a social community that many peoples of traditional societies, with all their poverty, were born to and could take for granted.

Trying to "make" a community was not an easy process. Watching the effort, I was struck with how readily our society provides us with so many things and how hard it is to find others. As social atoms, we can open the Yellow Pages and within minutes find beads from India, light fixtures of hand-made stained glass, truffles from France, llama rugs from Peru. But community?

What is on the menu determines how we order our lives.

The system tilts the social landscape, putting the private realm on the downhill side, while our public/community goods are uphill. One side is easy to get to—just let go. The other side takes hard work. Over time, it is not surprising to find our choices steadily accumulating on the downhill side.

Thus we find that combination, often noted in discussions about America, of private wealth and public poverty. The market creates a society rich in its fragmented parts but poor in its organic wholeness.

A system based on the free exchanges of social atoms gives one who loves to hike across the landscape a predictable combination of pleasures and pains. There is the pleasure of seeing so many lovely residences—well-made homes surrounded by beautiful landscaping, private gardens lovingly tended. Then there is the pain of the fractured landscape as a whole—the convenience stores and fast-food places that creep into our neighborhoods, the styrofoam cups and soft-drink cans that, with every rainfall, wash into our creek from the trashed-up public streets near those retailing conveniences.

The decade of the 1980s showed this skewing of our values most pronouncedly. It is no coincidence that at a time when the government of the U.S. was run by a group of especially committed market ideologues, the sale of luxury cars like BMWs and Jaguars increased manifold; and at the same time, as the decade closed, we heard about the deteriorated condition of America's infrastructure, about the need for many hundreds of billions of dollars to repair things like bridges and roads. Rich women bedecked by the finest of furs were on the streets, while huddled into the corners on those same streets were homeless men and women who had been discharged from underfunded institutions and did not have access to other community services that would assure they were taken care of.

The world created by the market is a distorted world because the market has no use for true community among people. Between the market and the web of our interconnection, a battle is fought.

WARRING AGAINST COMMUNITY

The ideology of the market represents its world as natural and right. But, as Marx pointed out, there are interests at work in ideology. The world of social atoms is not natural, and what it produces is not necessarily right.

According to the theory of "possessive individualism," as we saw in the preceding chapter, society is nothing but a network of exchanges among individuals who owe each other nothing. Though disguised as a definition of society, it is really an argument for a particular kind of society—a kind of society the world had not seen prior to its justification by the new ideology. Thomas Hobbes helped establish this ideology with an image of a "state of nature" in which human life was *solitary*. We now know, of course, that our ancestors were social animals long before we even began to be human. The solitary individual is anything but our natural state.

The image of our natural separation, and the idea of the 'natural liberty' of the market which our separation justifies, are useful fictions. These fictions are useful in that they further certain interests. These interests are those of a class, yes, but it is a class that is given power by a certain system of political economy. Thus, the interests served are those most essentially of the system.

And it is in the interest of that system that the bonds of community be fractured and that the system be able to deal with us as the social atoms pictured in its ideology.

In his powerful work, *The Great Transformation*, Karl Polanyi shows that the market not only is served by an atomistic society but actively works to create such a social order. In the land of its origin, he says, "the principle of freedom of contract" was not just an argument for noninterference. It was, rather, "the expression of an ingrained prejudice in favor of a definite kind of interference, namely, such as would destroy noncontractual relations among individuals and prevent their spontaneous re-formation."[1]

The market prefers us as social atoms. It is people who gather no moss who adapt most readily to the purposes of the system. It is in this light that we should seek to comprehend the observed correlation between mobility and "success" in the American market society. Blau and Duncan observe in their *American Occupational Structure* that "The data unequivocally show that migrants have more successful careers than men still living in the region of their birth. It appears that something either about migration or migrants promotes occupational success."[2] Part of that "something" may be that the willingness to move away from our "noncontractual bonds" facilitates our filling niches that the system regards as valuable—which is doubtless the authors' operational definition of "success."

A dramatic instance of the way noncontractual bonds impeded the creation of what the market ideology would describe as "rational economic behavior" comes from the record of European colonialism. The Western imperialists, to achieve their economic ambitions, wanted the natives to sell their labor to them like good "Economic Men." But in many places, the indigenous people were not sufficiently interested in "bettering" their condition. So long as they had enough to eat, they did not find the benefits of enriching themselves worth the costs. In many of the traditional societies of Africa and Asia, as Polanyi describes it, the colonialists came up against a barrier created by the cohesion of traditional community ties. For the individual in these societies "is not threatened by starvation unless the community as a whole is in a like predicament."[3] This made the traditional societies, in Polanyi's words, "more human than the market economy, and at the same time less economic."[4] The imperialists thus set about the work of tearing apart the fabric of native society, rending the bonds that support people but impede "progress."

At one level the imperialists were acting in their self-interest and, at another, as agents of a power system. What they clearly were not, however, were agents of "liberty," of the right of people to be "free to choose."

The market is likewise antagonistic to community when there is no coercion but only the unobstructed freedom of exchange. Where the market is not blocked, the interweavings of community tend to be severed. Where community remains strong and alert, the unfolding of the market can be impeded.

An intact community, with relations that transcend the exchanges of separate possessive individuals, constitutes a barrier to the extension of the market's domain. A friend of mine owns a home in Virginia, with a beautiful wooded backyard at the back of which a little creek wends its way. His backyard, in fact, is part of a wooded strip all along the creek, a strip that includes the backyards of all the other houses along my friend's side of the street, as well as the backyards of the homes on the other side of the creek. If this land consisted only of so many pieces of property to be disposed of as their autonomous proprietors wished, one can imagine how long this wonderful wooded strip would survive. Soon it would be dotted with swingsets, toolsheds, croquet courses, and so forth. But there is a covenant of sorts among the whole community of people to preserve the woods, a covenant that represents a *collective* decision to achieve a purpose that—were people acting one by one—would otherwise require that *all* agree *all the time*. Only by constituting themselves as a collectivity can these people exercise the choice of preservation.

A purely market society is far from free. Its fate is pretty well sealed by the atomistic structure of decision making. To the extent that society is reduced to so many autonomous proprietors coming together in "free" exchange, the fate of the commons hangs on a chain that is only as strong as its weakest link.

Imagine a community of people living in a bounded area, nurturing a way of life that is not accordance with the market's ways but is nonetheless fulfilling to the people. Imagine that a development company sees in this bounded area an opportune spot for building a shopping center, a development that would change the nature of social and economic relations in the community from its past, traditional form. What kind of "freedom" do the people of this community have—in the face of outside forces seeking to penetrate—to choose how their society will change and how it will remain the same? It depends on whether the choice is to be made by each person acting separately or by them all deciding together.

In my book *The Parable of the Tribes: The Problem of Power in Social Evolution*, I describe an analogous problem operating in the anarchic system of civilized societies. In such a system, so long as it is fragmented, the emergence of even a single aggressive actor can transform the whole system. The ways of power inevitably spread like a contaminant. Because of the system's fragmentation, "*no one* is free to choose peace, but *any one* can impose upon all the necessity for power."[5]*

Choice in a fragmented (atomistic) society can be foreclosed in the same way.

In our hypothetical community, if the people can make decisions about their destiny collectively, then, if most want to resist being transformed by the economic forces of the outside world, they will be able to protect their way of life. But if the decisions are made by each person acting as proprietor of his piece of the whole, then *any one* can compel the whole community to change. If the land, for example, is divided into autonomously governed shares, then it takes only one actor to open the community to the shopping center. A single individual can bring into the heart of that community enterprises that will change the culture forever.

Something of the sort was reported recently on ABC television news. The story came from Taylor, New York, which was described as a close-knit community, some two hundred years old. The roads running through this farming community bear the names of the families that live on them, that have lived there for generations. The Allen farm, which is located on Allen Hill Road, was about to change hands—and this was the problem. Mr. Allen, the owner of the farm who had worked the land all his life, was apparently feeling "burned out" and wanted to sell. He had decided to sell his farm to the highest bidder, which proved to be the state of New York. The state was paying him $1 million to acquire the property for use as a low-level nuclear dump. The other members of the community, the news article showed, were quite upset. They were adamantly opposed to having this dump in their midst and bewildered that a member of their community would sell out in such a manner, exposing the people who had long been his neighbors to such a fate.[6]

But with the market, with its atomistic order of possessive individuals, it only takes one actor to open the door when outside forces knock.

---

*The social evolutionary implications of this problem of power are discussed further in Chapter 6.

In a market society, acting individually is easy; acting as a collectivity is hard. In the absence of strenuous effort to protect a community—a commons, a way of life—from market forces, those forces will make changes flow in a predictable direction, like water draining off the land, downhill, to the sea.

Individuals get rich in market terms; as a human culture, and in nonmarket terms, they may become impoverished.

On the loss of wholeness in the face of market forces, one of our most sensitive contemporary commentators is Wendell Berry. In an article entitled "Does Community Have a Value," Berry describes the changes wrought, over the past half century, on the rural community of Port Royal, Kentucky. It was changed, he says, by "forces originating outside itself, that did not consider, much less desire, the welfare or the existence of such communities."[7]

Port Royal had been based on the "principle of subsistence" on family farms. He describes the life of this community, its work, its play, its ability to take care of itself. Without romanticizing that life, he declares it to have been successful. "Subsistence," says Berry, "is bad for the industrial economy and for the paper economy of the financiers; it is good for the actual, real-world economy by which people live and are fed, clothed, and housed . . . [With the penetration of the community by the market economy,] the 'standard of living' (determined evidently by how much money is spent) has increased, but community life has declined, economically and every other way."[8]

Without the firing of a single shot from imperialist cannon, the market breaks down the cultural obstacles that impede the expansion of the empire of commodity exchange.

Berry does not give an analysis of how economic forces wrought these changes, but he concludes that the community now exists "for 'the economy'—that abstract accumulation of monetary power . . . that does not concern itself at all for the existence of Port Royal."[9] Port Royal was changed, Berry says, "partly to its own blame." How to blame? Berry says of the process, "Somehow the periphery exhausted and broke the center."[10] Perhaps the community failed to take the "uphill" kind of steps that are required to protect the coherence of the whole—of the center which is the nexus of interconnections—from the countless "downhill" intrusions of outside market forces acting in collaboration with countless individual economic decisions. Thus the community beloved of Berry yields ground to a system that makes its own calculations of what is of value and what is not.

In America, the entrenchment of market assumptions has meant that a community needs real sophistication, as well as cohesion and vigilance, to be able to stop the "natural" course of market forces. Thus in some middle-class communities in the Northeast, collective action has helped preservation achieve occasional triumphs over development. Here is how Nancy Herndon begins a report on "land trusts":

> In 1985, Dutchess County was still a partly rural block of New York State, just two hours north of Manhattan. Land prices were rising, population was growing, and suburbs were reaching out from the Hudson River.
> Then two large farms went up for sale.
> You might think you can guess what Dutchess County looks like now. But if you guess that the farmland has been divided into subdevelopments, guess again.
> Local citizens took advantage of an increasingly popular conservation tool to preserve the green hills of their county. They formed a land trust—a private, nonprofit organization dedicated to preserving open space.[11]

The land-trust movement allows people who are unhappy with the way their community is changing to act as a community to stop it. The "noncontractual bonds" that, as Polanyi said, the market has worked to subvert reassert themselves: "Local land trusts are a network of people who can talk to landowners," an environmental official is quoted as saying, "because they are friends and neighbors."[12]

In the tropical forests of Bolivia, another drama is being enacted of change versus preservation. There is a wealth of lumber in those forests, fine woods like mahogany, for which the world market is hungry. A recent news article describes the way economic forces are devouring these woods.[13] "Bolivia's fine woods are rapidly disappearing into the bandsaws of the country's 175 lumber companies." In some areas, "mahogany has been harvested to virtual extinction," so the companies look into other areas. Along with the trees, there are people. These people, Indians for whom the forests are their ancestral home, want their land preserved. As the leaders of one tribe, the Moxos, put it in a letter to a ministry of the

Bolivian government, "we have learned to take care and maintain the ecology because we know that it guarantees our existence."

These Indians may understand what the uphill nature of preservation requires. The Moxos, the article says, "are asking for 500,000 acres to be owned and managed collectively." They say that only this way can they "preserve and protect their part of the Chimanes forest as an integral ecosystem." But those who want the trees also apparently understand, and they oppose the Indians' demand for a single, integral territory.

Divide and conquer, a maxim that served the imperial Caesars well, serves also the market, with its preference for a world of social atoms.

DIVIDED WE FALL

Market forces corrode community. James Fallows, in *More Like Us*, his book in praise of American mobility, declares that "Our individualism *is* our source of community. We're all doing our best for ourselves, but as players in the same game."[14] But this is not community. Participating together in a competitive game as social atoms does not bind us together: it does not give us the ability to choose together those aspects of our destiny that we wish to have in common, and it does not give us a feeling of connectedness with our fellows.

Pseudocommunity is what the market gives us. The need for a sense of interpersonal connection remains, but it becomes another force to be *used* by the market, more than a force that people can draw upon to control the market. Roland Marchand, in *Advertising the American Dream*, illustrates how the market exploits the very need whose fulfillment it undermines. Need a friend? American corporations will provide one. Earlier in this century, some manufacturers of consumer goods found it useful to create fictitious personalities with whom the customers could have a "personal relationship." Hungry for human contact, the customers wrote letters seeking advice from these imaginary figures. The advertisers "were amazed," reports Marchand, "at the credulity of people and their eagerness to discuss their personal lives and daily problems with invented commercial characters."[15] In the 1930s, Marchand reports, Sears, Roebuck and Co., in its radio commercials, asked its rural listeners for an opportunity "to pull up a chair and talk things over with you folks." All they wanted "is just to . . . visit. Are you going to be home?"[16]

A multimillion-dollar friend visiting in the hope that we will send our money their way. Unreal community in the service of very real economic power.

Against this criticism of the market, as a force that breaks apart community ties, the argument might be made that the market system is but one institution among many. The market may attend to a very simplified scheme of our points of contact—buyers and sellers making exchanges—but there are other social institutions that serve other purposes. There are churches that provide valuable community bonds to tens of millions of Americans. An enormous diversity of other private associations also prosper in America. Surely, this argument goes, it is not necessary for any single institutional system, such as the market economy, to take care of everything.

This argument, however, neglects the enormous power of the market system to bring everything into its orbit, unless effective steps are taken to block it. In the traditional societies before the rise of the market, "man's economy, as a rule, is submerged in his social relationships."[17] The emergence of a market economy, and of an ideology that serves to pry away from economic activity the restraints those relationships might impose, unleashed a dynamism of extraordinary potency not only to create wealth but also to mold all dimensions of a society. As we will see, particularly in part 2, a free market is not just one institution among many. Unless adequately restrained, the market tends to sweep up all the other institutions, all other cultural forces, and reform them in its own image. Society becomes an adjunct to the market, Polanyi argues: "Instead of economy being embedded in social relations, social relations are embedded in the economic system."[18]

Our society does have other institutions and other forces and values at work besides those of the market. These are important. (If I did not believe in their capacity, I would have no reason to write a book such as this one.) But so powerful does the market system remain in our society that it is able, in considerable degree, to determine our destiny. Driven by the engine of its dynamism, the vehicle of our society still lacks an adequate countervailing force to act either for steering or braking.

What make news are those instances of people successfully bonding together—like the land trust in New York, or the Bolivian Indians trying to save their forest. It is the triumph of the Whole over the logic of atomism that is the "man bites dog" story, because the usual news—the unremarkable "dog bites man"—is that market forces have run their "natural" course. The evolution of market society tends to entail the continual erosion of the fabric that holds things together and the expansion of the realms of private powers of production and consumption in a deteriorating social and natural landscape.

In cases like the land trust organizations, the collectivity that forms is "private" in nature. A free association of individuals enter into a complex contractual arrangement to achieve an objective that would be frustrated by the more simple, bilateral transaction the market specializes in. Milton Friedman would approve. The market's game of contracts freely made is not restricted but rather is extended. It is like the way a conference call, though a good deal more difficult to arrange than most calls, is still a phone call. The land trust is free of a coercive dimension.

But arrangements that are complex and difficult to make will never be able to counterweigh the gravity of the countless arrangements between buyers and sellers that are far more readily made. This is one reason that a market society cannot correct against the inherent biases of the market except by using the coercive arm of government.

Free marketeers seem to regard government as if it were an alien force, some kind of occupying power. But government, in a democracy, is the only means a people has to make collective decisions that are not subject to veto by *any* of the parties whose cooperation is required. If we were all entirely in separate vehicles, we could each take our own course. But there are important ways that we are all in the same boat. Without collective decision embodied in enforceable law, people are not free to choose their destiny.

4

Reining In the Market

Simply showing that the market's system of liberty is imperfect, the free marketeers rightly point out, does not prove that there is any superior alternative. In particular, it does not prove that state action will make things better. A good many of the nightmares of modern history have grown out of misguided, utopian strivings for perfection. The ideologues of the market are not given to such utopianism. They see themselves as clear-eyed realists, and it is this realism that makes them celebrate the achievements of the market's system of liberty and caution us against summoning the state to regulate our affairs.

Before we look at other dimensions of the market's tunnel vision (in the next chapter, "Devouring the Earth"), we might examine more closely the comparative virtues and deficiencies of the market and its principal alternative force, the state.

FREE PEOPLE AND
UNCHECKED POWER SYSTEMS

A prominent modern philosopher of the market system, Friedrich von Hayek, differentiates between two kinds of systems. There are systems governed by conscious human choice (for example, by laws passed by governments) and systems that unfold on their own from the net effect of countless individual decisions (for example, by free exchanges). Hayek calls these systems "organizations" and "spontaneous orders," respectively. The ideologues of the free market prefer the second kind of system.

The free marketeers have sound reasons for their reservations about allowing governments to rule our daily lives. For one thing, governments can be foolish. Human affairs are far too complicated for even intelligent human beings to understand and to guide wisely. Thus, command economies tend to be notoriously inefficient. For another thing, governments tend to be corrupt to a greater or lesser extent. There is peril, therefore, in giving one part of society too much power over society as a whole, for that power may not be used for the good of the whole.

Setting aside for the moment these reasons for distrusting government, let us look at the other side of the argument: the celebration of the spontaneous order. The free marketeers' clear-eyed realism, it seems to me, fails them when they assess the virtues of ungoverned systems, such as their beloved market.

The market is not the only spontaneous order, but it is the central one in this libertarian philosophy. Indeed, one begins to suspect that the whole ideological argument in favor of spontaneous orders is constructed with the sole aim of justifying the market and protecting it from governmental meddling.

Both Friedman and Hayek attempt to utilize other spontaneous orders to cast a certain benign light on the unfettered market. The unfolding of the market is likened, for example, to the development of language. No authority created, say, the English language—nor would any have been competent to do so. The incredible richness of words and meanings and images is, rather, the product of hundreds of millions of people, freely interacting over generations, over centuries, creating language as they needed it, perpetuating what they found useful and appealing, letting go of what seemed stale or obsolete.

So it is also with the development of knowledge. Friedman writes that

within any discipline the growth of the subject matter strictly parallels the economic market place. Scholars cooperate with one another because they find it mutually beneficial . . . They exchange their findings . . . Cooperation is worldwide, just as in the economic market.[1]

Once one has recognized the benign nature of the unfolding of these spontaneous orders, one should evidently be persuaded that the market economy is likewise benign. Friedman sees it as "one of the ironies of the situation," for example, "that many scholars who have strongly favored governmental central planning of economic activity have recognized very clearly the danger to scientific progress that would be imposed by central government planning of science."[2]

But is there necessarily a contradiction? When it comes to dangers, is the unfettered unfolding of the market system really analogous to the free creation of language by an entire culture?

The analogy holds in part. The market displays a creativity and an openness that are part of the dynamism and the wonder of American society. The liberty of the marketplace is probably organically connected with the vitality of American culture in areas like popular music, jazz, movies—expressions of the human spirit that have been adopted, freely and happily, by peoples all over the world as contributions to their own consciousness. And the opportunities presented by the market have also stimulated American inventiveness in technology, generating the innovations that have transformed the twentieth century—automobiles, airplanes, television, computers, and so forth.

What is missing from this analogy between the market system and the development of language is the recognition that the market is a power system. The market can be free, that is, only at the expense of people's freedom to choose how they want their world to be.

The real ironies in this situation are very different from the one Friedman cites.

There is the irony that the kind of liberty the free marketeers espouse leads to a kind of bondage. The defenders of the unfettered market are quite aware of how a ruler with the power to compel others to do his bidding strangles human free dom. But there are other ways to be unfree than to be subject to the will of another person.

And there is the irony that the sum of free human choices can create a world no one would choose. Our actions, even if uncoerced, are not necessarily free. Our actions take place in a context, and that context can channel how we choose to act. A system that subsidizes transactions and imposes a taxing burden on the web of our interconnectedness directs our energies and resources in directions of its choosing, rather than of our own. A system that is blind to the values of the natural world will inevitably lead people to devour the earth.

Freed of the yoke of another person's power, we can be ruled by a system as indifferent to us, in its way, as a tyrant. Escaping from the limited horizons of any human judgment, we can back our way into a landscape that no human being need have judged desirable.

A system can, at a microscopic level, be fueled by free human choice even when, in the larger picture of the society's development, that freedom of choice is just an illusion.

A MILL THAT GRINDS SLOW BUT FINE

How serious is the problem with the market? What proportion of the market's performance can be said to be as an instrument to facilitate human choices, and to what extent is the market driving our destiny according to a logic that is not our own?

The dangers of the market's power become fully visible only when we investigate the unfolding of the system *over time.* If we look only at one round of play, as it were, the market's bias might seem—in the phrase used earlier—just small change. Perhaps the market gives us $.98 on the dollar in each play of the game. But over many rounds of play, that $.98 has a cumulative, multiplicative effect. As human energies are channeled in not quite the right direction, as power flows toward those who embody the market's values and away from those espousing values to which the market is blind, as the landscape is shaped according to the dictates of atomism, each set of decisions takes a world already askew and bends it still further in that direction. $.98 × $.98 × $.98 × $.98 . . . leads over time to a product much less than 1.

Entrusting our destiny to the market is like playing roulette over a long stretch. Those two green spaces on the wheel mean that, on average, for every dollar we put on the table, we'll pick up less than a dollar on each turn of the wheel. Eventually, all we are left with is small change—the rest belongs to the house.

My earlier book on the evolution of civilization, *The Parable of the Tribes*, showed how a process of selection could exert decisive influence on how a system develops over time. Its power can be determining even if the selective process works slowly, so long as the criteria for selection are consistent. The market's warping of the evolution of market society is of this nature. In part 2, "We Are Driven: The Market as the Engine of Change in America," I will suggest the outlines of how the market's distortions have shaped the development of American society.

LANDSCAPE ROULETTE

For the present discussion let us consider what the contemporary American landscape shows about what happens when we play for a couple of centuries on the market's roulette wheel.

There are still places in America where one can get a sense of the American town of the eighteenth century. In Connecticut or in Maryland, one can walk out into a little village that still bears the basic contours of its origin—with its steepled church, its town square with tree-lined walkways across the grass and faced by little shops and homes. Few of us live in such places, but most of us have visited them. And we like to visit them, not just for their antiquarian interest, but because these places have a centering and healing feeling about them. The landscape is coherent, and the human figure fits well into their scale.

Around many such old villages, and even more so in the cities of the American West where less has stood in the market's way, the landscape has been carved according to very different principles. When I moved from the mountains of Arizona into the burgeoning city of Tucson, I saw Speedway Avenue there as typical. It is a wide thoroughfare with a jumble of commercial enterprises along both sides. I used to hear people in the region complaining about the Los Angelization of the Southwest, as though the sprawling and ugly pattern of development were being imported from the great metropolis of the region. But it was not a matter of importation, nor was it a matter of one place influencing another. The same forces that were molding the other cities and towns of the region had made Los Angeles, too, their creature.

What makes this region such a manifest exhibit of the sculpting power of market forces on a landscape is that the cities here—Phoenix, Tucson, Los Angeles—hardly existed before the full-grown market system, with its irresistible twentieth-century momentum, swept them up. The market can set its template of values down upon the land barely impeded by other considerations.*

The suburbs of America—even around those towns whose core was formed by other values, in other times—show a kindred kind of landscape, as land that once was farmed proves a malleable clay in the hands of the market system.

There is a little spot on the outskirts of Baltimore where one gets a glimpse of an earlier era. At the center of this grassy area, where a creek wends its way, is a stone building that once was a mill and that now houses a couple of shops and some offices. Walking into this place—if one tunes out the sounds on the nearby freeway and looks away from the adjoining parking lot—gives a poignant sense of a world lost, a world with a different pace, with a different balance between the human and the natural and perhaps a greater solidity at its core.

Perhaps this sense of loss is a fantasy. Perhaps it is simply a romanticization of the past, entailing a failure to recognize how much better things are now and to give proper respect to the achievements of the world that now rings this mill with its heavy traffic and commercial enterprises.

Perhaps. But how many Americans feel good when they contemplate what has happened to the landscape around them even in their own lifetime?

It is thirty-five years since I was in East Lansing, Michigan, the place where as a boy I first roamed the earth, finding

---

*Sure, there are zoning laws; the market is not the only force that governs the evolving shape of society. But the fragmentation of these landscapes, and the predominance of purely economic considerations in the use of the land, are signs of the comparative power of the collective versus the atomistic dimensions of "mixed" economy.

adventures in secret and wonderful places. I am afraid to go back there to see what has become of the place. (The most special spot for me in East Lansing was a pine forest that I heard was cleared years ago to make room for construction.)

What would we learn if we went around to all Americans who have lived for more than twenty-five years in the same place, asking them which they prefer: the landscape of today or the landscape of the earlier time? One does not suppose that a majority would choose today to yesterday. Further, it is probably less change per se than the *nature* of the change that discomfits us. A person returning to the place of his or her childhood would probably not lament upon discovering that, "where there was once a shopping center, there now stands a wooded glen."

Maybe this fragmentation of our landscape is the price we have to pay for other amenities, for being so well furnished with goods for our lives at home. Indeed, as much as it is my impression that most people prefer the "world" around them as it was decades ago, it is also my impression that these same people would choose their "home" of today over their own dwelling as it was in the past.

Maybe the benefit is worth the cost. But who can say? Who ever had a chance to choose? The market proceeds without letting us weigh the choice. Acting separately, we work to improve our separate lot, while we undermine our common environment. And the market facilitates only our acting separately.

So long as our destiny is created in the market system, the destiny we get is not necessarily one we would choose.

EVILS LESSER AND GREATER

When asked about democracy, Winston Churchill declared that it was the worst form of government, except for all the alternatives. Market society may be defended the same way. Even if the market is seriously flawed, the intrusion into the economy of the chief alternative force—the state—may only make things worse. Even if the market ideologues see their favorite system through rose-colored glasses, their "realistic" suspicion of government still warrants serious consideration.

Government has two major faults: incompetence and corruption. Incompetence refers to the inability of decision makers to *know* what is best for society. Corruption refers to the propensity of decision makers *not to do* what is best for society as a whole, even when they know it.

The incompetence of government reflects but a particular instance of the general limits of human intelligence. William Graham Sumner argued a century ago that people's knowledge is so inadequate that efforts to use political means to solve our problems usually do more harm than good.[3] Many of his fellow free marketeers of our time would still agree.

The failure of command economies, partisans of the market observe, demonstrates how the complexities of a modern society are far over the heads of human beings (even if they are aided by computers). The argument being made here, however, is not to replace the market but to use the government to fill in its blind spots. To those skeptical of government, even this may seem too ambitious. It could rightly be argued that it is often difficult to determine what the appropriate price should be, that is, how high a tax must be to reflect a cost or how much subsidy would correspond to a given benefit.

Although this is true, it hardly justifies continuing to leave pricing entirely to the market. Letting the market set prices has the appeal of simplicity, since impersonal forces rather than political decisions resolve the issue. But if we know the market's price is wrong, why treat it as though it were somehow sanctified? Our best guess may not be perfect, but it is surely likely to be better than no guess at all.* Incomplete knowledge should not be equated with complete incompetence.

Human intelligence, exercised through government, is surely capable of improving upon the information with which the market, with its identifiable blind spots, does its work. Taxes and subsidies do not replace the market; rather, they supplement it. The market with the lacunae in its vision

---

*The legitimacy imputed to the market price, and the general suspicion of taxation and subsidization, is one illustration of the market ideology's subtle claim on our thinking. The forces of the market, acting impersonally, are assumed to have validity even by many who disparage the ideology of the market, as though the invisible hand were God's.

corrected, is still in place to exercise its virtues with the adjusted information.*

More serious than the problem of incompetence is that of corruption. There are no more dangerous illusions, say the defenders of the market, than illusions about human nature. Utopians harbor such illusions and, believing people can be trusted with power, have tried to create heaven on earth. More often, the results are like hell.

To the ideologues of the market, the "realistic" assumption that people are fundamentally selfish is grounds both to celebrate the market and to suspect the state.

It was part of the original advertisement for the emerging market system, in Mandeville's famous *Fable of the Bees*, that the economy could transmute private vices into public virtues. The idea that private vice should be assumed and condoned caused a great outrage when Mandeville gave it voice in the late seventeenth century, violating as it did the sense of moral aspiration of the traditional worldview of our civilization. But by the following century, Adam Smith could appeal to a world of rationality and realism in assuming the selfishness of human behavior. "It is not from the benevolence of the butcher, the brewer, or the baker, that we can expect our dinner, but from their regard to their own self interest. We address ourselves not to their humanity but to their self-love, and never talk to them of our own necessities but of their advantages."[4] A paramount virtue of the market system of which Adam Smith was the greatest advocate was that it assumed no virtue in the human parts of that system.

But just as the market is based on liberty, the state is based on coercion. The selfishness that is fuel for the market, where each is supposed to look out only for himself, will inevitably corrode and corrupt the state, where a few are supposed to look about for the welfare of many. Power will be used corruptly, according to this realist analysis, not because power

---

*The nitty-gritty work of designing a process to assess what taxes and subsidies are necessary to correct the market, while very important, lies outside the scope of this work. My purpose, rather, is to fortify the principle that market prices are seriously deficient and that, as the consequences of these deficiencies are deleterious to social health and justice, they must be corrected by some appropriate political means.

corrupts, but because people are inherently too corrupt to be trusted to take care of anyone's interests but their own.

The market may be flawed, but putting economic power into the hands of the state will make things worse. "The combination of economic and political power in the same hands," Milton Friedman tells us, "is a sure recipe for tyranny."[5] Michael Novak praises the founders of democratic capitalism in America for their wisdom in separating the economy from the state: "They did not fear unrestrained economic power as much as they feared political tyranny."[6]

John Locke once punctured Thomas Hobbes's argument for an absolute ruler by saying that people would be foolish to take care "to avoid what mischiefs may be done them by polecats or foxes" while thinking it safety "to be devoured by lions."[7] To the free-market liberals, turning to the state to regulate the market is like creating a Hobbesean lion to devour us.

CAN WE TAKE CARE OF US?

Is it indeed reality to which the free marketeer's realism leads us? Is government power inherently dangerous to those who live under its coercive rule?

There are two levels in the realist's argument. First, there is the premise about human nature. Second, there is the argument from that premise to the conclusion that political power will be used corruptly.

The assumption about human nature—that it is inherently selfish--I will not challenge at length here, but defer that discussion to a subsequent book, *Nothing Sacred*. There I will try to show the ways in which the market's assumptions tend to be self-fulfilling. By setting up a system—both economic and political—predicated on human selfishness, we not only recognize but also encourage a selfish element in our nature, and thereby fray the moral fabric of our society. The capacity for altruistic feelings and actions—which are also a fundamental element of human nature—tends to atrophy under the influence of such a system.

But for now, let us assume the validity of that assumption and assume also what is doubtless true, that if we set up a system that *depends* on altruism to prevent corruption and tyranny, we are taking a big, and probably a losing, gamble.

But even if we assume self-interest to be at the heart of human motivation, must we jump from this premise to the "realist" conclusion that state power will be wielded corruptly and must be kept from intruding into our affairs?

As mentioned earlier, the free-market ideologues tend to speak of the government as though it were an alien force in our midst. But when we speak here of increasing the political input into the functioning of our economy, we are not talking about some Hobbesean absolute ruler. We are not talking, as in the Aesop's fable, about us frogs installing a stork to act as king over us. We are speaking, rather, about a democratic polity, a system of government presumably of, by, and for the people. In such a political system, how much sense does it make to warn against allowing *them* to intrude into *our* lives?

In our democratic system, it is supposed to be possible for people to work collectively through the agency of government to achieve their ends. We need not posit altruistic motives to imagine such a government acting justly instead of corruptly. For some of our own interests can be served only if we act in concert with the other members of our polity to make and enforce laws.

Government may still be unjust and corrupt, the advocates the free market will argue. There are two main gaps in the logic of government of, by, and for the people. First, even if a government is democratic, the will of the majority, backed by the coercive power of the state, can unjustly violate the rights of a nonconsenting minority. In such an instance, the majority, in the pursuit of its interest, makes state power corrupt. Second, in a complex society, it is never exactly we who rule but rather our ostensible representatives. Calling them our representatives only obscures the fact that they are separate individuals with self-interests of their own, interests not identical with those of the people they are supposed to represent. So, we are back to a "they" who wield power over "us."

GOVERNMENT LTD.

Concerning the first problem—which we might call "the tyranny of the majority"—the answer is that our democracy is a system not only of majority rule but also of "limited government." In limited government, there are built-in constitutional limits to the scope of state power. Beyond those limits, individuals are to enjoy their liberty as autonomous human beings. Exactly! free market ideologues would reply. Economic liberty should be part of that protected realm of autonomy beyond the limits set to the sphere of government action.

Is state intervention into the economy, of the kind recommended here, an unjust violation of the liberty of individuals? On the question of the limits to the proper role of government, Milton Friedman quotes approvingly a passage from Adam Smith. "According to the system of natural liberty," wrote Smith, the duties of the sovereign are quite limited. After protecting society in general from outside attack, the government has, "secondly, the duty of protecting, as far as possible, every member of society from the injustice or oppression of every other member of it."[8] Friedman regards both of these duties as "clear and straightforward," representing the second with the example of the armed robber from whose "coercion" we must be protected if we are to be truly free to choose. But is it really as straightforward as Friedman suggests to protect us from being the victims of "injustices" committed by our fellow citizens?

As we saw in the previous chapter, "Missing Our Connections," the exercise of what the free marketeer regards as liberty inflicts injustice on innocent parties. The market is a system that is more than fair to transactors and unfair to bystanders. As the citizens of Taylor, New York, discovered when they confronted the prospect of a modern nuclear facility in their midst, being accosted by an armed robber is not the only way one can have something of value taken away without one's consent.

Limited government is an essential idea, an invaluable barrier to tyrannical state power. But even the philosophy of liberty justifies the use of law and state power to correct the pervasive problem of the market we have been exploring.*

Even if *we* have a right to limit the economic liberty of some to protect the rights of many or of society as a whole, the

---

*In constitutional terms, the issue was largely settled in the United States, during the decades from the 1870s through the 1930s, settled in favor of allowing government intervention. The constitutional clause authorizing congress to regulate "interstate commerce" was made into a gateway to a vast network of power.

questions remains, will we be *able* to? Here we come up against that second challenge, of assuring that power in our representative democracy is wielded in accordance with the needs and interests of the people.

The view of government that corresponds to the market economy is pluralism, in which everyone seeks to achieve his self-serving purpose in the arena of politics. The whole Madisonian edifice of the American political system was based less on the hope that people would pursue justice than on the expectation that enough factions pursuing their own favorite form of injustice could prevent that most dangerous form of injustice, tyranny. Our politics, consequently, have been blessedly free of lions to devour us but rife with the polecats and foxes of special interests.

The corruption in our political system has two principal dimensions. One is *the reign of special interests*. The other is plutocracy, or *the dominance of the rich*. The two, of course, are related. But it makes sense to examine them separately, because they represent two different kinds of challenge to the task of creating a just democracy.

CORRUPTIONS OF PLURALISM

Some think of "special interests" as being rich corporate powers, which of course they often are. But on the subject of education, school teachers are a special interest, and on the question of national forest policy, the people who work in sawmills are a special interest.

Special interests exert undo influence in our democracy because, in a society as complex as ours, people simply cannot stay informed about all the issues and all the developments in the formulation and execution of thousands of government policies. People's ignorance is not, however, spread uniformly: about those few issues that impinge most powerfully on their own interests, they will know most. On these, too, they will be most intensely involved and best organized. Those in the government who make decisions quickly learn that the political rewards and punishments for themselves are determined not by how well they serve the interests of society as a whole on *all* the issues but by how well they serve the interests of those most intensely involved on *each* of the issues before them.

Even if power were evenly distributed among all the people, therefore, the uneven attention of groups would mean a pattern of public policy permeated with this pluralistic form of corruption. We end up, for example, with education policies that serve the education establishment at the expense of the public interest. Credentialing laws come to mind, not only in education but in a diverse range of other fields as well. In his discussion of "The Confucianization of America," James Fallows shows how professional associations get laws passed that protect their own control of their market, under the guise of protecting the public.[9] Milton Friedman makes one of his most telling arguments against government intrusion into the market as he relates the story of how the Interstate Commerce Commission became the instrument of the railway industry it was supposed to regulate. As the attorney general of the United States put it in a letter to a railroad tycoon in the 1890s, "The part of wisdom is not to destroy the Commission, but to utilize it."[10]

Thus it is that the picture of government regulation of markets and industries finds all too little of the image of the blindfolded woman with the scales and all too much imagery of foxes guarding chicken coops and of revolving doors.

With this pluralistic corruption, every group may "win" on its own special concern, but society as a whole inevitably loses. We vote for the congressman who gave us a hundred dollars on our big issue, even though he took a dollar away from us on each of two hundred other issues. For who notices one dollar? But we'll throw out of office the congressman who refused, in the name of the public interest, to give us the hundred dollars we wanted, even if he steadfastly refused all the others also and saved us two hundred dollars.

The amount we lose on all the "little" issues adds up to more than we win on our own big issue because, in the nature of human society, the whole is greater than the sum of parts. A thousand policies contrary to the needs of society as a whole lead to less, ultimately, for everyone.

What we have here, of course, is a perfect analogue of the corruption of the market itself. We benefit as transactors, and we are injured as bystanders. A system that cannot attend to its wholeness is doomed to deteriorate. The whole that is ignored will become less than the sum of its contending parts.

Is there a solution to this problem of pluralistic corruption? Of course, the better educated and better informed the citizens are, the more everyone will feel involved in the diverse issues that do have an impact on them and their world. (An article in a recent *Christian Science Monitor*, about the growing pressure on the Forest Service to be less of an instrument of lumber interests, has a caption reading: "The people of Cincinnati own the Willamette National Forest just as much as the people of Sweet Home, Ore."[11]) The educational system, the news media, and public interest groups have a vital role to play in helping to expand and intensify our vision as citizens beyond the tunnel vision of our own "special" interests.

More is needed, however. I have a modest proposal to offer. The problem might be ameliorated by establishing a special agency or commission of the government for this precise purpose. This "Commission for the Public Interest" would have as its sole responsibility to monitor government activity and to raise the alarm whenever it perceived that some part of the government had done or was about do something "conspicuously contrary to the interests of the nation as a whole." This Commission would have no powers save a moral power. (Perhaps the other branches and agencies of the U.S. government could be required, by law, to at least give public response to those announcements, made by the Commission, in which they are named.) This moral authority would derive in part from the nature of its mandate. The weight of its pronouncements would be further enhanced by insuring that the manner of its composition placed it, as much as possible, above politics.

If we look at those bodies that are least subject to special interests—the Supreme Court, the Federal Reserve Board, blue-ribbon presidential commissions—we get some clues about how the integrity of a "Commission for the Public Interest" might best be assured. Some possible measures could be: nomination by one branch and confirmation by another; long terms in office; appointment of people who are notable not for their political ambition but for their integrity and quality.

The press already serves, of course, as a warning system. But an official body—with this purpose and with high prestige—might help the press make abuses of the public interest so visible that the glare of public scrutiny would be politically unbearable. Officials might find that their own political self-interest requires no longer that they minister to the narrow interests but that they serve the public good.

GOVERNMENT FOR SALE

It is not just in the marketplace that dollars vote.

The premise of democracy is that each person is of equal intrinsic worth and that each person is entitled to an equal role in the determination of the collective destiny of the nation. But if wealth is unequally distributed among the members of a democratic society, and if wealth can purchase political power, the democracy will be corrupted. As in George Orwell's *Animal Farm*, some will be more equal than others.

The tales of how our democracy has been corrupted into plutocracy—of how it has become a government of the people, for the rich and by the rich—can be proliferated endlessly. One rather fascinating piece of this all-too-panoramic picture is described in Ivan Preston's book *The Great American Blow-Up: Puffery in Advertising and Selling*. Preston gives an account of centuries of legal evolution—from the medieval period in Europe through contemporary market society—concerning the rights and obligations of buyers and sellers. What he shows is the rise of "sellerism," the progressive erosion of the protection of buyers from the deceptions of sellers (an erosion reversed in some respects in our era).

Law in the Middle Ages held the seller responsible for deceptions both of commission and omission (telling untruth and withholding truth). But as "power in human affairs was transferred in great quantity to industrialists and traders,"[12] the age of *caveat emptor* (let the buyer beware) emerged. In the service of the wealthy class, the law applied a lower standard of good faith in the marketplace than in other areas of human affairs.[13] Preston goes on to describe the fundamentally deceptive nature of much advertising, deception that is both profitable and legally protected in American today.

Nowadays, it is not only their products that powerful corporations sell us with their advertising. In recent years, our great and wealthy corporations have used their riches to persuade the public of an image of themselves as responsible corporate citizens whose activities serve the needs of the nation. Dow Chemical Company's image was tarnished two decades ago because of pictures on our TV screens of idealistic young people protesting the company's role in supplying U.S. forces in Vietnam with napalm. Now the company spends millions to put before our eyes pictures of young idealists finding in Dow the means to heal the sick and feed the poor. "Dow helps you do great things," their song proclaims. In his book *Advertising, Politics and American Culture*, Philip Gold provides evidence that propaganda of this sort works.[14]

What is at stake in this ability of money to buy TV time to sell images is not just commerce and not just corporate images. It is also politics. People still glowing from images of Weyerhauser as "The Tree-Growing Company," from watching all those seedlings being lovingly planted into grassy ground, are less likely to mobilize from alarm at the way our national forests are being clear-cut, often by companies who, to get that right, are not even required to pay as much as it costs the government to construct the logging roads.

Just as money can create an image of idealistic youth grateful to Dow Chemical rather than outraged at it, so too will corporate wealth bankroll the Second Coming of Exxon. One can just imagine what Exxon will be telling us in a few years, when the image begins to fade in our memories of the oil-drenched carcasses of otters off the coast of Alaska. There we see the Exxon logo floating above the sparkling waters. A voice comes in to say, "At Exxon, we have always taught the rule: Do unto otters as we would have otters do unto us."

Exxon knows we do more than just buy gas. We also vote. And money buys the ability to mold the consciousness of voters. Because of the power of money, Exxon knows, our democracy is less likely to take the steps necessary to protect our collective interests against the giant oil company's unjust and irresponsible pursuit of profits.

Money enters into our politics in yet another, still more obvious way: through election campaigns. One need only pay the most superficial attention to the dynamics of our political process to recognize the truth of the famous saying that money is the mother's milk of politics.[15] So-and-so, we hear, has not decided whether or not to run—it depends on whether he can raise $x million dollars for his campaign. The top-ranking Democrat and Republican on the such-and-such committee of Congress both received so-many dollars in contribution to their campaigns from the such-and-such industry, the laws for which are drawn up by their committee. The victorious Senator You-know-who outspent his opponent three to one.

On election day, the patriot in us likes to hear the pundits say "The people have spoken." Gloriously, this is, in part, true. But in the back of our minds, we also recognize in the electoral process a validation of that fundamental idea of American culture: money talks.

The government, as it is presently constituted, thus appears as a rather imperfect instrument to rein in the excesses of the market system. For to the extent that those who have money can make the government the instrument of their purposes, and to the extent that the market system determines what kind of people it is who get the most money, then it is the market itself that governs the government.

Of course, it is not money alone that talks in our system. We have a cross between plutocracy and democracy. But it seems clear that the translatability of money into political power is the greatest source of corruption in our body politic.

What does this imply for the argument, made in this work, that our politics must do more to circumscribe the power of our economic system?

It does *not* imply, in my view, the conclusion that Friedman draws: that we are more likely to get justice for the weak from the market than from our government.

Friedman believes, for example, that it is the rich more than the poor who are the beneficiaries of environmental protection: the poor would "benefit most from the lower cost of things that would result from permitting more pollution."[16] This does not sound like the world I live in. I watch the news and I see an article about a poor neighborhood in Baltimore, where cancer and other deadly diseases are occurring in unusually high frequencies, evidently as a consequence of toxic chemicals that local industries spew into the air and dump onto the ground and into the water. The owners of the industries do not live in neighborhoods adjoined by chemical dumps. My father, an economist, once explained to me as we explored some of the nicest neighborhoods of the Twin Cities, west of Minneapolis, that it is typical to find the wealthiest residents of American cities living to the west of the cities, since in most areas the winds come from the West. They make their money in the cities, in other words, and head home to the west where they won't have to breathe the city's fumes.

A few years ago I had the pleasure of being invited to speak at a conference that was being held at the beautiful estate of the Harriman family in upstate New York. The house was, of course, quite fine. But what was really wonderful were the extensive grounds in which the house was situated. This estate helped me grasp one of the great advantages of wealth in our society. In proportion to one's wealth, one can afford to create around oneself a microcosm that has been purged of the ugliness, chaos and poisons that may be ascendant in the macrocosm of society. The middle class home achieves this to a degree. Those whom the market rewards most abundantly—like the Harrimans—can escape even further from the mess the market also creates.

The great Harriman fortune was made a century ago in the railroad industry, as the iron horse was unleashed to extend and bind together the growing empire of industrial capitalism in America. The locomotive figures in the marvelous opening metaphor of Leo Marx's book *The Machine in the Garden*. Marx traces the motif, in nineteenth-century American literature, of the train as the harsh intruder into the serene and bucolic landscape, as the "engine of progress" whose unwelcome noise "arouses a sense of dislocation, conflict, and anxiety."[17] Here, even today, on the Harriman estate, the sound of motors could not be heard. Footpaths wended their way along a sylvan landscape where, if one were still, one might see deer grazing. On the pond created by a little dam on the brook, majestic swans were swimming. The Harrimans commanded enough money to create a little world in which one could forget the noise and smoke from which that same money came.

It is not the rich, therefore, who stand to benefit most from environmental legislation.

In addition, the market's bias in favor of transactors has clear implications for the question of justice between rich and poor. Even if we assume that the market's distribution of income is just, as soon as people start to spend their money in an uncorrected market, the poorer people will begin to suffer from injustice that favors the rich. Whenever we spend, we enjoy the benefits of the market's subsidization of consumption and its disregard of third-party effects. The poor, for want of money, get to play the role of transactor less often than the rich and are compelled to play the role of bystander more often.

92 ♦ Tunnel Vision: A Radical Critique of the Market

They are therefore more often the victims than the beneficiaries of the market's inherent injustice. Abandoned simply to the market system, therefore, the poor have little hope of justice. Through the political process of our partial democracy, there is at least the hope, the possibility, that those who are weak in dollars can make themselves powerful enough in votes to enforce justice. American history of the past century shows this in abundance. Despite the "socialism for the rich" that we often see—in the railroads, in agribusiness, in import quotas for various goods—the overall effect of government action has been to protect the vulnerable more than the mighty.

THE POSSIBILITY OF DEMOCRACY

Even if our corrupt government is better than no government, it is still far from good enough.

Embedded in the critique of government is the assumption that the problems we see now are inherent and inescapable. (The "reality" of the realists is always grim.) Milton Friedman says that those who favor an FDA without its present faults are like someone who declares, "I would like to have a cat provided it barked."[18] The problems are simply the nature of the beast.

The deficiencies of the market we have explored *are* indeed the nature of the beast. Within the market system alone, it is impossible to find the means to rectify them. But with the problems of our democracy, such as its corruption into plutocracy, there is no such inherent inevitability.

If we "chickens" who are citizens of the country could ourselves become more clever, we would not be so vulnerable to the foxes who guard our coop (or co-op). But our becoming better informed and organized, less gullible and manipulable, would assuredly be a long-term process, and recent trends in American education and politics give scant assurances that we are even moving in the right direction.

With respect to institutional structure, there is surely no reason to assume that we have achieved the limits of attainable democracy. There are public interest groups like Common Cause that continue to work to strengthen the integrity of our political process, to insulate our democracy from the corrupting effects of money talking. In this process of reforming government to make it more representative of the public interest, we have only begun to try the promising ideas that have been formulated and proposed. So long as this remains so, we cannot know that a government uncorrupted by money is like a cat that barks.

We need first to commit ourselves to the idea that our polity is premised on equal division of political power among the citizens. One person, one vote—this should be the central principle of political power and justice in America, even as refracted through the lens of our representative system. So long as inequalities of political power issue from inequalities of wealth, our system is violating its citizens' constitutional right to "equal protection of the laws." (How can we be equally protected by laws that we have an unequal voice in formulating?) Justice does not require equality in other arenas of life, but if it is missing in the area of political power, there can be no justice of any other kind. (How can the results of any of the other games of our society be fair if the rules of political power, by which the rules of the other games are made, are not fair?)

The protection of that equality, therefore, should be our first priority, even if that requires some sacrifice of other important rights. Two general principles would advance our democracy.

First, access to political speech must not be apportioned according to wealth, at least in the publicly licensed broadcast media. If a corporation like Exxon buys time to broadcast a message with political import, there should be equal time provided (perhaps at Exxon's expense) for an opposing point of view. Defining political speech might not be easy, but it should not be impossible. Our legal system continually solves definitional problems of this nature. The right of free speech is sacred, but there is no reason it should be defined in a way that subverts one of its primary purposes: the protection of democracy. Exxon has the right to be heard. But let us hear also the voices of other people, though they lack Exxon's billions, on the same policy-related questions.

Second, our political campaigns need to be completely insulated from private wealth. This is not easily achieved, but this, too, should be possible. Perhaps it could be achieved with some combination of free air time, public financing in proportion to registered voters signing petitions, and automatic public financing. In any event, it is incompatible with the principle of democracy for a candidate to have an advantage over an opponent because the supporters of the one are rich and those of the other are poor.

Let us not despair of the possibility of democracy. We have yet fully to try it.

MASTERS OF OUR DESTINY

What is at stake is whether we can create a future of our choosing or whether our destiny will be governed by a machine beyond our control. Though we may see some human beings in positions of power, if it is the dynamic of the system that selects its own governors, then it is the system that governs itself.* Plutocracy is defined as rule by the wealthy. But more fundamentally it is rule by money. And underlying that is rule by the system that apportions wealth.

The market system has its own criteria according to which money is distributed. As we have seen, those criteria only partly overlap with the entire spectrum of what is of value to us human beings. To allow our future to be shaped by such a system is to assure that the future we get is different from the one we would choose.

To the extent that we can act only as atomistic pieces of the market machine—and of the pluralistic polity that is the market's political analogue—we as people cannot be masters of our fortunes.

There is indeed a wonderful complexity and creativity in the "spontaneous order" of the market system. But that order is not altogether "spontaneous" in the sense of human spontaneity, which is a sign of the vitality and freedom of the human spirit. It is spontaneous in that it is unchosen by its human members. But central, and not altogether desirable, characteristics of that order are foreordained by the nature of the machine.

Willingly to turn over to a mechanical system the question of how our living culture will develop is a form of idolatry. Not impersonal forces, but their only real alternative—collective human decision—should govern our destiny.

---

*On this point, see the section in *The Parable of the Tribes* entitled "Choosing the Choosers: The Historymakers," pp. 60–63.

5

Devouring the Earth

We have already seen that there are important categories of value to which the market, by itself, is incapable of attending. Most especially, the market cannot take into account the web of our interdependency, all those ways that our individual activity has an impact on others even when we are not dealing with them directly. This selective inattention breaks apart the wholeness of a human community. The market thus exerts a disintegrative force that can be rectified only through the agency of collective decisions, in particular through what free marketeers (and to a degree, members of liberal society generally) regard as intrusions into the realm of economic liberty. Intrusions they may be, but unless collective action—for example, with a legally instituted system of corrective taxes and subsidies—supplants this tunnel vision of the market, the market system will, over time, end up giving people an extremely skewed mix of goods. The atomistic system gives us a mixture of a superfluous private abundance and an impoverishment of the public realm. Indeed this distorted mix is in some important ways already quite evident in American society.

It is time to explore another, somewhat related domain of value to which the market is blind. This is the domain of nature. The market, by its nature, treats the earth like dirt.

WORTH WHAT WE PAID FOR IT

The value of what nature supplies is systematically undervalued because, at bottom, no one has to be paid for it. It took the evolving systems of life on earth some three and a half billion years to produce the living systems over which human beings began exercising an unprecedented control some ten thousand years ago. This was when human societies initiated the domestication of plants and animals. With the emergence of modern market societies during the past three centuries or so, the empire of human domination over nature has grown exponentially. In a system predicated on the notion that something is worth what you have to pay for it, what the industrial capitalist could pillage from nature could be regarded and treated as though it were of no worth. What from a more enlightened point of view would be conceived as invaluable capital that we have inherited from our Mother, the earth, are treated in a market system as "free goods" and worth only what we paid for them.*

The assumption that the value of natural resources can be disregarded is embedded in some of the philosophic foundations of liberal society. That labor of theory of value which, as I noted in the introduction, proved so useful to Marx, was put to rather different uses a century earlier by John Locke. In the chapter "Of Property," in his famous essay *Civil Government*, Locke explores the relation between labor and land, asserting

---

*I say "more enlightened," but I would say that even that perspective is not very enlightened. To regard nature even as invaluable capital is to misapprehend our own place in the order of things. It is to fail to recognize that other creatures also have rights, even if they do not have the capacity to compel us to recognize them. It is to be unaware of the wholeness of living systems.

But for the purposes of this critique, the rather narrow and self-serving assumptions of our specio-centric economics will be granted—that nature exists for our use, and that our use of the natural world for our self-interest should be restrained only to the extent of being enlightened.

two principal points: first, that it is labor that creates value in the goods of nature (some 99 percent of that value he figures); and, second, that as a man owns his labor, whatever in nature to which he applies his labor becomes his property.

Locke clearly does not intend to rationalize the pillaging of the planet, but even against his intention his logic can serve that purpose.

His view of the right relation between human property and the natural world refers continually to two suppositions to define and limit what is justified. First, he would confine the right of ownership to what a person is able to enjoy: "As much as anyone can make use of to any advantage before it spoils, so much he may by his labor fix a property in; whatever is beyond this, is more than his share and belongs to others."[1] But he is undone by his second presupposition—the assumption of abundance: he speaks always of a situation "where there is enough, and as good left in common for others."[2] He speaks always of that time when there was, of the goods of nature, no scarcity, of a world that remains in large measure an "America," that is, so vast in relation to the population that scarcity is no issue. "For he that leaves as much as another can make use of, does as good as take nothing at all."[3]

But the logic of Lockean property leads beyond the limits of what a person can use. If a man owns whatever he can join his labor unto, because he owns his labor, then by the same logic he can own all to which he can apply the capital he owns. The limits of personal use and enjoyment form a flimsy barrier to block the imperial logic of property. Additionally, the inevitable expansion of empires of property, along with the growth over time of populations, mean that an argument based on the supposition that there will always be "enough and as good left" must ultimately fail to recognize the true economic value of nature.

In a world where resources were truly infinite, the Lockean argument that it is labor that gives value, and therefore also rights, to nature's bounty, might work (in the strictly economic terms of this discussion). But the world is finite and does not remain "America" for long. Locke's calculus of value cannot guide an economic system in such a world; over time it can rationalize the market's insensitivity to the essential importance of the natural world in which we are embedded.

AFTER THE HORSE IS GONE

The defenders of the market, in their steadfast refusal to recognize the market's severe disability in this area, maintain that the price of resources is not a problem because, when a desired resource becomes scarce, its price will rise. ("As a much-used resource becomes scarce," writes market apologist Michael Novak, "it tends to become more costly [like oil]."[4]) But the market's response to scarcity is an inadequate solution to the problem—a matter of too little too late.

Lateness is a frequent failing of the market, when things change. If the future brings a new set of needs different from those of the present—even if those needs can be foreseen—the future gets short shrift. As economist Tibor Scitovsky writes, "market prices . . . reflect the economic situation as it is and not as it will be."[5] Nowhere is the truth of this more evident than in the market's undervaluation of natural resources that are not yet scarce.

In the 1950s, the U.S. took pride in its energy independence. While other industrial economies depended on imported oil and used taxes to discourage its consumption, the American economy grew into a form that depended upon the assumption of cheap energy. Treating oil as though it were worth little more than it cost to pump the oil out of the ground, the U.S. employed a policy that two decades later, during the time of oil shortage, was dubbed "Drain America First." Once the time comes that oil is scarce or difficult to obtain it will be too late to undo the profligate spending of what (like Lockean land) has always been in finite supply.

In the U.S. now, we are beginning to approach another threshold of the awareness of scarcity—in the area of landfill space for our throwaway society. Until the space has virtually run out, we treat it as though it were infinite. The price begins to rise, in the market system, only when the well starts to run dry. The market is slow to recognize the reality, always present, even if not yet encroaching, that the world is finite.

The market's foolish disregard of the value of what the earth provides us subsidizes the recklessness of the present at the cost of the future. The reassurances we get from the free marketeers call to mind an image, suggested by Ezra J. Mishan, of the sanguineness of a man falling a hundred stories, after passing the ninety-ninth.

PROFLIGATE HEIRS

The market encourages us to treat as income what is the capital of our inheritance. The foresters stripped the wonderful hardwood forests of Minnesota, in the century before this, until the rivers were choked with the floating carcasses of those trees. All the trees cost the foresters was the cost of cutting and transporting; nothing compelled them to respect the value of the treasure furnished us by nature. As if there would always be the Lockean "enough and more" for those who were to come later. In the southern plains of this country, farmers have for decades been draining the Ogallalah Aquifer, a wealth of underground fresh water, as if it would go on forever. It won't. Meanwhile, the farmers treat the water virtually as a free good, and we who consume their produce pay nothing extra to reflect that a scarce resource is being consumed.

Recently, the *Washington Post* ran an article on the devastation of the Great Plains of the United States. The authors, Popper and Popper, call for the area to be turned into a "Buffalo Commons," citing the inability of "private interests" to last for long. "Responding to national market imperatives, they overgrazed and overplowed the land, overdrew the water."[6]

The prairies, because of their comparative fragility, are but a more obvious instance of a more general problem. The topsoil of these "American steppes" was shallow, but that of the hills of Iowa was rich and deep. Yet in the century or so that the market has been cultivating that land, the riches of that soil have been depleted substantially. It still is not "scarce" according to the market, however, so when we buy a bushel of Iowa corn we pay no premium to acknowledge the expenditure of the bushel of Iowa topsoil that was washed and blown away in the grain's production.

The market encourages us to be profligate heirs, counting only the costs of writing the checks and disregarding the value of the account from nature we are rapidly drawing down. We have, says Wendell Berry, "an 'economy' that leads to extravagance."[7] In the mid-1970s, the president of the United States vetoed a bill to regulate strip-mining, to impose on those who profit from the mining operation the costs of restoring the land rather than leaving it ravaged. We could not, said President Ford, "afford" such a bill. As Berry says of our extravagant economy, "Labor is expensive, time is expensive, money is expensive, but materials—the stuff of creation—are so cheap that we cannot afford to take care of them."[8]

The market, in its tunnel vision, creates a warped system of accounting. Robert Repetto, of the World Resources Institute, notes the destructive effects of such accounting. Though we subtract from GNP the depreciation of man-made assets, our failure to treat as similarly valuable the capital assets of our natural environment creates "a confusion likely to end in bankruptcy." This confusion is now worldwide, embedded in a national-income accounting framework—used by international institutions like the World Bank and the United Nations—that "fails to distinguish between the destruction of natural resource assets and the creation of income."[9]

Thus, for example, almost half of Indonesia's ostensible "economic growth" from 1970 to 1984 was really the depletion of the country's stock of resources. For the quarter century between 1965 and 1980, the economic growth of the Philippines appeared to average almost 6 percent per year. But this obscured what was being done to the land; it counted as pure profit the harvesting of almost 90 percent of the country's old-growth forest but disregarded the effects of denuding more than twelve million acres that, as Repetto describes, "now release floods and sediments into irrigation systems and waterways, damaging local food production and local fisheries." Here, not only is the expenditure of capital counted as income but also the destruction of the "web of interdependence" is counted as having no cost.

Repetto recommends a change of accounting to insert into the calculations the true costs in natural resources. Such a change, he argues, would help bankers, citizens, governmental officials, to evaluate possible investments and economic policies more realistically.

This change in accounting would help foster an important change in awareness, but such a shift by itself would be far from enough to discourage the prodigal waste of nature's bounty. Accounting is not all that needs to be changed.

Ultimately, it is probably necessary to change our entire concept of property and the rights that adhere to property where the resources of the earth are concerned. Native Americans thought bizarre the white man's notion that pieces of the earth could belong to people, when it seemed so clear that it is people who belong to the earth. This planet is apparently such an extraordinary, special place for life among the countless places of this universe, it hardly makes sense for individuals to have the *right* to bulldoze down tropical forests for their own immediate enrichment with no regard to future generations. Our future cannot be protected while those tilling the breadbasket of the nation have the right to erode the soil away to increase their short-term yield.

But what is needed first is a change intermediate between Repetto's revamping of national-income accounting, which would expose the problem without remedying it, and a fundamental change in our system of property rights, which might solve the problem but is not now within reach.

CORRECTIVE LENSES

What Repetto's proposed changes in accounting help clarify should be obvious in the first place. If the world has become blind to it, it is because the market with its blindness has warped people's perception of value. Though a useful heuristic measure, the change in accounting would be unavailing so long as individuals could still make a profit by engaging in economic activities whose costs they don't have to pay. Only if the prices in the market are made to reflect the real values involved will individuals make the necessary adjustments in their behavior.

The most available lever to move us from our wastrel ways is the pricing system: move the prices and you move economic activity. If there are costs, real though unmeasured by the market, to cutting down forests, then taxes should be imposed to install these costs in the price of wood and virgin paper. Correspondingly, the recycling of paper could be subsidized. If certain kinds of tillage result in soil erosion while others do not, some means must be found to tax and subsidize appropriately. We should not use strip-mined coal if we cannot "afford" to heal the injury to the land and water that the mining process inflicts. In some cases, destructive practices may need to be banned outright.

Correcting the distortion in the market's prices would improve our behavior in two ways. First, it would allow people to make choices that are now foreclosed. Second, it would encourage people to make choices that, though already available to us, we are dissuaded from making by the temptations placed before us by the present system.

First, the new options. In a competitive economy, producers must generally be as efficient as their rivals to survive. Sometimes, a producer can choose to be inefficient and poorer, still staying afloat. A doctor can spend more time, even though it is not well remunerated, talking to patients instead of performing more procedures or seeing more patients. Such a doctor can still make a good income, even if it is less than that of some of his or her colleagues. An artisan can make furniture by hand, even if the extra price the resulting goods command does not fully compensate him or her for the extra labor that goes into the handmade, in contrast with machine-made, product. But there are many areas in which an inefficient producer cannot survive. Although a producer can choose to pay himself less for his own labor, for many other factors of production the efficient and inefficient must pay the same price.

Consider a farmer who wants to till in an environmentally responsible way, and assume that this way is not efficient in terms of yield per acre and per investment of other inputs. (It might also be: an egg farmer who wants to let his chickens live a life worthy of a bird; a forester that wants to respect the integrity of the forest, and cull out only the really mature trees on the land; a fisherman that wants to use techniques in fishing that do not lead to overfishing; and so forth.)

In a economy that ignores the genuine inefficiency of spending topsoil, the price a bushel of corn commands in the market may well be less than the cost of producing the grain in a way that conserves the soil. A well-intentioned farmer—having to pay the same price as his competitors, who do not protect their soil, for an acre of land, a gallon of gas and a tractor—may well have no viable choice but to produce corn the environmentally destructive way. If he loses money, he will soon be out of business and will readily be replaced by someone willing to follow the market's dictates about what is valuable and what is not.

A producer of steel is similarly constrained. Imagine a steel-maker whose concern for acid rain has led him to utilize a technology that costs more per ton of steel produced but is more respectful of the cost—ignored by the market—of fouling the earth's atmosphere. Such a manufacturer will not be able to charge enough for his steel to make a profit. So long as his competitors are utilizing the market's subsidization of methods that disregard the value of the natural environment, the responsible path is not a viable option.

The examples could be multiplied endlessly.

Then there are the good options that we are free to choose, but are led away from by temptation. Recently, I spoke to a group of high school students about the environment. After my initial remarks about the importance of turning around the ongoing destruction of the living earth, we got into a lively discussion. Some argued that environmental concern was just a trendy thing, and too "easy" compared with attending to other social issues of our day, like homelessness. It is fun, some said, it's clean, it's no real bother to get together with your friends and take the bottles to the recycling depot.

I replied that the work of making our society sustainable had many aspects, not all of them easy. It was at this point that I got the most electric response of the day—a gasp—when I asked them to imagine going into their rooms and their closets and asking, "Do you find there just what you really need or is there a lot more?"

Subsequently, when the students were pondering among themselves whether they would be willing to give up any of their "standard of living," that is, their rate of consumption, they admitted that as much as they wanted the environment to be OK, they were not ready to change their habits. They were hooked on their ways of consumption, they said, and would change only if prices forced them to. There would have to be, the students felt, some kind of "environmental impact tax" to compel them to resist the temptations that the market, ignoring such impacts, places before them.*

---

*I must confess my own succumbing to temptation. Early in the 1980s, I needed a piece of furniture. Shopping around, I found the best value was a piece in a Scandinavian store—good-looking, well-made, and above all, well-priced. I bought it.

The problem is, the piece was made of teak. I could say—and at times I have tried to persuade myself—that in 1981 I didn't understand the significance of encouraging the manufacturing of furniture from the trees, such as teak, from tropical forests. But in fact, I was not so ignorant. Feeling financial pressure, I turned away from what I knew. Following the temptations afforded by the messages from the market, I contributed to a global process I knew should stop.

There are some areas where the ignored costs of the production or use of products is much greater than others—for example, the styrofoam popcorn in which fragile articles are shipped. But it can be said that the market's inattention to the value of the natural world constitutes a general subsidization of production and consumption. A proper balance can be achieved in a market only if taxes and subsidies are used to correct the market's inherent bias.

DON'T WORRY, BE HAPPY; OR, WOULD YOU BUY A USED PLANET FROM THESE PEOPLE?

The advocates of the free market and of unfettered economic "growth" often argue that the concerns of environmentalists are overblown, if not altogether misguided. These arguments offer a clear window into the tunnel vision that characterizes the market's worldview.

One such argument is a version of "you never had it so good." Milton Friedman, for example, says that "If we look not at rhetoric but at reality, the air is in general far cleaner and the water safer today than one hundred years ago."[10] About what air and water is he thinking? He can't be thinking of the totality of groundwater in the United States, since the amount that is polluted now is vastly greater than the amount that American industry and agriculture had managed to contaminate a century ago. Nor can he be talking about the condition of the atmosphere over the continent: a century ago, the woodfires and industrial furnaces of America had barely begun to spew the volumes of particulates and toxins that are disgorged into the air now in countless tons. Friedman is probably ignoring the big picture, with its accelerating—and cumulative—despoilation. In that statement, he is probably focusing only on the water that an American gets from the tap to fill his glass and on the air a resident of Liverpool breathes today as she walks along the streets that a century ago were clouded in noxious vapors. If the air isn't entering our lungs, and the water isn't going down our throats—if there is no transaction being made—what difference does it make? If we're still doing all right passing the ninety-ninth floor, why worry about the larger picture that suggests we're still falling and that a bottom lies somewhere below?

This leads to another, much more central argument employed by the market's growth worshippers to assure us that business as usual is prudent policy. This is the argument that there is nothing wrong with our using up resources because we can count on human ingenuity to create new technologies to replace whatever we have destroyed. Oil, so precious to us today, was worthless until comparatively recently. It is only the progress of science and technology in this century that have made uranium a "resource." "Nearly all the things which we today call resources," argues Michael Novak, "were not known to be resources fifty, one hundred or two hundred years ago."[11] Julian Simon's book of a decade ago, *The Ultimate Resource*, made this case as a defense of the growth cult against the movement, then gaining strength, to make our economic activity more circumspect in relation to natural resources. Don't worry, be happy. The problems technology creates, more technology will solve.

This argument clearly has some validity. But it would be folly to buy it wholesale. It may be that by the time we have used up all the earth's petroleum, we will have found a way to power our cars on sunlight or on water. It may be . . . But there are two main flaws in this kind of thinking.

The first is another aspect of tunnel vision. Maybe in the little picture of particular economic processes, we will find substitutes for old resources that are depleted and create altogether new categories of resources. But in the meanwhile, there is accumulating evidence that the big picture is deteriorating, that the precious balances of the biosphere are being upset. The evidence that climatic patterns are being disrupted, the loss of topsoil, the disappearance of the ozone layer in the stratosphere, the spread of deserts, the rapid extinction of species—all these are signs that the overall living systems of the earth are being undermined.*

---

*Another good example of tunnel vision was provided by Julian Simon on the PBS television program on the stock market, "Wall Street Week." Simon was advocating an open-door immigration policy for the U.S. Asked by the program's host, Louis Rukeyser, what he would say in reply to those who object to more immigration because we already have an overcrowded, polluted environment and so should avoid increases in population. Simon gave his customary sanguine reply. Since natural resources are "products of our minds,"

The processes of life are not just a matter of finding specific materials to perform specific purposes at specific times and places. All these little junctures of our conscious purpose and activity rest upon a larger network of intricately interconnected flows—far beyond our comprehension—that characterize the living system. The interdependence among living creatures far transcends our visible transactions.

The growth lobby is quick to seize upon any uncertainty in the alarming scenarios of environmental destruction. As the problem of global warming emerges as a threat to our continuing with business as usual, the apostles of unlimited growth ask: Is the climate really going to get warmer because of the volume of carbon dioxide we are putting into the air? If it did, would it really be that much of a problem? On another issue, the growthologists bring out their technicians to demonstrate that we can thrive without topsoil, that topsoil is fast becoming a superfluous atavism, a relic of how plants used to be grown in the age before the appearance of wondrous new technogies for raising crops without soil.

Here we come to the second part of the folly: *how much do we want to bet* on these "don't worry, be happy" propositions? It is like Pascal's famous wager:[12] he thought it more prudent to act *as if* there were a God who rewarded the good and punished the wicked, though he didn't feel certain of it, since if he acted on that supposition and it were false, the cost of his error would be small; whereas, if the proposition were true, but he had acted as if it were not, he would pay dearly in hell through eternity. If the growthologiosts are right, our being unncessarily cautious might make us a bit less fabulously wealthy than we could have been. But if they prove wrong, and we have imprudently followed their reckless counsel, we will find ourselves roasting in a hell of our own making.

Not only is banking on optimism in such matters inherently risky business, but the case for optimism seems especially suspect because of its source. The "don't worry" crowd with their technological fixes are coming from the same cultural current that promised a generation ago that nuclear energy would mean safe electricity so cheap it would not need to

---

he said, "immigrants help us with their ideas, help us increase our supply of natural resources." The undoubted power of the human kind is here inflated to swallow up the reality of ecological limits.

be metered. Would we want to let all our topsoil blow away on their assurance that it won't matter?

In addition, my experience in the world of Washington think tanks showed me that ideas often become prominent not so much in proportion to their intrinsic merits but in proportion to the wealth of the interests the ideas serve. When Julian Simon's book appeared, there surfaced an enormous constituency in our market society supportive of this thesis that resources needn't be treated as scarce. This constituency was enormous not in numbers of people but in power and influence. When someone makes a "case" for a proposition that can help big monied interests get their way, those ideas are adopted as a brief for those interests, and they get their day in the court of public opinion to a degree far beyond what other ideas, even superior ideas, can get. Future generations and even life on earth are not constituencies capable of buying their advocates similar prominence.

So when the contest is between limits and growth, between those scientific findings and ideas that weigh on the side of applying the brakes and those on the side of putting the pedal to the metal, the arguments we hear are skewed by the inequalities of power that arise from the market system. It is as though the two sides of the argument are being viewed through two different ends of the same telescope, magnifying the point of view that would keep the market unfettered and diminishing those arguments that would persuade us to rein in our destructive excesses.

It seems that the people who talk about a glorious future of technological marvels are the same ones whose way of conducting business shows little regard for the future (sometimes not even for a future beyond the next annual report). It seems that many of the same people who say we cannot limit "growth," lest we consign the poor of the world to their impoverishment, forget their concern for the poor in other contexts, where helping the poor runs counter to increasing their own wealth.

The market produces rationalizations for its *idee fixe*—the indefinite expansion of the economic empire—and it creates and empowers people disposed to voice them.

6

Not Just the Market

Why blame the market? Even if the obvious is conceded—that we are despoiling our environment—it is clear
that societies of all kinds are participating in this headlong
rush toward environmental disaster. The Communist countries
of Eastern Europe have a disgraceful record on the environment, and some of the lands being most rapidly degraded today are found in the Third World. What are the implications,
for my indictment of the market system's inability to place
proper valuation on what nature provides, of the evident fact
that the kind of environmental destruction the market inflicts
is found today in non-market societies as well? Does the ubiq-
uity of the problem suggest that the market is not really the
problem?

In a word, yes and no. The market's blindness is a substantial part of the problem of why human activity is out of
joint with the biosphere. But it is far from the whole problem.

The recent transformations in Eastern Europe have brought
to the forefront the shameful ecological record of communist
economies in Europe. If market societies can become environmentally responsible only when collective—governmental—
action intrudes into the economic system, why is it that collec-

tivist, command economies seem afflicted with the same disease? Surely when the rivers of Poland flowed with toxins, when the air over East Germany was filled with grime, it was not the fault of an atomistic economic system. Why is it that economies run by rulers who presumably *could* choose to safeguard their environment have been in some ways even more reckless than industrial market economies?

One possible explanation would have rather pessimistic implications: that the problem is a function of inherent characteristics of *human nature.* Human beings, according to this argument, are always going to choose their own immediate well-being over all other considerations—certainly over other species, over the needs of future generations, even perhaps over their own well-being in a future whose reality pales next to the palpable present. Are we inherently incapable of acting for the good of the whole?

To this, too, the response is yes and no. Yes, life on earth has indeed embarked on a dangerous experiment in unleashing upon the planet a creature with the capacity to rearrange the ecosystem to suit its purposes, rather than being confined, like all the other creatures, to an ecological niche foreordained in its genetic endowment. It would, indeed, inevitably jeopardize the integrity of the biosphere for an element of the system to achieve godlike powers without the corresponding godlike wisdom and virtue. "If men were angels," James Madison says in a very different context. But we are not angels, merely creatures of flesh and blood that have not evolved the built-in restraints to substitute for the age-old checks and balances of the ecosystem from which we began to escape some 10 thousand years ago.

But no, the history of those 10 thousand years does not suggest that human beings and their cultural systems are inevitably as wanton as those we see set loose on the earth in our times. Traditional societies have typically had a very different attitude toward nature than modern societies, an ingrained sense that there are limits to how much exploitation of nature is permissible and appropriate. The biblical institution of the sabbatical years, which enjoins the people to let the land lie fallow one year out of seven, is indicative. In his book *The Primitive World and Its Transformations,* Robert Redfield describes the deep feeling in the peasant societies of the Yucatan that when something is taken from nature something must be given in return. Native American societies felt that their relationship with the natural world was of spiritual significance. They felt a bond with the living systems of the earth from which they drew their sustanance. In so-called primitive societies generally, the natural world was a "thou," not just an "it."[1] And their relationship with nature was seen as one of reciprocation, of give and take.

The perception of nature as a mere object is a modern one. With this objectification, a reciprocal relationship gives way to one of unbridled exploitation. As the world become just an "it," modern societies can treat even living animals as mere mechanisms. Chickens are rendered into egg-laying machines that never get to walk around or to peck the earth, and cows are reduced to four-legged factories for producing milk, condemned (in the most "advanced" facilities) to solitary confinement except for regular elevator rides to the milking parlor.

Our modern consciousness, therefore, should not be mistaken for our inherent nature, and our current environmental destructiveness cannot be adequately explained by reference to human nature. Is it perhaps something about *modernization* that has made all industrial societies—Communist as well as capitalist—reckless with nature?

In his insightful book *All That Is Solid Melts into Air,* Marshall Berman seems to suggest something of the sort, depicting modernization as a force that sweeps all old orders—natural and man-made—aside in the drive toward the creation of ever-new worlds. In a brilliant analysis of Goethe's *Faust* as a "Tragedy of Development," Berman puts new substance into the old idea that the character of Faust is emblematic of our modern ("Faustian") civilization. Faust is shown as the archetypal developer, embodying the modern economy's compulsion to create a world where "all that's solid melts into air." The spirit of Faust's relationship with the natural world is part of this.

In part 2 of Goethe's *Faust,* the hero and his ally, Mephistopheles, begin in a state of depression, at an impasse. Then, as Berman tells the tale:

> Faust begins to stir. He contemplates the sea and evokes lyrically its surging majesty, its primal and implacable power, so impervious to the works of man.
> So far this is a typical theme of romantic melancholy, and Mephisto hardly notices. It's nothing personal, he

says; the elements have always been this way. But now, suddenly, Faust springs up enraged. Why should men let things go on being the way they have always been? Isn't it about time for mankind to assert itself against nature's tyrannical arrogance . . . He goes on: It is outrageous that, for all the vast energy expended by the sea, it merely surges endlessly back and forth—"and nothing is achieved."[2]

To Faust, this is unacceptable: nature must be tamed and harnessed to human purposes, transformed into grist for his mill. Nature—in this case, the energy of the sea—is reduced to a resource for Faust to use in the realization of his ambitions.

Development, says Berman, has followed "authentically Faustian forms" in the industrial economies of the world. Not only nature but all "people, things, institutions and environments" are of necessity under a continual process of reconstruction. Whatever fails to make the necessary, mandatory transformations "will be swept away." "The climactic clause in Faust's contract with the devil—that if he ever stops and says to the moment, 'Verweile doch, du bist so schoen' [Linger, you are so beautiful], he will be destroyed—is played out to the bitter end in millions of lives every day."[3]

But from whence comes the mandate that compels these changes? Berman seems to personify "modernization" and "development," making them into forces that could drive a society with a will of their own. But what is the source of this force? Missing from Berman's otherwise fascinating depiction of the modern world is any real engine behind the drive toward change. He describes the modern cosmos wonderfully, but he gives us no prime mover.

We are exploring how an unfettered—or, more pertinent to our present circumstance, *an inadequately fettered*—market economy is an engine of transformation with a thrust of its own. It was to the market, also, that Karl Marx referred when he wrote—in the line Berman employs—that in the world of the bourgeoisie, "All that's solid melts into air." The figure of Faust, moreover, is probably connected in its origin with that spirit of capitalism, coalescing in Europe as the modern world took embryonic form within the late medieval. With respect to that modern view of nature as a resource to exploit—epitomized by Faust's raging at the unharnessed sea—Chandra

Mukerji associates this specifically with capitalism. The cultural force that has made our environments "almost entirely a reflection of human will," Mukerji writes in his book *From Graven Images*, "expresses the sense of dominion over nature felt as early as the seventeenth century." It arose as a result of "the systematic outcome of the interaction of capitalism and materialism."[4]

My analysis here may explain how the dynamic of capitalism can foster, indeed make mandatory, the Faustian exploitation and despoilation of nature. But neither this analysis nor reference to modernization can explain the Faustian record of the Soviet Union, where rivers are diverted from their course (with severe, destructive consequences), where the land is dotted with potential Chernobyls. Even if the inherent dynamic of capitalism can explain the origin of the Faustian relation to nature, we are still compelled to search for an explanation of its spread throughout the modern world, even to societies whose economies are controlled by different principles.

FLATTERING OURSELVES: THE MYSTERY OF IMITATION

A commonsensical explanation is available, and is indeed implicit in the way most of us think about the spread around the world of productive technology of the West. Our ways spread because people *emulate the superior.*

It was the market, according to this view, that showed the way. As the system able to liberate human creativity, the market discovered the escape route from the age-old human condition of poverty. The exploitation of nature was an essential component of that escape. As people in more backward societies witnessed the higher standard of living demonstrated by advanced market societies, they imitated Western technology without necessarily adopting the market system.

Upon inspection, this hypothesis about imitation can be seen as an elaboration on the explanation by human nature. People, by nature, choose the course that better meets their needs. When a new way of relating to nature became available, a way that offered relief from suffering and deprivation (even if at the cost of some long-term environmental deterioration), people quite understandably and predictably emulated the technology of the more advanced societies.

Like the explanation by human nature, this explanation of "emulation of the superior" has considerable validity. But it also has important limits.

This explanation is doubly comforting to us. For one thing, it confirms us in our belief in the rightness of our ways; being imitated is not only flattering, it stills whatever lurking doubts we may have about ourselves. For another thing, it bolsters the reassuring idea that we humans are in control of our destiny. The cultural ways that spread are those that people freely choose because they find them the most attractive.

Let us consider first the assumption that our being imitated proves that our ways are superior to the backward ways our imitators are abandoning. Unfortunately, what is imitated is not always the better way. Imitation is more complex than that.

A marvelous glimpse into this complexity is afforded by a passage quoted by Ashley Montagu in his book entitled *Touching*. The story is told by a former director of the World Health Organization, Dr. Brock Chisholm. He was being taken on a tour of a hospital in Pakistan:

> As we were going along a corridor which was a sort of balcony on the side of the building, we passed the screened door of a ward. Suddenly someone pointed out to me, with great enthusiasm, something away off on the horizon in the opposite direction. Now, to any old Army inspecting officer, the situation was perfectly clear; there was something nearby they didn't want me to see. If you see only what people want you to see you will never find out anything.
>
> So I insisted, at some risk of offense, on seeing this ward, and when I insisted, my guides began apologizing, saying that I really wouldn't like to see it at all. It was of a very old pattern; they were ashamed of it; they hoped to get it changed; they hoped that the World Health Organization might help them get the money to adopt modern and new patterns for this particular ward, because it was very bad indeed. It was a pattern hundreds of years old.
>
> However, I still insisted that even as an antiquity I would like to see it. I went in to see this ward, with the reluctant accompaniment of the train of people with me, and I saw the best maternity ward I have ever seen in any

country, far better than I have ever seen in North America. Here was a big maternity ward with beds down both sides. The foot posts of each bed were extended up about three feet or so, and slung between the foot posts was a cradle. The baby was in the cradle, and I noticed as I looked down the ward that one squeak out of the baby and up would come the mother's foot, and with her toe she would rock the cradle. On the second squeak, she would reach into the cradle and take the baby into her arms, where a baby is supposed to be most of the time.

. . . They wanted to get rid of that perfectly beautiful arrangement, to put their babies under glass the way we do, and to keep them in inspection wards where they can be seen at a distance by their loving fathers whenever they visit, and taken to their mother if she is good and does as the nurse tells her![5]

"Progress" is not always movement in a better direction. The more "advanced" is further along in a direction we might be better off not going.

What would lead people to imitate what is not necessarily better than what they already have? Dr. Chisholm concludes: "They wanted to do all that because we Westerners had given them the impression that all our methods are superior to theirs." It is not, of course, just a matter of Westerners working to "persuade," but also of other peoples being disposed to see all our characteristics as superior.

It is a matter of *prestige*. Prestige led lower-class French women of the nineteenth century to prefer "a shoddy, mass produced silk to a sturdy handsome cotton," Rosalind Williams reports in her study of the rise of French consumer society, because silk had the aura of the monied class.[6] It is prestige that, as Russell Belk describes it, leads residents of Third World societies to prefer poor Western products even to superior and cheaper alternatives produced locally. In Kenya, "multinational soap brands greatly outsell local soaps, even though they are more expensive and functionally inferior. Similarly, Kenyans now prefer refined maize to less expensive and more nutritious unrefined grains."[7]

It might seem that the very fact of the West's prestige demonstrates again our superiority. This prestige may spill over even onto the more regrettable aspects of our culture, including the shoddier products of our market system. Yet if it were not for an overall superiority of Western ways, this argument might run, the West's aura of prestige would not exist, and the pattern of emulation of the West (even if it is insufficiently discriminating) would not develop.

Again, like imitation, prestige is more complex than that. Prestige is not just a function of superiority; or rather, superiority is not just a matter of *worth*. Here we come to the nub of the issue: the problem of power.

THE PROBLEM OF POWER

We will be less reassured by our being emulated around the world when we remember that abused children tend to imitate their parents and become child abusers. Identification with the aggressor can lead a Georgian boy who hated his Russian oppressors to grow up to become the "Father of all Russians," and to change his name to the Russian word for steel, Stalin. Through such emulation, he became a hyperbolic extension of the Russian tyranny that he and his people had endured and hated.

Third World countries were introduced to the wonders of the West not through some free market of ideas, but through the aggressive and exploitive intrusion of Western imperialism. Superior? Superior in power at any rate. It is because of the superiority of Western arms and productivity that the grandparents of those Pakistanis—who were ashamed of the wonderfully human, nontechnological, unforgivably "backward" maternity ward—lived their lives under the gaze of European masters. Under the boot of the technologically advanced, capitalistic English, the proud tribal peoples of Kenya learned the harsh lesson that "backwardness" has its costs, that their traditional culture—whatever other virtues it may or may not have had—was impotent to protect them from humiliation. Is it any wonder, in such circumstances, that local products cannot compete with the brands produced by their prestigious former rulers?

Third World "development" has been notoriously wasteful and inappropriately grandiose in many of these former colonial societies. Ruling elites, often educated in the West and eager to become respected players on the world stage, have opted to channel resources into huge industrial showcase projects rather than to nurture the more organic development of the indigenous economy and culture. Often environmentally unsound and unsustainable, as well as unsuited to the local society, these massive projects like dams and factories seem to express, among other things, the urgent emotional need to escape from the status of the little guy, the one who gets pushed around as if he were too insignificant to warrant consideration. The drive for material wealth is not universal in these Third World societies. I am told that away from the cities, in the places where the traditional culture remains more intact, the imperative of a "rising standard of living" is not strong.[8] It is at those nodes where power has entered and shaped the system—in the cities and among the elites—that the impetus to emulate the West is strong.

The identification with the aggressor, the attribution of prestige to those with the might to compel others—these are psychological aspects of a problem of power that operates at a larger level as well to shape the apparatus of our civilization.

When we unfold the implications of this idea, we will find yet another reason we cannot draw comfort from the emulation of the West. Not only does the imitation not guarantee the intrinsic value of our ways. It also, as we will now see, does not substantiate the image of humankind freely choosing its destiny. More fundamental than the psychological analysis of prestige is another framework that explains the contagion of the technologies that characterize modernization and that now threaten us with ecological disaster. It is the dynamic of the struggle for power in the intersocietal system.

THE PARABLE OF THE TRIBES; OR, THE IMPERATIVES OF POWER

Producers working within a market economy are not the only ones who are compelled, if they wish to survive, to adopt certain technological practices. Throughout history, there has been a still larger arena of competition, where survival of a much more fundamental nature has been at stake. In the anarchic system of sovereign societies, a ceaseless struggle for power has been inevitable, beyond the capacity of any of the actors to stop or to avoid. As a result of the operation of this competitive process over time, of all the cultural options apparently available to civilized humankind, only those ways of organizing society that confer sufficient power can survive. All other options—however harmonious they may be with human needs or with the biosphere—if they make a society vulnerable to predation from surrounding societies, are ultimately swept away. The ways of power inevitably spread throughout the world so long as the global system remains anarchic, lacking any order that can protect the weak and the cultural options they embody.

This is the core idea of my theory of the evolution of civilization, developed in my book *The Parable of the Tribes*. And it is pertinent to understanding the particular issue at hand here: the spread of modern, environmentally destructive technology.

If one society discovers and adopts a way of exploiting nature that magnifies that society's power, other societies will feel compelled to emulate it. Those that fail to emulate it will be vulnerable to those empowered by the new technology. Millennia ago, our hunting-and-gathering ancestors confronted this technological imperative when they faced the power of the early agricultural civilizations. And in recent centuries, the rise and spread of modern industrialization has again demonstrated this grim edict of social evolution.

After a case-by-case overview of the conditions in which the process of industrialization was launched among the nations of Europe, W. W. Rostow concludes that "in all cases, reaction to foreign intrusion, actual or threatened, is relevant to the domestic thrust towards modernization."[9] Even in its place of origin, England, the movement toward industrialism was spurred by a fear of France. And once the English had embarked on the Industrial Revolution, the new technological system's manifest implications for power among the contending nations of Europe led to its spreading like a contagion across the continent. When the Japanese later "observed the rest of Asia being carved up and apportioned by the various European powers," says David Kaplan, they felt they had little choice: "it was industrialize or be gobbled up like the rest."[10]

The problem of power helps explain the degradation of the natural environment worldwide in our century, including in Third World and Communist societies. On the level of the intersocietal struggle for power, what are seen as the imperatives of security have driven *all* societies to move toward adopting the technology of the mightiest nations.* These mightiest nations—Great Britain in much of the nineteenth century, then gradually overshadowed by Germany and the United States as the nineteenth century gave way to the twentieth—utilized market economies to harness the potential energy and resources of the natural world to an unprecedented extent, greatly magnifying the wealth and power of their societies. It was specifically to make itself a greater power that the Soviet Union under Stalin launched its relentless drive toward industrialization, with its specifically militaristic cast. In the rush to compete with the West, Communism's industrial drive compelled managers to meet production targets, regardless of the costs or the hazards for people's health or the environment.[11] And, of course, the industrialization of the Soviet empire was geared specifically to military purposes, not to the imitation of Western consumer society. In market societies like the U.S. and Britain, the military implications of productive power, though relevant, were comparatively much less central in driving the process of industrialization.†

---

*On a different level, the play of power *within* communist and third world societies can determine the *kind* of people whose decisions govern the course of these societies' development. In many of these societies, power has been gained by violence and exercised as tyranny, subjecting the people to repression and exploitation of greater or lesser cruelty. Even if, theoretically, a political decision maker enjoys a freedom, not available to an actor in an unfettered market, to choose a course of environmental harmony, the people who rise to power in such systems are unlikely to exercise such environmental care. The kind of men who are willing to brutalize their own people to preserve and to extend their power are not likely to treat the biosphere with any more regard. Concomitantly, those who live under oppression are unlikely to be in a spiritual place to care for the earth. It can be observed, even in the United States, that around the places where the most powerless and hopeless live, the surrounding landscape is likely to be strewn with a long accumulation of litter.

One may hope that the liberalization of Eastern Europe will, by changing both the nature of the leadership and the frame of mind of the population, allow a real, progressive change in environmental policies.

†As the Soviet Union moved away from its centralized economy and more toward the economic institutions of the West, the demands of power may still have been playing the role of prime mover. "It was largely in response to economic stagnation" write Cabot and Fuller, "with its negative implications for military preparedness, that reform [perestroika] was begun in the first place. Gorbachev was chosen to carry out those reforms with the blessing of senior

Similarly, in attempting to explain two decades ago why the nations of the Third World are "hell-bent" on "following the technology of the West," Arnold Toynbee said that it is "because they feel that unless they get even with us in technology, which means in material power, they will be at our mercy, and we shall continue to abuse our power and exploit them."

The problem of "the illusion of choice" has, therefore, more levels than one. Our principal concern here is with the illusion that the market system allows us to choose our destiny: the inherent dynamic of the system itself drives us toward outcomes of its own determination. The larger perspective, provided by the social evolutionary theory I call "the parable of the tribes," shows how little choice humankind as a whole has had in determining fundamental aspects of our cultural evolution in general. These interlocking levels of the challenge we face in trying to create a more humane and viable civilization will be explored further in part 3: "Out of Control."

For the present discussion exploring the reasons behind humankind's current destruction of the biosphere, what needs to be emphasized is that in both kinds of competitive systems—in the free market and in the global arena of societies struggling to survive the anarchy that obtains among them—the nature of the system *mandates* a relationship to the environment we would not, if we were wise, freely choose. If one competitor—a firm, a nation—gains a distinct competitive advantage by utilizing some new technology, the others must imitate or be eliminated. This is true even if that new technology is not, in the long run, sustainable.

Consider our tropical-forest-killing hamburgers, an even more extreme example than the corn raised on Iowa's eroding hillsides. If one of the McBurger chains gets its beef more cheaply, even if it is through the one-time and short-term expedient of destroying the fragile soils of the tropical forest, it puts competitive pressure on the other burger chains. In this example, indeed, the market and the intersocietal levels converge: for it is the blindness of the market that rewards the destruction of the forests, and it is those rewards that drive the powerful society of modern Brazil to overwhelm and destroy

---

military and KGB leaders, who understood that a competition-based, technologically modern economy was in the long run essential to a superpower" (Cabot and Fuller, p. 54).

the native tribal societies that were there first, living in the Amazonian Basin.

These tribes, like indigenous peoples enduring a similar fate in other places, such as the Philippines, had developed a way of living in harmony with the living systems of their jungles. Their sustainable technology can be eliminated by a new technology that, in the short run, reaps more wealth and power from nature.*

So long as these competitive systems are fragmented, with each actor compelled to do what competition demands, human wisdom will be unable to govern. In bondage to the dynamic of competition, actors are compelled to be short sighted. Long-run viability is necessarily sacrificed to short-term power, for we cannot make it to the long run if our competitors eliminate us in the short run. So the intrinsically viable is rendered unviable, and the intrinsically moribund becomes the mandatory form for survival.

In both levels of competitive system, the bearer of the advanced technology can be like a rabid dog—infected with the seeds of its own destruction, yet able by its bite to spread its disease. Thus it was within the host bodies of market societies, with their potent dynamism, that the radically more powerful technologies of modern industrialism were incubated. And now, even though these technologies increasingly menace the integrity and even the survival of the biosphere, they appear to offer the only path open to humankind.

It is only by overcoming the fragmentary nature of these systems—which means exercising collective choice—that we can remedy the diseased aspects of the technological thrust of modern civilization.

---

*Nowadays the argument is heard that the preservation of the integrity of the tropical forest makes most sense even in the terms of economic profit in the reasonably short term. Gathering the produce of the natural forest is said to be more profitable than other, more destructive uses to which the land can be put.

I don't know whether this is true or not. It certainly simplifies things whenever the right and the expedient things to do are identical. But we can be sure it will not always be so, that short-run profit and the long-term preservation of the environment will not always be in harmony. And it is frightening to think—as some of those who make this argument for the rain forests (such as a fine organization named Cultural Survival) appear to—that environments will inevitably be used in whatever way is economically most advantageous.

PART II
WE ARE DRIVEN

THE MARKET AS THE ENGINE OF CHANGE IN AMERICA

It is astonishing to contemplate how profoundly we have altered the face of the American continent in a comparatively short period of time. Only three centuries ago, it is said, a squirrel could traverse the territory from the Atlantic to the Mississippi without even lighting on the ground, so dense and uninterrupted were the forests. Now a thick web of roads overlies the land, the trees reduced in a great many areas to hedgerows by the fields cleared for crops and to ornaments along the avenues of cities and next to the homes of suburbanites. Scarcely more than a century before I played as a boy by the banks of the Red Cedar River in Michigan, the whole territory belonged to Indians, among whom were sprinkled a mere handful of whites who, like the Indians, were hunters. Now so great is the pace of history that the area falls under the appellation of Rust Belt, indicating that great edifices of productive enterprise have had time to be erected and to get corroded in a few generations. Looking down through the window of a transcontinental flight, one can see that this continent, so recently new, has been wholly transformed by the uses to which the American civilization has put it.

While this astounding transformative process is obvious, what has governed the process is not. Is the America today the one our founding foreparents wanted to create? Is it a clear reflection of their values? And if the same determinants continue to direct our social evolution, will the America of a century hence be a fulfillment of the ideals that animate *us*?

Of course, there is a correspondence between American values and the way American society has evolved. The outward face of America is, in important ways, the sign of an inward and spiritual American worldview. Most Americans take great pride in the spectacular achievements of our nation. We measure progress along scales that are aligned with the direction of our historical evolution. Our values, in other words, largely ratify and affirm our history.

Even if the America of today corresponded perfectly with our contemporary values, however, it would not prove that our America is the one that its apparent creators chose. It is our values that govern our choices. But our values, in turn, are governed by a great confluence of forces. A preponderance of these forces come from the society we live in.

A reciprocal relation therefore operates. Our values shape our society, and we therefore get the society we choose. At the same time, our society shapes our values, and it therefore gets the people it chooses.

A naive psychological reductionism might assume that since a society is ultimately *only* the product of its members, the whole reciprocal pattern can be reduced to the terms of human values and choice. But when the systems of society possess a dynamic of their own, such reductionism must collapse. We can drive our own car "freely," but if we are traveling on a grid where all the north-south streets are one-way streets going north, our choice of destination will be limited.

In part 1, "Tunnel Vision," we have seen that the market economy does indeed have a logic of its own. Once the market system is in place, the people in it are no longer wholly in charge of their destiny. Without comprehending that the system they are adopting will make all roads head north, people can unwittingly foreclose southern destinations they might have preferred.

It can meaningfully be asked, therefore: To what extent is the face of America an expression of the choice of the American people and to what extent has it been shaped by the workings of the nation's economic system? To what extent is our socio-economic system an expression of our values, and to what extent have our values been formed by socioeconomic forces beyond our control?

The answer to these questions is doubtless extremely complex. In part 3, "We Are Driven," two main points will be argued. First, of the different visions of America that have contended throughout our history, the determination of which vision would prevail has been made in large measure by the power of the market system. Second, American values have undergone a transformation in which the market system has molded human consciousness to make our view of the world, and of human life, more like its own tunnel vision.

7

A Black Hole in American History

The material accomplishments of American society are staggering. Our achievements in the realm of economic development doubtless far surpass the expectations or even hopes of any of our civilization's seventeenth- and eighteenth-century founders, even of those whose vision for this nation was the most materialistic.

Our founders had other dreams, however, of what America might become. Their vision of America had more to do with the godly virtues of Puritan simplicity and the republican virtues of public spiritedness and justice than with opulent wealth.[1] In these areas our achievements would not overwhelm them. Indeed, they might be deeply disappointed to see what kind of city we have built upon their hill.

America remains the embodiments of several visions of the good. The morality of our Judeo-Christian heritage remains alive. A presidential candidate caught cheating on his wife is drive from the race. The ideals of the just republic survive also. A president caught flagrantly violating the rules of power is hounded from office in disgrace. There can be little doubt, however, that of the competing visions of America, the materialistic vision of the good life has prevailed. Analysts of American elections say that people "vote their pocketbooks," that with few exceptions the rates of economic growth and inflation can predict which party's presidential candidate will be victorious.[2]

Ever-increasing material prosperity is the God of our society. It dominates our sense of the good. How did it happen that economic growth became the purpose of American society?

From our vantage point, through the prism of our worldview in a modern industrial capitalist society, it may seem perfectly natural, inevitable, that this would be how we would understand the "good life." But the materialistic vision has continually been confronted by alternative, opposing visions of America. These visions, too, seemed to have great power—power to inspire individuals and social movements. American history can be seen, in fact, as a drama in which major cultural currents repeatedly confronted, but again and again proved unable to contain, the advancing tide of materialism. Seen in terms solely of the values of the people, the triumph of the materialistic vision seems far from preordained.

The course of American history confronts us with something of a mystery. In astronomy, when what is visible fails to explain the course of a body's movement through the heavens, astronomers posit the existence of some invisible body as the source of the unexpected force. The inexorable advance of the materialistic component of America's possibility may be regarded as a movement of this unexplained and mysterious kind. And the dynamic of the market system may be seen as the invisible but powerful black hole in our social universe, a force warping the course of our society's development.

ALWAYS HEAD NORTH

Throughout American history, as materialistic and nonmaterialistic values have clashed, it seems as though our country has, indeed, been on that hypothetical grid where the rule was "always turn north." Inexorably, American society has magnified the values conducive to economic expansion and the accumulation of wealth. This pattern could admit of many possible explanations, besides the one I am advancing here. But before we concern ourselves with what the pattern signifies, let us sketch some of the highlights of this historical confrontation.

The conflict between different possibilities for America goes back virtually to its beginnings. The materialistic possibility was always there, even at the genesis of the Puritan colony in Massachusetts. John Winthrop "posed the issue to his congregation," says Robert Bellah, as "the choice between adhering to God's covenant or pursuing 'our carnal intentions seeking great things for ourselves and our posterity,' seeking 'our pleasures and profits.' "[3] If we are to believe the Puritans, however, materialistic values were not the ones they wanted most to actualize in their society's development. The Puritans saw the love of riches as a powerful threat to the achievement of their ideals, and they agonized to see Mammon gaining ground on God.

One of the great spiritual battles over what kind of vision and what set of values would animate the soul of America is represented by the Great Awakening, the powerful religious revival in the first half of the eighteenth century. In his study *The Simple Life*, David Shi writes that "the causes of the Great Awakening were many and complex, but a central concern of many of the revivalists was to halt their society's headlong rush toward impious materialism and to restore felt religion and simple living among the colonists."[4] A minister in 1733 declared the need for piety and a "slighted" religion to rein in the "powerful love of the world, and exorbitant reach after riches."[5]

A generation later, as the time of the American Revolution approached, leaders like Benjamin Rush and John Adams agreed that "American society was racked with the disease of materialism."[6] But Rush was optimistic that the problem was remediable, "since the ailment 'has advanced but a few paces in luxury and effeminacy.' "[7] Many other leaders of this revolutionary generation also articulated the hope that simplicity and republican virtue would prevail over the love of pleasure and the drive for wealth.*

---

*My concern here is not with the important, and by no means self-evident question of what kind of values it would be *preferable* for a nation to embrace. Rather, the present point is simply to establish that there was a struggle over

Two pairs of men stand as classic embodiments of the dichotomous possibilities for the evolving American society.

One pair is presented by David Bell, drawing on Van Wyck Brooks's famous dualistic image from early in this century. The essence of the American character, Bell suggests, is part "the piety and torment of Jonathan Edwards, obsessed with human depravity," and part "the practicality and expedience of Benjamin Franklin, oriented to a world of possibility and gain."[8] Of this same pair of men, virtual contemporaries of one another, Robert Bellah says that though Franklin's influence has been more spectacular, Edwards's has been just as persistent.[9] Nonetheless, if we lay Edwards's sermons down next to the maxims of *Poor Richard's Almanack*, there can be little doubt as to which kind of counsel has most guided the course of the evolution of American civilization.

Similarly, America "turned north" when the nation, needing to define itself in the generation after independence was declared and achieved, faced two great visions of American possibility. This is the famous dichotomy between the Jeffersonian and the Hamiltonian visions. Thomas Jefferson's vision was quite different from Edwards's Puritanism, but they shared a belief that the most important dimension of a people's way of life is not material wealth and economic empire but its moral and spiritual quality. Alexander Hamilton's vision, articulated in his *Report on the Subject of Manufacturers* in 1791, extends the calculus of Franklin's "time is money" to provide a scorecard for national achievement similarly denominated in the currency of economic power.

Jefferson's image of a pastoral America with virtuous yeoman farmers has long since been swept aside by the Hamiltonian design for an expanding industrial economy. Wealth and power triumphed over simplicity and virtue.

The ideals predominant in the minds of those who founded American civilization were not those that held sway in the lives of their descendants. The "almighty dollar" was

---

values, and that the outcome of that struggle may not be a clear reflection of the wishes of those who strove to create the civilization of America. A couple of reasons for rejecting some traditional antimaterialistic value assumptions are considered briefly in the section North May Be the Way to Go, in chapter 10, pp. 158–159.

not the deity that Winthrop and his shipmates intended to govern their city upon a hill.

It was not just in America that materialistic values relentlessly overcame competing moral and spiritual perspectives as the market system gathered power.

Max Weber's *The Protestant Ethic and the Spirit of Capitalism* shows not only how the religious values of Protestantism—the ethic of hard work combined with frugality—were well suited for establishing the dynamism of capitalist investment. In that classic study, one can also discern how, over time, the Protestant values progressively lost their spiritual and moral content, increasingly becoming merely mundane and pecuniary drives toward wealth. This can be illustrated not only in America with the teachings of Franklin, a descendant of Puritans, but also with the evolution of the "protestant ethic" in such foci of capitalist development as England and Germany.

The relations between religious values and the economic system are quite complex, but throughout the capitalist world the power of religious convictions about the good life proved wholly inadequate to restrain the rising momentum of the pecuniary values embedded in the ascendant market economy.

In capitalist Flanders in the sixteenth century, the Christian humanists stressed the dangers of the love of luxury. Illustrating this recurrent warning, Simon Schama describes a picture that "featured Opulentia [luxury] riding Fame, accompanied by all the usual undesirable traits associated with her victory. Her charioteer was Guile, her steeds Fraud and Rapine, her attendants Usury, Betrayal and Lust. At the rear, in front of Idle Pleasure (Vana Volupta) walks the figure of False Joy blowing the bubbles of her ephemerality."[10] This same theme was echoed throughout the seventeenth century in Calvinist Holland.

While the Puritans were struggling to keep Mammon subordinate to God in America, back across the Atlantic, in the bustling commercial cities of Holland, the Calvinists were engaged in a similar, and similarly futile, effort. In his fascinating study of Dutch culture in the Golden Age, *The Embarrassment of Riches*, Simon Schama describes how religious leaders inveighed against the materialistic values they saw as undermining the life of virtue. "How can it be," asked Trigland in Amsterdam in the middle of the seventeenth century, "that

God's people could be so ornamented with silver and gold?"[11]
Yet all the while the pursuit and display of luxury grew.

The fruits of our labors are not always those we intend. Although Weber may be right that the Protestant Reformation provided a religious outlook conducive to the development of capitalism, the world of capitalism with its pecuniary values was far from what the religious leaders of Protestantism intended. The Calvinist clergy, Schama says, "spent far more time denouncing gain than in praising it."[12] They fought against the tide. "Sermons that explicitly contrasted the profane greed of finance with the humility of the Elect rained down on well-heeled congregations."[13] Yet the tide continued to roll in.

Why was the future that (according to Weber) the Calvinists helped to usher in so different from the one they wanted? Why did the culture of Puritan piety evolve into that of Yankee shrewdness?

The question of our ability to choose our future arises also regarding the unfolding of the market society in France. In her study of the rise of consumer society in late nineteenth-century France, for example, Rosalind Williams describes the coming of a future at variance from the goals of diverse groups struggling to shape France. The future that came to France was one where "consumer goods, rather than other facets of culture, became the focal points for desire," where the people were invited into "a fabulous world of pleasure, comfort, and amusement."[14] Of this future, Williams writes: "This was not at all the future that a conservative nationalist like Talmeyr wished; it was not the vision of a worker's society that socialists wanted; nor did it conform to traditional bourgeois virtues of sobriety and rationality."[15] If this was not the future they wanted, why is it the future they got?

I will maintain that an important part of the answer lies in the power of the market system to override human choice in the unfolding of the future. But there are other possible answers as well—answers that also help to illuminate the question. Let us look first at these.

8

The Will of
the People

$\mathbf{D}$id Americans get the future they chose? To my thesis that, in important respects, the rule of choice is an illusion, alternative interpretations are variations on a theme that says: we got what we wanted.

DESPITE OBJECTIONS

One variant would maintain that the opposition to the advance of materialism represented merely a minority opinion. Clergymen may rail against this sin or that, and communities may give such men respect, but the preachers' priorities are not necessarily those of the people. Prophets may be deputies of God, or of what they take as the will of God, but the customary posture of the prophet in our tradition is less as the representative or spokesman of the popular view than as the one who sets himself against the predominant tendency of the people, upon whom he rains down his jeremiads. The majority, according to this argument, are generally happier to work in the service of Mammon.

This argument probably contains a good amount of truth. Yet the power, within the hearts of the people, of the values mitigating against the materialistic path was probably considerably greater than this view suggests.

The people who braved persecution in England for their religious beliefs, and who risked everything to establish in the New World a community governed by their religious vision, must have had more than a casual commitment to the righteous path as they understood it. John Winthrop was not just some voice crying out in the wilderness. As this community set out on its errand into the wilderness, Winthrop was its leader. A Jonathan Edwards's place in his society is not to be confused with the place of a Protestant minister in an upper-middle-class Protestant American community today. (Indeed, the shift in power over two or three centuries from religious leaders to economic leaders is part of the transformation that calls for explanation.) The Great Awakening was a powerful religious upsurgence infused with the deepest passions of a great many Americans.

It is not clear how we can establish what the will of the majority was. But the voices raised against making materialism and economic expansion the chief end of American society do not seem to have been peripheral.

In the political realm, Thomas Jefferson's goals for America were not obviously less representative of the body of American opinion than Hamilton's. Jefferson was certainly not on the fringe in terms of the esteem of his countrymen. Hamilton's views, certainly, were congenial to many of the most powerful commercial interests in the new nation, and it may be said that these interests prevailed. But to establish that there were *some* who chose our future is not to refute the notion that the power of human choice is illusory. For, as we said earlier (p. 94) about historymakers, if it is the structure of the system—in this case, the market system—that determines who shall choose, then at the most fundamental level, it is the system itself that chooses.*

---

*Something similar should be observed concerning that consumerist society that emerged at the turn of the twentieth century in France. Although the consumerist society that arose was not the one desired by various political movements whose values were contending in the struggle to shape the future of France, the creation of such a society was the result of the successful

LIP SERVICE

Another serious, and probably at least partially valid, counterargument to my thesis about the power of the market is that people's pronouncements about their values cannot be taken at face value.

It is in the nature of our inner dynamics as moral beings that we tend to represent ourselves as being what we believe we should be, to identify ourselves with the part of ourselves that speaks with the voice of moral authority. But that does not mean that what we really want is what our morality tells us we should want.

Even if the early American religious leaders who decried the love of riches were representative of their flocks, the materialism that took hold in the New World may have represented the real choice of those communities. If we look at the lives of these moralists, we discover that many of them did not themselves practice what they preached.

Among the Puritans, for example, Cotton Mather held up for emulation the "primitive principles and primitive practices" of those who had founded the Massachusetts Bay Colony a few generations before. But, says David Shi: "His own spacious three-story house on Hanover Street in Boston, some argued, befitted more a merchant prince than a minister. It was adorned with classic pilasters and lavish ornamentation."[1] A similar contradiction between public preaching and private practice is to be discovered in the life of William Penn. "Despite Penn's sincere pleas for living among [the] colonists of his Quaker Pennsylvania," Shi writes after describing Penn's "magnificent country estate, "he himself clearly lacked a sense of economy."[2] As Shi demonstrates, both Quakers and Puritans placed a high value on simplicity, but both groups found it anything but simple to live up to their ideals.

The gap between professed belief and actual practice is a ubiquitous problem in human life. Such hypocrisy raises questions about the genuineness and power of people's stated beliefs. Did the founders of American society really want to live

___

strategy of businessmen working to stimulate demand for their products. To say that the businessmen chose this future does not mean that, ultimately, it should be understood as the people choosing their destiny, if it is the system that conferred on those few the power to override the goals of many others.

the kind of simple and pious lives they said they valued? Or are the preachings about piety and simplicity merely lip service to values they did not really hold?

The relationship between honesty and hypocrisy is more complex than the dichotomy of possibility would imply.

Sometimes, the hypocrite seems to be simply a liar. In our own time, when a Jim and Tammy Bakker fleece their flocks of millions in the name of spiritual concerns and use the proceeds to put gold handles on their bathroom fixtures, to some the hypocrisy may seem sheer dishonesty. It is possible to doubt whether the Bakkers care much about the values they preach. In other instances—and perhaps even with the Bakkers—the question of the sincerity of the hypocrite is more difficult to unravel.

Hypocrisy raises questions not only of the sincerity of belief but also of the power of competing desires. Another aspect of our moral systems is that from the strength of the prohibition can be inferred the strength of the impulses our commandments forbid. Morality spends no time telling us not to poke our fingers into our eyes. It is our lusts and temptations that we are warned against. All the strictures against cupidity and greed are like so many signs at ground level telling us that the well of those vices is richly fed by underground springs of desire.

In our moral struggles, which side is "really" us? Consider the passage in the book of Romans, when Paul says:

> For the good that I would, I do not; but the evil which I would not, that I do . . . For I delight in the law of God after the inward man; But I see another law in my members, warring against the law of my mind, and bringing me into captivity to the law of sin which is in my members.[3]

Are we to believe that Paul really wanted the good but not the evil? No, Paul's rhetoric shows that he identified with only a part of himself. His action reveals which desire is the stronger. The moral will is only part of the will.

Paul wrote honestly about his own failure to follow his "higher" will.* Here the question of honesty is translated,

---

*Another contemporary hypocrite comes to mind. Jimmy Swaggart—the fundamentalist minister who was disgraced a few years ago by public revelation of his consorting with prostitutes—confessed only when he was ex-

rather, into one of integration. That the different parts of the self war with each other signifies a failure to reconcile the different elements on terms that make consistency possible. Hypocrisy, in such an instance, is a sign that the war continues within the person and that neither side consistently prevails. Additionally, hypocrisy is a sign that only one of the person's governors is allowed to give public utterance, and so the testimony of his words is the truth, but not the whole truth.

We can impute honesty to values, therefore, even in the face of hypocrisy if we understand that values that are held sincerely are not necessarily held wholeheartedly. Such a hypocrite simultaneously means what he says he wants and wants to do what he does, even though the two are in contradiction.

The greater the gap between profession and conduct, perhaps, the more we may be entitled to infer that the unuttered wants are stronger than the moral commitments that are declared but violated. This raises a question about my earlier statement that the materialistic society that emerged in America is not what the Puritans wanted: from which wants ultimately gained satisfaction, can we infer which wants were the stronger? Perhaps they did not do the "good" that they "wanted" because in their members dwelt a stronger law that held them captive.

If such were the case, then we might say that Americans did not get the future they chose only in the sense that Paul did not want to commit the evil he did. The problem of choice would involve not our failure to control our evolving economic system but our failure to integrate our psychological system. The only illusion surrounding our choice would derive not from the hidden autonomy of the market but from our identifying only with a part of ourselves, while another part takes us where "we" don't want to go.

There is one more facet to the question of hypocrisy that is pertinent to explore. We have seen that the hypocrite may be a liar, or he may be, like Paul, an honest witness of his inability to achieve his moral aspirations. He can also fool himself about what he is really doing.

---

posed, and even then the theatricality of his confession cast doubt on his public honesty. But perhaps in his private life he had, like Paul, fought to follow sincerely held values, but nonetheless lost to what Paul called the law in his members (or evidently, in Swaggart's case, one in particular).

With self-deception, the failure to integrate may remain covert, so that a person is governed by unadmitted desires that appear to act within the person's moral government like so many spies, or moles, from the other side. I tell myself that I stand for what I call virtue even while I, unnoticing, practice what I call vice.

It may be that Americans have had some capacity to fool themselves regarding their own materialism. After describing the disparity between pronouncement and action in William Penn, Shi observes that "Penn saw no contradiction between his espousal of material moderation and his own princely style of living."[4] In his book on attitudes toward consumer society in America during the final decades of the nineteenth century and the early decades of the twentieth, Daniel Horowitz describes some apparently similar self-deception in the American middle class. In the period before World War I, writes Horowitz, the middle class in America "may have behaved like dedicated consumers but tended to see itself not as incipient Babbitts but potential Thoreaus or cultivated citizens."[5]

The question arises: what does it mean to say that someone *believes* in a set of values if those values do not notably restrain or channel his actions? Horowitz describes both the importance and the limitations of the influence of Henry David Thoreau—the great nineteenth-century embodiment of simple living—on subsequent American culture. "Thoreau's impact on the imagination of successive generations of Americans," Horowitz says, "was out of proportion to his ability to affect the decisions people made in the marketplace or in the corridors of power."[6] Perhaps ambivalence is played out by giving each set of values a realm in which those values hold sway. According to Horowitz's formulation above, Thoreau and the nonmaterialistic values for which he stood evidently exercised dominion in the realm of the imagination, while in the real world of action the love of wealth could rule.

Dividing the world into different spheres can thus allow some people to hold contradictory convictions without having to reconcile the opposing elements, or even to confront seriously their mutual inconsistency. Separating one of the spheres from the realm of one's own actual conduct in the world—creating an arena of moral rhetoric and imagined or vicarious lives—provides a convenient way to remove troublesome values from one's path without rejecting them. One can bow to God and then get back to living in the service of Mammon. Moral commitments—such as nonmaterialistic values—can be reduced to gestures.

As gestures, the nonmaterialistic strain of moral values remains alive and well in America today. "Money can't buy happiness," we are told; "Money Can't Buy Me Love," the Beatles sang. Yet the juggernaut of the acquisitive society rolls on. Philip Slater sees not just a contradiction but an organic relationship between these opposing currents in American culture. The gesture of rejecting money, according to Slater, helps us survive in a society dedicated to wealth. The "sentimental rejection" of our dominant materialistic mores in popular songs and in films, Slater says in *The Pursuit of Loneliness*, acts as a "safety valve" for our dissatisfactions. "[s]uburbanites who philosophize over their back fence with complete sincerity about their 'dog-eat-dog world', and what-is-it-all-for and you-can't-take-it-with-you, and success-doesn't-make-you-happy-it-just-gives-you-a-heart-condition—would be enraged if their children paid serious attention to such a viewpoint."[7]*

---

*Another investigator of the rise of consumer society also sees an organic connection between such apparently contradictory elements in our culture's values. In his work *The Romantic Ethic and the Spirit of Modern Consumerism*, Colin Campbell sees Puritan asceticism and what he regards as romantic consumerism to be two sides of the same coin. "Puritans" and "romantics," he says, "have the same personality traits; they merely value them differently." (pp. 222–23). The two types, which he regards as "complementary rather than contradictory," "jointly [compose] one overall 'purito-romantic' personality system." (p. 223).

Campbell suggests another interesting way that, in our culture, both sides of this personality can gain expression. In his formulation, rather than the division of realms that I proposed above, Campbell suggests that in the middle-class life cycle there is "a serial form of integration," in which the life of the person is "divided into a Bohemian youth followed by a bourgeois middle age." (223).

This dichotomy corresponds better to some other polarities in our values about life-style—such as the opposition between leisure and work, between conventional and unconventional, and between what Campbell calls "sentimental" and "utilitarian" values—than it does to the nonmaterialistic versus materialistic values with which we are concerned here. For the Bohemian life-style of youth, more self-indulgent in some respects, also tends to be less consumerist in many ways than the bourgeois life-style of the older generation.

Because of these contradictions and hypocrisies that can attend people's espousal of nonmaterialistic values, I need to concede some important points.

When people declare what they believe in, what they regard as good, what they want, their declarations cannot necessarily be taken at face value. Even if their commitment to those values is sincere, it may be far from wholehearted. With respect to moral statements especially, we are justified in suspecting that what is gaining expression could be but a vocal minority among the contending elements of the personality. The moral element tends to be vocal because it is approved, because it wears the gown of respectability. But it can still be outvoted in the arena of behavior if there are passions that, though mute, are still more powerful than the moral commitment. This calls into some question what it is that the early Americans, for all their moral declarations, *really wanted*.

But even if it is conceded that the full articulation of what the Puritans and Quakers and so forth "really wanted" would be more complex, less strictly spiritual and moral, than their sermons, there is still reason for believing that the drive toward materialism was not wholly of human choosing. This reason is the *change over time* in America toward those values in which the market system deals.

Our discussion of hypocrisy could serve to explain why *each generation* would tend to live more materialistically than its moral statements would lead us to expect. But it cannot explain why, over the course of *successive generations,* the values of the society overall would grow more materialistic.

When a group of people embrace wealth more energetically than their values would suggest, we might surmise that their actions give us a clue absent from their words about what they really want. But if a nation's values change continuously in a certain direction, even contrary to many of the culture's stated values, we are justified in seeking forces that lie outside the psychological nexus.

Hypocrisy alerts us to the possibility that people want something other than what they say they want. A consistent, long-term transformation of values in a culture's values alerts us to the possibility that what people want is being shaped by forces operating at the societal level.

THE GOOD OLD DAYS NEVER WERE

We began our investigation by noting the enormous transformation that American civilization has wrought on this virgin continent, erecting a huge productive apparatus that allows most Americans a degree of material wealth that is opulent by any historical standard. The next step was to note an apparent discrepancy between the materialist thrust of our society's development and the values to which a great many, perhaps a preponderance, of Americans were apparently devoted during the generations that our civilization took form. After acknowledging that Americans were probably more committed to Mammon than their godly preachings would suggest, the conclusion was that the transformation of American values over time nonetheless may constitute evidence for the operation of that social evolutionary black hole, the power of the market system to shape society according to its own logic.

An interesting counterargument to this thesis arises here. Our investigation has come to fix its focus on the question of how the transformation of American values is to be explained. But *what if no such transformation occurred*?

Defenders of the market often complain that modern capitalist society is often condemned for being unusually *materialistic*, whereas what is remarkable about it is only that it is unusually *rich*. Greed was hardly invented by market societies. It was declared one of the seven deadly sins long before Adam Smith counseled us to appeal to the cupidity rather than the altruism of our brethren to get our needs met. In his work *The Quest for Wealth*, Robert Heilbroner presents portraits of some of those through history who have been most avid, and most successful, in the pursuit of riches. Avarice did indeed have a long pedigree before capitalism developed. While people have bemoaned the materialism of Western market societies in Europe and North America, other Westerners traveling to traditional societies elsewhere in the world have found many in these nonmarket societies as greedy as a John D. Rockefeller or Howard Hughes.

According to the psychological assumptions embedded in the concept of 'Economic man,' the market is simply an extraordinary instrument for delivering the goods that, as a direct function of human nature, people inevitably wish to have:

more and more of all the things that satisfy their limitless wants. (My critique of this view of human nature will await another book.)

As for American society in particular, we have already seen that the pious pilgrims had not been long off the boats before they began to struggle with the eruption of their avaricious impulses and the desire to flaunt their wealth by wearing fancy clothes and constructing imposing houses. By the time of the American Revolution, we recall, a love of luxury, disturbing to some, was already well entrenched. Well before the Civil War, which is to say before industrial capitalism in American commenced the explosive phase of its development, a Whig journal, the *American Review*, commented that "To get, and to have the reputation of possessing, is the ruling passion . . . of nine-tenths of our population."[8] At the beginning of this century, Henry James observed that in his native America the will to grow economically was "everywhere written large, and to grow at no matter what or whose expense."[9]

Whether materialistic desires predominate in human nature or not, this argument could conclude, there is ample evidence that Americans were inflamed by the passion for wealth from the beginning. If material wealth is what Americans always wanted, what mystery is there in the materialistic form our society has taken? Rather than look to the market system as the engine of our materialism, one might more reasonably join Chandra Mukerji in declaring the "materialism helped to shape the patterns of capitalist development."[10] The market would seem to be an engine that simply took us where we always wanted to go.

The good old days of a less materialistic America, in other words, never were.

This argument is persuasive up to a point, but that point falls short of negating my thesis. It is not that the market is wholly master, rather than servant, but only that it is partly master, partly the shaper of our destiny. It is not that the market created materialism, but that it tends to make materialistic values more dominant, less held in check by other competing notions of value.

This indeed did happen in America. Materialistic desires were always a factor, and, early on, their strength was alarming to people whose goals for this civilization were in a different direction. But even evidence of intense alarm in the seventeenth and eighteenth centuries does not demonstrate that the materialism of their society was as intense as that we find in the late nineteenth and the twentieth centuries. To people of fervent moral concern, a few steps down what they regard as the wrong path can seem catastrophic. If such people condemned the materialism around them more strongly than we hear it censured today, it may still be that contemporary America has proceeded a good deal further down the path of Mammon than the society that elicited those earlier denunciations.

Even while our foreparents may have succumbed to materialistic temptations, the vision of spiritual possibilities was alive within them. Their failure fully to embody their godly ideals, as they understood the will of God, is not to be equated with our society's possession by the spirit of Mammon. Cotton Mather can stand both as an emblem of their shortcomings and as a measuring post to gauge the ebb of a vital dimension of our culture. While acknowledging the tragic dimensions in Cotton Mather's life, Robert Bellah goes on to say: "But unlike so many in the generations to follow, he knew who he was, why he was here, and where he was going. That precious cup of meaning, *which has been draining away in America every since*, was, for him, still full."[11]

There has been a transformation of values in America. It is time now to delineate that transformation.

9

The Transformation
of American Values

In the first century and a half of our nation's existence, two profound and parallel changes took place. In the economic realm, a vast national market system developed, with enormous wealth and productive power becoming concentrated in industrial enterprises. At the same time, a shift occurred in American values, a shift that brought the way people evaluate their lives into considerable congruence with the way the market system keeps score.

In the first four decades of the nineteenth century, Daniel Horowitz writes, economic and cultural forces "gathered enough strength" to create a new kind of person. "There emerged," says Horowitz, "a personality type built around ambition, a sense that time was money, and an appreciation of progress."[1] From one point of view, the values of this new man can be seen as useful equipment for his succeeding in the market. Perhaps more fundamentally, a plentiful supply of such men was essential equipment for an economic system seeking rapid, even limitless expansion.

In this transformation of the values of the nineteenth century American, two main dimensions particularly warrant our exploration. First, there arose a worship of *success*. This success meant the fulfillment of ambition in the arena of economic competition. And second, there was a tendency to enshrine *wealth* as the essence of value.

THE WORSHIP OF SUCCESS

The question of the purpose of human life is one that every culture must address. The answers are not identical from one culture to another (though certainly there are cross-cultural themes). And even within a given culture, over time, the predominant answer can change. That is what happened in American culture with the rise of the ethic of success.

From Weber's *The Protestant Ethic and the Spirit of Capitalism*, we learn that the emphasis on the quest for success was in some ways prefigured in the earlier Protestant way of life. Diligence and discipline and frugality were cherished virtues in the early Protestant worldview, and they also constituted a good recipe for success in economic terms. Thus a person's prosperity in the pursuit of his calling might be regarded as outward evidence of a favorable spiritual state of the inward man.

During the course of the nineteenth century, however, the spiritual core of this worldview seems to have broken down, leaving but the dry husk of material success to define the purpose of human existence. No longer focusing on the progress of the pilgrim's soul toward virtue or salvation, the new worldview fixed its constant gaze on simply "getting ahead."

Two works describe this transformation in remarkably similar language. In his book *The Dream of Success: A Study of the Modern American Imagination*, Kenneth Lynn identifies among "the most widely accepted concepts in nineteenth-century American society" the equation of "business success with spiritual grace."[2] "A tendency to equate success and salvation" is discussed also in a most telling account of these transformations of values, John Cawelti's *Apostles of the Self-Made Man*.

In the late nineteenth century, Cawelti shows, there emerged a literature that "treated failure and success in terms that the Christian tradition had reserved for damnation and salvation."[3] Cawelti chronicles the displacement during the nineteenth century of an older ethic, focusing on virtues of character, by a new ethic concerned only with outward success. In the first part of that century, the American middle class adhered to a religious set of values embracing industry and honesty and piety. In this Protestant tradition, success was a matter essentially of self-improvement. By the second half of the century, success is defined in terms external to the self: getting ahead in the competitive market has become central. In this Vincelombardian tradition, where winning is the only thing, the religious virtues give way to such "secular qualities as initiative, aggressiveness, competitiveness, and forcefulness."[4] In the new literature, "success requires, above all, the will to win."[5]

The old worldview was about the relation of one's soul to God; the new one is about getting and keeping an edge on one's competitors. The religious terminology remains, but is transformed. "You've got to feel the same personal solicitude over the bill of goods that strays off to a competitor," wrote one of the apostles of success, John Graham, "as a parson over a backslider, and hold special services to bring it back into the fold."[6]

For centuries, a great struggle was waged between a religious set of values and the gathering forces of economic expansion. With the rise of the new ethic, there is peace—a peace on the terms of the economic system. "To make money honestly," said Russell Conwell, another proponent of the ethic of success, "is to preach the gospel. The foundation principle of godliness and the foundation principle of success in business are one and the same, precisely."[7] No longer do the demands of virtue act as a restraint against the unbridled pursuit of wealth. The latter, which earlier ages had regarded as an evil, is now represented as the very school for moral improvement.

> The very labor a man has to undergo, the self-denial he has to cultivate, in acquiring money, are of themselves an education. They compel him to put forth intelligence, skill, energy, vigilance, zeal, bring out his practical qualities, and gradually train his moral and intellectual powers.[8]

The displacement of the old ethic of character by the new ethic of unrestrained material ambition was, of course, gradual. (Indeed, the old ethic has never vanished entirely.) Even in the early years of this century, the two sets of values could be seen contending, as Cawelti shows, in the pages of a single publication, a journal called *Success*. In its first few years, proponents of the different worldviews appeared in the same pages, different voices espousing a confusing mix of old Protestant values and new commercial ones. "But, by 1907, . . . *Success* dropped the traditional gospel. One sign of the change was the appearance of a regular feature, 'Hints to Investors,' in a magazine that, only five years earlier, had stated that speculation was more contemptible than gambling."[9]

Moral values had acted as a brake upon the dynamo of the market. But so powerful was that engine that the brakes, eventually, could not hold. Lo! a new set of moral values, and these, far from being a brake, helped to make the human will a more potent additive in the system's fuel.

THE VALUE OF THE DOLLAR

A closely related aspect of the same transformation was the enshrining of the dollar as the measure of all values.

Just as success became equated with salvation, says Kenneth Lynn, so also did Americans in the course of the nineteenth century come to equate "the pursuit of money with the pursuit of happiness."[10] Making material wealth the standard of human fulfillment led the way to the twentieth-century practice of officially measuring how "well" we live by the dollar cost of the volume of goods and services we consume.

For centuries, the religious teachings of Western civilization had inveighed against the love of riches. Robert Heilbroner shows that the first cracks in this girding against cupidity appeared early in the process of the emergence of the modern economy.[11] But in America it is when the power of the market mushroomed during the nineteenth century that the moral and religious restraints against the single-minded devotion to moneymaking fell away. Reminding us that "The great Puritans, Winthrop, Mather, Edwards, however much they emphasized the value of hard work, were deeply sensitive to the tension between . . . God and Mammon," Robert Bellah notes the later moral transformation. "In the late 19th century, the tension in many quarters was almost gone."[12] He cites a widely used ethics text book from the 1880s by D. S. Gregory, which declared: "By the proper use of wealth man may greatly elevate and extend his moral work . . . The Moral Governor has placed the power of acquisitiveness in man for a good and noble purpose."[13]

Cawelti notes the same transformation in the American moral perspective. "You ought to be reasonably ambitious to have money," the extremely popular lecturer, Russell Conwell, told his audiences. "You ought because you can do more good with it than you could without it."[14] The head of the Chicago, Burlington, and Quincy Railroad articulated the new gospel of the morality of wealth, saying:

> History and experience demonstrate that as wealth has accumulated and things have cheapened, men have improved . . . in their habits of thought, their sympathy for others, their ideas of justice as well as of mercy . . . Material progress must come first and . . . upon it is founded all other progress.[15]

"Godliness," said the Episcopal Bishop of Massachusetts in 1901, "is in league with riches."[16]

The new moral leaders of America—men like Napoleon Hill, Dale Carnegie, and Norman Vincent Peale—related to wealth and to greed in a way unknown even among the philosophers of self-improvement a generation or two before them. They "frankly sanction the desire for hard cash and assume that material wealth is an ultimate human motive."[17] Napoleon Hill told his readers "you can never have riches in great quantities unless you can work yourself into a white heat of *desire* for money."[18] Coming from the author of *Think and Grow Rich*, this is clearly not a condemnation of excessive greed.

THE CASE OF THE VANISHING PROTESTANT ETHIC

One other dimension of the moral transformation of America deserves examination. Over time there has been a shift from values emphasizing productiveness to values that promote consumption. The asceticism of the Protestant Ethic was ideal for the accumulation of wealth. But as the productive power of the economy expanded, some believe, the continued growth of the system depended on assuring a sufficiency of *demand* for the goods produced.

The idea that the system required people to become consumption oriented "as production caught up with demand" has been proposed in different ways by a number of scholars.[19] In the case of England, McKendrick, Brewer, and Plumb place the beginnings of the shift as far back as the eighteenth century. In *The Birth of a Consumer Society*, McKendrick says that "the consumer revolution was the necessary analogue to the industrial revolution, the necessary convulsion on the demand side of the equation to match the convulsion on the supply side."[20] In the case of the United States, Daniel Horowitz sees the transformation beginning a century later. On the basis of his study of the shifting patterns of belief about *The Morality of Spending*, Horowitz observes: "In the late nineteenth century a shift started from self-control to self-realization, from the world of the producer, based on the values of self-denial and achievement, to a consumer culture that emphasized immediate satisfaction and the fulfillment of the self through gratification and indulgence."[21]

It was in the aftermath of World War II, however, that the economics and psychology of demand, rather than supply, of consumption, rather than production, seemed really to take over. After two decades of depression and war, Americans unleashed a torrent of demand that had been long pent up. Daniel Bell describes the ascendancy of the new ethic:

> The culture was no longer concerned with how to work and achieve, but with how to spend and enjoy. Despite some continuing use of the language of the Protestant ethic, the fact was that by the 1950s American culture had become primarily hedonistic, concerned with play, fun, display, and pleasure.[22]

The new ethic not only replaced frugality with spending, but even encouraged people to spend money they did not have. John Kenneth Galbraith devoted a chapter of his work *The Affluent Society* to lamenting the rise of consumer debt. Describing "the process of persuading people to incur debt" as being an essential "part of modern production," Galbraith declared that the "Puritan ethos" was "overwhelmed by the massive power of modern merchandizing."[23]

If we regard the market as merely an instrument for meeting human needs, and particularly if we understand human needs in terms of the calculus of the insatiable and materialistic Economic Man, the development of an economy of consumerism requires no special explanation. Consumption, which is equated with human fulfillment, is simply the market system achieving its ultimate purpose of providing satisfaction for the human beings acting within the system. But if we see the market also as a power system that uses human beings to achieve its purposes, then we must address the question: How does this transformation relate to the requirements of the economic system?

The relationship is not so self-evident as it may at first appear.

Without escalating consumer demand, some interpreters of our economic system apparently assume, there would be no way to sell what is produced. With no demand, there would be no supply, and the system would begin to break down. The reason this argument is not airtight is that consumerism is not the only possible source of demand: production can also go into investment, that is, into creating the means for more production. Factories can labor to equip more factories.

That sounds irrational, of course—production for the sake of more production, ad infinitum (if not nauseam). To what end would we want all these means of production? Yet irrationality of this kind is evidently not an insurmountable barrier to the limitless expansion of the wealth system. Many individuals who already possess more wealth than they could consume in ten lifetimes are nonetheless obsessed with acquiring more. In part 3 of this work "Out of Control," we will explore the irrationalities of the cult of economic growth that retains a nearly unchallenged grip upon the political economy of the United States (and other countries). A system of production for the sake of more production, without the goods ever taking a form suitable for direct human enjoyment, is not really so much more irrational than other visible aspects of our wealth system.

The case of contemporary Japan, indeed, may be said to approach such a system. A number of observers have noted that the Japanese economy, quite unlike ours, is oriented toward the production sector in considerable preference over the consumption sector. Japanese policies have lead to the creation of the huge and prosperous corporations that have come to dominate much of the world's industry and finance, while the Japanese people consume like members of a much poorer society. James Fallows has written that "The per capital income in Malaysia is about one tenth as high as in Japan, but by most of the measures of basic human comfort—housing space, clothing, food, leisure time, recreation, and amusement—the difference between the two societies is not very large."[24] The Japanese pay eight or ten times as much for rice, the staple of their diet, as the world price. In their asceticism, their savings rate is many times higher a percentage of their income than that of Americans. Though Japanese prosperity derives from selling to *foreign* consumers, the system itself is organized as production for the sake of production. And the Japanese rise to economic preeminence proves that such an economy can thrive.

To achieve unlimited economic expansion without correspondingly rising consumption might demand more insanity* than the consumer society we have developed for the past century. Or perhaps it would require the practice of slavery, where the asceticism of productive workers is compelled by force. But it is not logically impossible.

If the stimulation of consumer demand is not a logically inescapable requirement of an indefinitely expanding economic system, in what way can the rise of consumerism and the erosion of the Protestant ethic be understood as a manifestation of the power of the market system to mold human consciousness to suit its purposes?

The answer rests on an understanding that the market system is not teleological, but *opportunistic.* It grows not with a plan or a purpose, but wherever it can. Like water running wherever there is a gully, the market will flow to wherever there is money.

As the market system developed, money inevitable ended up not only in productive enterprises, but also in households.

---

*After two generations of comparative personal sacrifice amid exploding national wealth, the Japanese are showing some signs of reluctance to continue to be energetic in production and ascetic in consumption. To the extent that a people is free, an economy of increasing production for production's sake is probably difficult, for psychological reasons, to sustain over the long term.

The people who ran the enterprises, and increasingly also those who labored in them, were rewarded by the market for their valuable contributions. As households gained wealth, the opportunity arose for a market in goods made for those households. This opportunity could best be exploited by those best able to persuade people to think and act as consumers. A part of the market system, therefore, sent some of its power and resources flowing on an educational mission to create the consumer values and images that would lead people to part with their money in exchange for the goods produced by the system. (The Japanese economy has, by contrast, been effective in recent decades in persuading households to put their money back into the system, buying such investment vehicles as publicly-traded stocks.) The gathering momentum of the efforts of corporate America, earlier in this century, to indoctrinate the American public in the consumerist world-view is described by Roland Marchand's *Advertising the American Dream*. The power of advertising as an educational process in contemporary American society has grown still greater in recent decades.

The creation of the consumer society, and the corresponding weakening of the Protestant ethic, are therefore at least partially the work of the economic system, or at least parts of it. The system fostered these new values not because the system as a whole requires them to continue its expansion, but because parts of the system inevitably would emerge to exploit the *potentiality* for a market implied by the existence of widely distributed private wealth.* Indeed, as far as the long-term expansion of the economic system as a whole is concerned, this transformation of American values is proving more a hindrance than a help.

It is becoming increasingly evident that the stimulation of consumer demand that so many have regarded as an economic necessity actually undermines the foundations of economic growth. This is what Marx would have called a

---

*The inevitability of the market's exploiting such a large potential niche may seem to be irreconcilable with the slowness of consumerism's rise in Japan. But the skewing of Japan's economic development toward production during its post-war "miracle" was made possible by politically determined interferences in the market's functioning. It is because of politics, not the market, that the Japanese pay excessively for rice, and that an automobile made in Japan costs more in that country than in America.

contradiction in the evolution of the capitalist system. The system that teaches people to spend now weakens as a result of their failure to save.

In recent years, as the economic supremacy of the United States has declined in the face of competition from industrial societies more disciplined in their spending, the Protestant ethic has begun to make something of a comeback. Do the Japanese work longer hours and take fewer vacation days? We'd better buckle down to work as well. Do the Germans (and Japanese) save more than we? Then we too had better become more frugal.

The question of what the game of life is about is, of course, one of the most profound we confront as human beings. But so long as our world's way of keeping score says that whoever controls the most wealth wins, then the Protestant ethic of hard work and thrift—as the non-Protestant, but hardworking and frugal Japanese have reminded us—remains the winning strategy.

Saving, we are nowadays being reminded, is not a failure to consume. It is *investment*. And investment is what magnifies productive power for the future. So we are admonished in the *Washington Post* in 1989, in an article entitled "Why America Won't Save," that "Americans have been saving at rates low enough to cheat our future."[25] The old morality—which Samuel Butler once observed "turns on whether the pleasure precedes the pain or follows it"[26]—is again being promoted. "Think of undersaving as cholesterol: Both are the by-product of immediate gratification, neither involves short-run cost, both accrue slowly with real dangers in the future."[27]

This is one transformation that the proponents of the economic system may be coming to recognize as a cul-de-sac turning off from the road to wealth without limit.

A CIVILIZATION OUT OF BALANCE

What are the values around which our civilization is organized? There are, of course, many. But some values have come to dominate, and they are the values in which our economic system deals. As E. F. Schumacher put it, "The development of production and the acquisition of wealth have . . . become the highest goals of the modern world in relation to which all other goals, no matter how much lip-service may still be paid to them, have come to take second place."[28] It was not always thus. A balance has shifted. As the modern market society began to take shape in Europe, many protested. They advocated medieval values to constrain the free play of the market, "particularly those precepts that limited the pursuit of profits or declared that economic matters must be tied to some socially integrative function."[29] But, says Mukerji, the power of the market soon overwhelmed the old system of values. In early modern Europe, he writes, "As the new system of trade grew to the extent that it overshadowed other social institutions and became the central organization force in social life, the value placed on accumulation began to gain priority over other cultural values."[30]

Our society in America is an extension of that European civilization. As a new society, however, it has formed a more pure laboratory for the expression of the particularly modern forces of the market system. For in American society, far fewer remnants of an old social order—such as the interests and values of an entrenched aristocracy—stood as obstacles to the unfolding of a new order built on modern lines. This new start made it easier to establish a democratic polity in the New World. It also has allowed market forces a freer hand in molding both the continent and the people.

But even in America, as we have seen, our civilization sprang forth out of other visions of the good and virtuous life. In the first couple of centuries of the development of American society, the pecuniary values of the emerging market economy were poised in an uneasy balance with other sets of values also fervently held by the American people. But the dynamic of history did not sustain that balance. As Cawelti describes it, the growing "authority and prestige" of the mighty industrialists and financiers, who were knitting together a national economy in the latter half of the nineteenth century, led to a shift in popular moral teachings. This shift was "away from the earlier balance of political, moral, religious, and economic values and in the direction of an overriding emphasis on the pursuit and use of wealth."[31]

Just as the market system, in its growing power, could remake the land, rendering the bounty of the continent into so many exploitable natural resources, so could it also remake the minds of men. The market's values triumph over its competitors. It *subordinates* them. As wealth-values become the highest, Schumacher says, "all secondary goals have finally to justify themselves in terms of the service their attainment renders to the attainment of the highest."[32] The other domains of value become as colonial clients of the conquering domain of value.

In the history of imperialism, we see repeatedly how the cultural ways of the conqueror are adopted by the vanquished. The languages of France and Spain reflect their subordination millennia ago to the Roman empire. The elites of India are fluent in the language of their British former overlords. Robert Heilbroner describes how, with the ascendancy of the economic sphere over American culture, the language of the conquering sphere spread: "In government, in education, in fields far removed from the sphere of the market place, 'business thinking' was now held to be the criterion of sound thinking, while even in the selection of pure ideas, the ultimate in justification was that a proposal might be a 'money-making proposition.' "[33]

Whole domains of value collapse, becoming subsumed under the aegis of the economic realm. In 1990, the president of the United States declares that environmental concerns must be balanced with "the economic factor, the human factor," his intonation clearly implying that the "economic factor" *subsumes* the "human factor." Over the generations, one tends to become the Economic Man the system's theory propounds.

Over time, the transformation of values reflects and helps create a civilization out of balance.

10

In the Image of
Our Creator

On the face of it, the dramatic resculpting of the features of this continent over the past couple of centuries was done not by "forces" or some other intangible abstraction but by the concrete activity of actual human beings pursuing their own ends.

At the same time that the material features of the New World were being altered, however, so was human consciousness. While factories were being built, canals dug, fields cleared, stones quarried, from generation to generation the values of the American people were shifting also. So when we speak of people pursuing their own ends, it is necessary also to examine how it is that people end up committed to such ends.

The changing face of the American continent and the changing minds of the American people form a congruent pattern. The idea of a pattern, itself an abstraction, suggests the possibility of systematic forces at work. Such forces, though not tangible and seemingly removed from the reality of our lives, can have a more fundamental reality than the concrete events of our day-to-day lives—more fundamental in the sense of having more power to determine the shape of things. If you place a magnet under a paper on which iron filings are scattered, the filings will align themselves in a predictable pattern. The notion of lines of electromagnetic force seems like an abstraction; the intangibility of such a force makes it seem less than real. But the reality of the electromagnetic field is sufficient to dictate the disposition of countless concrete bits of ferrous metal. Likewise, both the changes in the material arrangement of nature and civilization on this land and the shift in the balance among values in American society are in alignment with the forces of an expanding market economy.

What does it mean to say that people *choose* their destiny? If we are driven north by being mercilessly whipped whenever we head south, then clearly our decision to go north is not freely made. But even in the absence of such a whip, even without brute coercion, our going north may not be freely chosen.

Oscar Wilde wrote a fable entitled "The Magnet." It goes like this:

> Once upon a time there was a magnet, and in its close neighborhood lived some steel filings. One day two or three little filings felt a sudden desire to go and visit the magnet, and they began to talk of what a pleasant thing it would be to do. Other filings nearby overheard their conversation, and they, too, became infected with the same desire. Still others joined them, till at last all the filings began to discuss the matter, and more and more their vague desire grew into an impulse. "Why not go today?" said some of them; but others were of the opinion that it would be better to wait till tomorrow. Meanwhile, without their having noticed it, they had been involuntarily moving nearer to the magnet, which lay there quite still, apparently taking no heed of them. And so they went on discussing, all the time insensibly drawing nearer to their neighbor; and the more they talked, the more they felt the impulse growing stronger, till the more impatient ones declared that they would go that day, whatever the rest did. Some were heard to say that it was their duty to visit the magnet, and that they ought to have gone long ago. And, while they talked, they moved always nearer and

nearer, without realizing that they had moved. Then, at last, the impatient ones prevailed, and, with one irresistible impulse, the whole body cried out, "There is no use waiting. We will go today. We will go now. We will go at once." And then in one unanimous mass they swept along, and in another moment were clinging fast to the magnet on every side. Then the magnet smiled—for the steel filings had no doubt at all but that they were paying that visit on their own free will.[1]

Here is a fanciful, but clear and compelling, image of *the illusion of choice*. In the evolution of America society, the market system has functioned as such a magnet. We Americans have been like those filings—surely not altogether like them, but still in large measure—in the choices we have made that created the American civilization we now see.

NORTH MAY BE THE WAY TO GO

Again, the issue here is not what direction we *should* go. The point is, rather, what *governs* our direction.

Going "north," it could be argued, is a good move. According to this somewhat reasonable view, we are well rid of those medieval ideas condemning wealth. It may be that cautions against our greed and paeans to simplicity made sense in an era when the productive impotence of the economic system condemned the great mass of people—of necessity—to poverty. Morality as sour grapes. Now the grapes are within our grasp, and there is no further reason to deny their succulence.

The asceticism of the Puritans, moreover, seems to reflect an antagonism to our humanity. A worldview founded on the assumption of human depravity is antagonistic to the pursuit of happiness. We need hardly lament our civilization's movement away from a revulsion against the flesh and toward a celebration of life's pleasures. Our liberation from the dark and joyless spiritual prison into which earlier eras of our civilization's evolution had led us, according to this argument, is cause for rejoicing.

To a considerable degree, I would endorse that argument. Whether or not our present materialistic cultural approach to life represents liberation, there was much in the antimaterialism of the past from which we should be glad to be freed.

Though our society today seems beset by a kind of gluttony, I do not mourn the passing of the cult of spiritual anorexia that characterized much of the morality of the past.

My own view is that the human creature should be nourished, not deprived; our needs should be regarded as sacred, not sinful. The more fulfilled we are—the more our needs are met—the more we are enabled to achieve our potential as moral and spiritual beings. These views strongly differentiate my worldview from those of many who have inveighed against the materialistic and hedonistic course our society has taken. On the other hand, I cannot endorse that materialistic course. Our present society provides a rather skewed menu, depriving us of much that truly nourishes us.

The central point at issue here, however, is not so much which way is *better* for us to go, but whether we are and have been *free to choose* to go the way we want to go.

If the market system governs our destiny, taking us in a direction of its choosing whether we want to go that way or not, that is worth our knowing. Even if we judge that the path it compels us to take serves us well in some ways, we would not be wise to entrust our fate to a machine.

OTHER DYNAMICS OF CHANGE

The case—that the market has governed our destiny—remains unproved. Even if it is granted that our founding foreparents wanted a different, less materialistic kind of society (their hypocrisy notwithstanding), even if it is granted that a significant transformation of values occurred in America toward the values of the market, it would still need to be established that it is the market system itself that has been the engine of change. Other explanations are possible.

Intense spiritual orientations in a culture, for example, have an intrinsic tendency toward erosion. History is full of charismatic religious movements that, within a few generations, degenerate into something much less than their original form.

Dostoyevsky's famous story (embedded in *The Brothers Karamazov*) of "The Grant Inquisitor" represents one form of this tendency. The inquisitor, supposedly the representative of Christ on earth through the Christian church, comes face to face with Christ himself and recognizes that they are enemies. The charismatic savior, who resisted Satan's temptation in the wilderness, saying that "man does not live by bread alone," is lectured by the powerful leader of the Christian institution who says that by giving the people bread, "we shall give them the quiet humble happiness of weak creatures such as they are by nature."[2] The inquisitor maintains that the higher aspirations of freedom that Christ offered are above the reach of the mass of humanity.

Every religion, every religious movement, faces the challenge of how to keep alive the spirit of the experience, the intensity of vision, from which it first arose. Even within a single life, the moments of epiphany that one might hope would guide one's whole life are not easy to sustain. In the passing of life from generation to generation, this problem is compounded.

The erosion of the original vision of the early spiritual disciplines of America might be explained in such terms. David Shi writes that both the early Puritans and the original Quaker settlers "failed to transmit to their children their own religious zeal and social ethic."[3] Perhaps the inflow of more materialistic values can be seen as a kind of spiritual entropy. You can pump all the water out of a well shaft, but as soon as you turn off the pump, or the pump stops working well enough, the groundwater starts seeping back to its natural level. Keeping the water out takes real work, and maintaining a good pump from generation to generation is a cultural task beyond most groups' capacity.

In this perspective, the way the envisioned city upon a hill was overtaken by materialistic growths could be likened to the way nature reclaims any abandoned edifice, the way jungle trees overgrow ancient Mayan temples. The materialism of our civilization might be seen as a downhill place to which ambitious spiritual aspirations would inevitably slide.

Though once called to higher visions, over time the people of a culture will tend to submit to the dictates of their lower natures. The force of materialism's attraction to Americans could thus derive from the gravity of our human inclinations. The market's role could be simply as the supplier of temptations to indulge those inclinations. Shi, for example, describes in terms of seduction the course Americans took. "Seduced by the seemingly limitless economic and social opportunities available to them," Shi writes, "more and more Americans chose the individual pursuit and enjoyment of plenty over the cultivation of piety, plainness, and the public good."[4] The market may act like Satan in the Garden, in this view, but it is original sin and not Satan that explains the choice. It is still the discourse of free will.

BEYOND FREE WILL

The role of the market as the engine of our society's movement is still unproven, and so it will remain. All that can be established is that the market's impact on the context of human decision making inclines choices toward certain directions. Whatever the natural level of human nature in relation to human aspiration, the operation of the market system powerfully tilts the playing field of our activities. Whatever the "attractions" of the materially good life, it can at least plausibly be shown that the market's pull—like that of Wilde's magnet—could be a significant part of the attractive force.

There are several ways in which the market, rather than free human choice, can dictate our course. Some of these we touched upon in part 1. But it would be useful to underscore here the various mechanisms of the market's power.

Raw Power

In some respects, the path of economic "progress" has been opened not by some consensus of free men and women but by the exercise of coercive power of some people over others.

In part 1, we looked at the Faustian myth as emblematic of the dynamism of Western society. Faust also enacts the coercive element in the story of modern economic expansion. At one crucial point in this "tragedy of development," the hero and his agents resort to brute force to finish the task of creating "a whole new society . . . in his image."[5] The one remaining piece of land that embodies the old values is occupied by an old couple who, says Berman, "are the first embodiments in literature of a category of people that is going to be very large in modern history: people who are in the way—in the way of history, of progress, of development; people who are classified, and disposed of, as obsolete."[6] Faust cannot tolerate this remaining piece of an old world, this one clouded spot in a plane that otherwise serves as a mirror of Faust's ambitions. "That aged couple should have yielded, I want their lindens in my grip, Since these few trees that are denied me Undo my worldwide ownership . . . Hence is our soul upon the rack, To feel, amid plenty, what we lack."[7] Faust tells his diabolical companion, Mephisto to get the old people out of the way. In his desire not to see or to know how the deed is done, Berman suggests, Faust's "self-consciously evil act" represents "a characteristically modern style of evil: indirect, impersonal, mediated by complex organizations and institutional roles."[8]

When Goethe wrote, the process of development was already well under way in the more "advanced" European nations. In England, for example, the creation of the modern economy was accomplished with the forcible dispossession of whole classes of poorer people. In the land of the "mother of parliaments," most people were long denied any voice in Parliament. The coercive arm of the law could thus be wielded, by those who desired the economic revolution, against the many disenfranchised people who held other values. It was, says Karl Polanyi, "only when the working class had accepted the principles of a capitalist economy and the trade unions had made the smooth running of industry their chief concern [that] the middle classes concede[d] the vote to the better situated workers."[9] This strategy of withholding power helped in the "spreading of the market forms of existence," says Polanyi, "since it helped to overcome the obstacles presented by the surviving organic and traditional forms of life among the laboring people."[10]

In the perspective of our contemporary American capitalist democracy, Faust's indirect murder of those who stood in his way, and the English capitalists' government *of* the people *by* the dominant classes *for* the spread of their economic system, seem extreme. The U.S. government does not nowadays send in troops, as the Korean government did in the spring of 1990, to break up a strike by workers. A century ago, however, it did. Those industrialists, whose growing power, as Cawelti has suggested, helped to make pecuniary values outweigh all others in the American worldview, were also in great measure able to make the political system of the country an extension of their empires.

Fundamental choices about the destiny of this country have been shaped in corporate board rooms and implemented by the coercive power of the state.

Throughout the history of civilized societies, powerful elites have compelled the many to conform to social arrangements of the elites' choosing. The United States, because of its democratic institutions, has mitigated but hardly eliminated that injustice. And to the extent that the market can determine the distribution of power in American society, it is the market that chooses our destiny.

Shaping Choices

Even in the absence of coercion, the economic system places other kinds of power in the hands of its human captains who can bend the society to the market's will. More subtle than imposing one's will on others is molding the will of others to conform to one's own.

Of the various ways the market system helps to fashion human consciousness into the form it desires, the most clearcut and deliberate is advertising.

The idea that advertising seriously infringes upon fundamental human choice is scorned by some. George Will, for example, claims that "nowadays no serious person believes the hoary liberal theory that advertising annihilates consumer sovereignty."[11] Not wishing to forfeit my claim to seriousness, I might begin my response by noting that this hoary theory originated not with liberal critics of the institution of advertising but with the advertisers themselves. Early in the 1920s, the prominent advertising firm of Barton, Durstine and Osborn proclaimed that:

> The product of advertising is something . . . powerful and commanding—it is public opinion; and in a democracy public opinion is the uncrowned king . . .
>
> Archimedes asked for a lever long enough and strong enough to move the world. We have a suspicion that if he lived today he would apply for work in an agency.[12]

Of course, such a pronouncement could be dismissed as self-serving: the agency is claiming that it can deliver the public to its clients. But equally self-serving are the more recent protestations of the market's defenders who, wanting to maintain that the market satisfies our needs, find it inconvenient to concede that the market also fashions our needs.

What are we to believe? As American society is now mobilizing against the evils of addiction to nicotine, the tobacco industry and its advertisers have come before Congress (in

1990) to testify that their marketing efforts are really innocuous. We are not trying to create new smokers, they claim (even though they lose a thousand customers a day to death from smoking-related diseases). The advertisements, they maintain, are merely the way the different companies compete for existing customers. Each company is simply trying to get the customers of other brands to switch to their own. Therefore, there is no public policy justification for interfering with the free play of such commercial speech.

To believe that argument, one must either be stupid or believe the tobacco industry to be stupid. If all they think they are doing is fighting over a fixed and finite number of customers, then their battle is an expensive, zero-sum struggle, in which the industry as a whole has significant costs but no gains. If that were the case, and if they were smart, they would welcome laws banning all such advertising. Like nations in a costly arms race that can increase no one's overall security, these companies would be stupid to oppose a treaty that would terminate their fruitless expenditures. Whatever other shortcomings the tobacco industry has manifested, folly in figuring out where their own self-interest lies is not one of them.

From their desire to continue their advertising campaigns, the most plausible inference is clearly that these companies believe the ads can persuade nonsmokers to begin smoking. Evidently, the tobacco industry, too, believes the hoary theory that ads can create demand.

Advertisement does not create "needs," for our needs come with our natural human endowment as human beings. But advertisement can channel our needs in ways that serve its purpose. From the ads for cigarettes, we can infer what needs are being so channeled—the need to be desirable and attractive, to be in convivial contact with friends, and so forth. Channeling human needs is something all cultures do. By the use of various inducements, cultures take the package that comes from nature in the form of a baby and molds it into a form that corresponds with the demands of the surrounding society. As advertising has become more and more pervasive an influence in our culture—even Will reports that "the typical American is exposed to approximately 3,000 commercial messages—from newspapers to billboards—a day"[13]—it has become a major enculturating agent. Advertising has become a principal teacher in our culture system.

As a system of teachings, advertising imparts a vision not just of specific products but of a whole way of life. Cigarettes constitute but the filter tip of the consumption iceberg. As people are taught to smoke to gain conviviality, so also has advertising persuaded people to see the whole quest for fulfillment in terms that serve the expansion of the power system.

At a crucial juncture in American history, says Roland Marchand in his study of the workings of the institution from 1920 to 1940, advertisers functioned as "apostles of modernity." They sold the American people a way of living, fast of tempo and focused on private consumption, that fed the expansion of the economic system. Many Americans were deeply suspicious of such a way of life, but "advertisers paid close attention to signs of consumer resistance to their messages" which gave them "a particular sensitivity to certain consumer discontents with modernity."[14] Addressing people's anxieties about the world the market was helping to create, the advertisers created images that, however little they reflected the realities of their circumstances, could assuage their fears and enlist their participation in the world of consumption.

Again, every culture shapes people, finds ways to teach its way of life. What is unusual about advertising is the cultural teacher's unrelenting manipulativeness and fundamental dishonesty. Has there every been so powerful a cultural institution to whom the human beings it molded were so much merely means to an end—the end being their surrendering their money—and so little ends in themselves?

Advertising is thus a powerful weapon for the market in the struggle for control between the human and the system. In our society, enormous wealth is controlled by corporations and by the people who run those organizations. But it is the market that governs what kind of organizations will get this wealth and, in turn, each corporate system quite nonrandomly selects which individuals will hold positions of control.* This wealth, placed in hands chosen by the system, confers a power to indoctrinate that is not available to other cultural institutions animated by competing systems of value. The market thus gains considerable power to create the kind of people it wants.

---

*See Chapter 11, "Automatic Pilot," for further discussion of the nature of corporate systems.

Are we a materialistic society? Do most of us believe that what the present system gives us is what is really valuable? It is no wonder. Since before we were born, American society has been inundated by cultural teachings promoted by our materialistic market system. These teachings, conveyed through mass-media ads, says Jonathan Rowe, promote "an ideology of consumption."[15] As Ernest Dichter, "one of the fathers of modern advertising" cited by Rowe, said in 1956, the aim of advertising is to convince the average American that "the hedonistic approach to . . . life is the moral, not the immoral one."[16] No wonder we think we are getting what we want. We have been taught to want what we get.

Taking options away

A third way the market shapes our choices—beyond coercion and persuasion—is by arranging our world so that it is difficult to choose anything but what the market offers.

This is the skewed menu discussed earlier. It is easy in our society to find communications equipment but difficult to find community. The Yellow Pages tells us where to find bottled water, but it cannot tell us where to find clean rivers. If it can't be bought and sold, before long, in a market society, it can't be found.

This connects with advertising. Advertisers, says Michael Schudson in his book *Advertising: The Uneasy Persuasion,* claim that they "have the consumer always in mind." But, Schudson points out, "marketers do not actually seek to discover what consumers 'want' but what consumers want *from among commercially viable choices.*"[17]* Thus, even where the market does not, by its action, eliminate choices, it continually holds before our eyes only certain of the choices we might conceivably want to make.

---

*A perfect illustration of this is the infamous case, from the early 1980s, of Nestlé's campaign to persuade Third World mothers to buy infant formula. Breastfeeding was a better choice—better both for the women and for their infants. But this superior and naturally available option involves no sale and makes no companies rich. So the Nestlé company traded upon the prestige of the West and upon the desire of these women to provide for their children the most advanced care to entice these women to make a choice that endangered the lives of infants but filled the coffers of the rich corporation.

The system also shapes our choices through its atomistic structure. So long as we each make our decisions separately, we may each contribute to outcomes different from those we would choose if we could choose together. Recall the leaf blowers that make sense for each user, but not for the neighborhood; and the rock salt that is inexpensive, but imposes high costs. Barry Schwartz, in his book *The Battle for Human Nature*, provides another example:

> Imagine two bookstores, side by side. One is a discount chain with little selection but good prices. The other is an old-fashioned bookstore with seemingly everything in stock and a knowledgeable proprietor but list prices. A current best seller is available at both stores, but it costs fifteen dollars at the old-fashioned bookstore and ten dollars at the discount chain. A rational purchaser will, of course, go to the chain. So will everyone else. The old-fashioned bookstore will go out of business. Faced with the choice between spending a few extra dollars and keeping the old-fashioned store alive, or saving money and putting it out of business, would everyone still have chosen to save the money?[18]

But, as Schwartz understands, people acting in an atomistic system are not faced with such a choice. Such a choice can be made only if people create a forum in which they can act in concert. So long as each act is a solo, these acts will combine in discordant ways.

In a market society, decision making tends to gravitate to the level of autonomous social atoms. The capacity for collective choices is undermined. "Rational" choices made in an unbalanced system lead to undesired outcomes.

WHAT'S THE USE?

So great is the manifest power of the market system that one can reasonably wonder if there is any point in attacking the problems it creates. Whatever we might try to do, one might think in despair, it will be futile. The juggernaut will roll on.

Somehow, the market makes everything into grist for its mill.

Is there another locus of value that could compete with the market? The market will find a way to harness it for its own purposes. The Ewens, in their book *Channels of Desire*, describe a sales strategy of the Sears company in 1905. "The company wrote to all of its current customers in Iowa and asked each to pass on catalogs to friends and neighbors. The customers, in turn, sent the names of people given the catalog to the company."[19] Iowa in 1905 represents, no doubt, a world of greater innocence about market forces than the world of late twentieth century Americans. But we have gained our greater awareness, our cynicism, at a cost. Part of the price of learning to see more clearly what we were up against was the sacrifice of some of the social resources we might have used to protect ourselves. About this "Iowaization scheme," the Ewens observe:

> Customary rural networks became pathways along which modern channels of commerce were established. In the process, social relations themselves were metamorphosed. Originally built on patterns of mutual reliance and barter, now these relationships provided an arena within which people became individualized agents and consumers of goods.[20]

Even our antagonism toward the system, even our suspicion and skepticism can be grist for the mill of the market system. I recall seeing, in the midst of the youth rebellions of the early 1970s, an advertisement in the *San Francisco Chronicle* for a new style of clothing which was recommended for "the revolutionary look." If the market has its way, revolution will mean simply coming full circle. Do people seem to sense that there is a lack of substance in what they are getting? Madison Avenue will come up with a highly successful advertising campaign to draw upon this very feeling: "Where's the beef?" asked the cute and feisty old woman in the Wendy's commercial. Are people fed up with all the deceptions and manipulations to which they have been subjected by ads? Here's another highly successful ad campaign, featuring Joe Isuzu and telling us out front that their man is lying to us.

Judith Williamson explains the title of her book *Consuming Passions*, which discusses popular culture, saying that she is not concerned only about the passion for consumerism. More than that, "what I am concerned with is the way the passions are themselves consumed, contained and channeled into the very social structures they might otherwise threaten."[21] The market system is indeed adept at blunting all threats to its continued dominion.

A master of a kind of social aikido, the market society can control us without appearing to restrain our movement. We are free to do our own thing, but it seems it's the market's thing we end up doing. "Energies fired by what might be, become the fuel for maintaining what already is."[22]

Our system is both wonderful and frightening in its way of being simultaneously open and closed, receptive to change and inexorable in its progress. Our liberal society does not, for the most part, eradicate options by force. Seizing the lands of the indigenous peoples of this continent and sending gunboats to pry Japan open in the previous century are not typical of the way our system uses power to further its economic expansion. If our vision does not conform to the dictates of the dominant orthodoxy, we need not fear that secret police will whisk us away in the night. Voices speak more or less freely here. Shi's book is full of voices that have cried out over the centuries for values neglected by the market. But the system rolls on—(almost) never silencing those who would stand in its way, but never blocked from its expansionary course either.

What's the point of trying to understand the ways the market uses us for its purposes? Is it possible for ideas to help us craft a more whole world, or is it all so much water off a duck's back?

Russian writers coming to America have been greatly disillusioned in a way they never imagined. Living under tyranny, they have yearned for the freedom to express themselves without fear of reprisal. As emigrants to America, they have found that freedom—but they also find that in America no one really cares what anyone says. Words, so sacred and so powerful in a country ruled by terror, are trivialized and made impotent, they find, in the land of free expression and free exchange.

Ideas, however impassioned, are rendered by the market's process of social aikido into mere commodities. The talk-show host turns from selling laxatives to talking to his guest about the survival of the planet, and back to perfume, and then on to the guest who has written a book about Donald and Ivana Trump.

So, what's the use? Why write, why read, about the power and the flaws of our economic system?

GETTING HOLD OF
THE STEERING WHEEL

It is not futile. Accomplishing change will certainly be difficult, but it is not impossible.

In the first place, history already suggests that the market's power over our worldview has its limits. The full flowering of the ethic of materialistic success, described by Cawelti, passed its prime some time ago. Our innocent acceptance of the system's good intentions has broken down under the impact of repeated unsatisfying encounters. The system remains formidable, and its subtlety continues to develop. But our humanity remains our abiding asset. As our experience raises the alarm that something has gone awry in our social universe, our worldview bends away from old orthodoxies in the search for an understanding that will give better succor to our real needs. During the course of this century, as the excesses and the inadequacies of the materialistic system have become increasingly visible to Americans, other values have asserted themselves. Our attitudes about pollution have changed. Our assumption that the system's expansion means our own betterment is no longer so confident.

For many years, the orthodoxies of communism continued to prevail in Eastern Europe even while the fervor of genuine ideological belief died out. Perhaps in America the edifice of belief that helps maintain the capacity of our system to resist adequate reform has also started to become hollowed out. The passion is no longer there. It is for lack of any vision of another way to go that we continue, as if on automatic pilot.

The time may be ripe, therefore, to take on this juggernaut. The market system has been a powerful and, in many ways, a fruitful experiment in humankind's social evolution. But it is not the end of history. The system's failure to align with the forces of life makes its eventual transformation inevitable, for those forces will continue to seek fulfillment. The scars being inflicted on the earth will compel us to learn to harmonize with the rest of life or perish. The frustration of our needs for real fulfillment will continually pull us to seek other paths. The need for succor is born every minute.

American values can be transformed again. This is both essential and insufficient. Only if we see and feel the need for change will we make the changes that need to be made. There are signs of growing awareness of the need for new values. A few years ago, the *Washington Post* ran an article entitled "Free Market Economics, Old Testament Morality." It portrayed an orthodox Jew from Israel, Meir Tamari, who is teaching the need to bring traditional moral beliefs into one's conduct in the free market. "Market efficiency is very important," Tamari is quoted as saying, "but I don't think we want it to be more important than morality." "It is impermissible to waste resources even when they belong to you," says Tamari, reminiscent of John Locke's arguments about property.[23]

But changes in our values are not enough. We had other values before, but the force of the market overwhelmed them. "We receive natural resources from God," argues Tamari, "not just for us, but for future generations. There is something to be said for placing limitations on consumption."[24] If these limitations remain solely in the realm of moral teachings, they will be inundated by the wealth system just as we saw that Locke's sense of limits was stripped from that part of his teaching that served the system (see p. 97).

The transformation of values must go hand in hand with a transformation in the economic system. While it is true that unless we understand the need for change, we will not make the needed changes, it is also true that so long as the system remains with its power unchecked, the worldview of the American people remains captive to the system. The systems that teach us what life is about can impede a change in our orientation.

In 1979, the president of the United States went on national television to tell the American people that "in a nation that was proud of hard work, strong families, close-knit communities and our faith in God, too many of us now worship self-indulgence and consumption."[25] About this famous and politically disastrous speech, David Shi rightly observes that in implying that "the national malaise was solely the result of individual selfishness and secularism," President Carter "totally ignored the fact that the country's dominant institutions—corporations, advertising, popular culture—were instrumental in promoting and sustaining the hedonistic ethic that he decried."[26] Perhaps the president underestimated how much he was up against in seeking to reverse this historic movement. At any event, his speech encountered great resistance. Addictive patterns and addictive belief systems are not readily broken.*

For us, the realm of ideas and values is an indispensable point of entry into the system as a whole. It makes sense for us to seek to understand why the system must be transformed and what kinds of modifications will set us free.

Only when this understanding creates movement toward actual institutional change, however, can we begin to gain real control over our destiny. Without such changes, in so long as we live in the field of the system's magnetic force, like Wilde's filings, we will, continue to "choose" to embrace it. We will embrace a world in which human needs, rather than being the principle around which society is organized, are bent to serve the system's requirements.

---

*There is an emptiness all this "stuff" helps to cover over. Facing this emptiness may be a necessary part of this healing. But people tend to be reluctant to give up something for nothing. An essential part of the process of liberating the American people from our materialistic addictions will be strengthening the knowledge of other, more nourishing realms of experience. We will be more able to relinquish our gluttony when we have some taste of what is really, in the phrase of the ad, "real food for real people."

PART III
OUT OF CONTROL

The issue is human freedom. Are we masters of our destinies? Or are we the servants of systems that are our creations?

The idea that our creations might run amok, wreaking havoc with a will of their own, has a powerful presence in our imaginative lives. Much earlier in the process of economic and technological expansion, this image came alive in the form of Mary Shelley's *Frankenstein*. As the new dynamo of power took shape in Europe, the figure of the Frankenstein monster arose from the romantic imagination. In our own time, science fiction movies have reiterated the motif of the machine, once unleashed, rising up to destroy its inventor.

The market is, in some ways, like Frankenstein's monster, running out of control.

The legends are emblems of the tragical paradox of power. Overreaching for power, men render themselves powerless. As in the still-older story of the sorcerer's apprentice, the protagonist is overwhelmed by forces he himself has conjured up. The image applies, certainly, to the explosion of scientific knowledge and technological power through which, in our effort to become the lords of creation, we threaten to bring about our own destruction. The relation between freedom and power we find to be rather more complex than we imagined. A similar paradox afflicts the dynamism of our economic expansion, by which, in our pursuit of limitless riches, we also, in some ways, impoverish ourselves. The relation between the rich life and material wealth also turns out to be less than—or perhaps more than—straightforward.

Is the machinery of our productivity an extension of our will, or are we just human parts in a vast machine? Charlie Chaplin's most famous comic image—of the worker on an assembly line whose repetitive motions become involuntary and who becomes physically caught up in the enormous gears of the factory—expresses a part of our experience of this relationship. But there can be no doubt that, for the most part, this is not how most of us, most of the time, experience *Modern Times*. Despite the disturbing intuitions embodied in some of our mythic symbols, most of us offer our allegiance to the productive apparatus we have created.

The system is seen not as some monster, run amok, but as a benign embodiment of our collectivity. A social psychologist, Alex Inkeles, describes the modern factory in quite un-Chaplinesque terms. "A factory guided by modern management and personnel policies will set its workers an example of rational behavior, emotional balance, open communication, and respect for the opinions, the feelings, and the dignity of the worker, which can be a powerful example of the principles and practices of modern living."[1] This factory stands in relation to the worker as good parents to the child they are socializing. About this passage, and about the "modernisms of the futurist tradition" of which it is representative, Marshall Berman comments that the problem "is that, with brilliant machines and mechanical systems playing all the leading roles—just as the factory is the subject in the [Inkeles quotation]—there is precious little for modern man to do except to plug in."[2] But people, accustomed to familial and cultural systems into which often, in large measure, one must simply plug in, do not always chafe at such a subordinate role.

An "iron cage" is how Max Weber described the constraints of this rational and bureaucratic order of the modern capitalist economy. But most people are not aware, most of the time, of a sense of imprisonment. This is our world, we think. We identify the forces at work in it as our forces. The wave we ride into the future, even if it is overwhelming, we regard as ourselves. The glory of our impressive system shines on us.

If we see the system as us and ourselves as the system, the question of human freedom in relation to the systemic forces we have unleashed becomes difficult to confront. We must therefore look at the roots of this identification.

In part, it reflects the ubiquitous human tendency to identify with the collective culture, whatever its nature and dynamics. In part, it reflects the benign aspects of the system, which is, in part anyway, an instrument of our needs and desires, and which also, like Dostoyevski's inquisitor, knows how to feed and enslave us in the same gesture. But in part, also, something still more dark and painful may be going on.

It is called "identification with the aggressor."

In his book on "the experience of modernity," Marshall Berman discusses the vision of the architect Le Corbusier, whom he calls the most influential architect of this century. Berman is discussing the transition from the boulevard of the nineteenth century to the highway of the twentieth, describing the former as "a medium for bringing explosive human and material forces together" and the latter as "a means for putting them asunder."[3] In a world dominated by the highway, the machines take over and the human figure is squeezed out. What is interesting about Le Corbusier is the glimpse his history provides into how the human being becomes the willing agent in his own undoing.

By his own account, Le Corbusier's vision is precipitated by an experience on an evening in 1924, as he goes out for a peaceful walk. The rush of automobile traffic, however, drives him from the street. "It was as if the world had suddenly gone mad . . . To leave our house meant that, once we had crossed our threshold, we were in danger of being killed by passing cars."[4] Berman notes how similar is this starting point of Le Corbusier, the twentieth-century architect, to that of Baudelaire, the nineteenth-century poet. But whereas Baudelaire's modernist vision was to fill the city landscape with human meaning at the human scale, Le Corbusier suddenly makes a leap in a very different direction.

In response to his shock and fear from the assault by the traffic, Le Corbusier indulges in some nostalgia for the Baudelarian world the hurtling machines have sundered. "I think back twenty years," he writes, "to my youth as a student:

177

the road belonged to us then; we sang in it, we argued in it, while the horse-bus flowed softly by."[5] But at the next moment, he has his vision in which, as Berman says, "he identifies himself totally with the forces that have been bearing down on him."[6] By virtue of an imaginative leap, in Le Corbusier's own words:

On the 1st of October, 1924, I was assisting in the titanic *renaissance* of a new phenomenon . . . traffic. Cars, cars, fast, fast! One is seized, filled with enthusiasm, with joy . . . the joy of power. The simple and naive pleasure of being in the midst of power, of strength. One participates in it. One takes part in this society that is just dawning. One has confidence in this new society: it will find a magnificent expression of its power. One believes in it.[7]

Assaulted one moment, and identified the next with the very agency that has threatened one's destruction. This is an imaginative leap one encounters wherever one studies the cycling of violence.[8] The abused child shows, when he later becomes an abusive parent himself, how he had identified with the parent who beat him. Joseph Stalin, born Iosif Dzhugashvili, the Georgian boy who hated the Russians oppressing his nation, changes his name to the Russian word for steel, becomes "the Father of all Russians," and feels nothing but contempt for the culture of his origin. Hostages held in terror come to identify with those who held them captive, who held guns to their heads. Some of the inmates of Auschwitz came to feel a bond with the SS guards.*

Identification with the aggressor is a form of magical self-defense. If it is too terrifying to experience one's powerlessness, through the magic of identification one can change places. Afraid to be oneself, one becomes what one fears.

---

*About Le Corbusier, who as a student had loved when "the road belonged to us," Berman says, in a subsequent note: "Le Corbusier was never able to make much headway in his indefatigable schemes for destroying Paris. But many of his most grotesque visions were realized in the Pompidou era, when elevated highways cleft the Right Bank, the great markets of Les Halles were demolished, dozens of thriving streets were razed, and substantial and venerable neighborhoods were turned over to 'les promoteurs' and obliterated without a trace."

In exchange for an immediate amelioration of terror, one transforms oneself into a channel for the forces of destruction. The weakness of the human victim feeds the strength of harmful systems.

In a world hurtling out of control, to experience our powerlessness can be frightening. Where the human element is being assaulted and exploited by mighty machines of power that unfold according to their own logic, following a course not chosen by human will, then a full experience of our humanity might be too painful to bear. One way out of that pain is to make the system's cause one's own. One way to escape terror is to run away from the vulnerability that comes from being a creature of flesh and blood.

As Stalin became "steel," architects make modern cities out of shafts of steel erected beyond the human scale. As the abused child perpetuates the injurious pattern he incorporates through identification, many in modern society adopt the values of a system that exploits and manipulates them. *Arbeit macht frei* (Work makes you free), says the sign over the entrance to Auschwitz. And Chaplin's pathetic assembly-line worker in *Modern Times* returns to us a half century later employed by International Business Machines in ads to sell systems that can make production more efficient.

The system represented as our tool wields us skillfully.

It is frightening and painful to confront how much we are not masters of our destiny. But it is still more frightening to contemplate the destiny we will have if we fail to confront the realities of our condition.

11

Autopilot

Things are in the saddle,
And ride mankind.
Emerson

THE PROBLEM

Private property. To many people, private property is the essence and foundation of liberty. What we own is ours to do with as we please. A man's home is his castle. Freedom of the press is enjoyed by those who own a press. In the absence of the institution of private property, many ideologues of the market argue, all of our liberties would be in jeopardy.

For American society, the pressing question is not whether liberty would die in the absence of private property. It is, rather, whether freedom can survive the institutions of private property we now have.

The problem is the modern corporation. Our society is dominated by entities that are running on automatic pilot. Many of our corporations are, in a meaningful sense, virtually beyond human control.

Such an assertion violates our commonsense understanding. The law might treat corporations as if they were persons, but they are really just the instruments of real, flesh-and-blood people. Right? Not necessarily. Not with the huge, publicly traded corporations that play such a preponderant role

181

in our economic system. In the case of these companies, the *structure of the system* makes it virtually impossible for the organizations to behave in a socially and environmentally responsible fashion.

Most corporations begin as the creatures of an individual or small group who realize their entrepreneurial vision and who can control their creations. Doubtless these entrepreneurs are not a random selection or representative group of the population at large. The single-minded devotion to material success that is often required to become a John D. Rockefeller or a Henry Ford means that other, competing values are less likely to sway their choices. Even if being socially responsible was not high in the priorities of such men, however, no one could prevent them—if they wanted to—from making Standard Oil or the Ford Motor Company an instrument of other values than those rewarded by the market. But with most of today's Fortune 500 companies, it is quite otherwise.

Take Exxon. (Please!) This is the company that in one year (1989) gave us the disastrous oil spill in Alaska, a huge refinery fire in Louisiana, and yet another mess in New York harbor. Exxon's response to the Valdez spill was a combination of half-hearted indifference and fraudulent public relations, and the corporation at its 1990 annual meeting soundly defeated several stockholder efforts to get the company to adopt an environmentally more responsible posture in the world. Is Exxon's course determined by the free choice of flesh-and-blood people, and if so whose?

On the face of it, it is *management* that chooses. These are the people—the *men*, more specifically—who run the company. So we might venture that a corporation will behave responsibly when and if its managers are people whose values lead them in that direction. But this is only superficially true.

At a deeper level, the management is the instrument of a corporate system, rather than the other way around. People do not just happen to arrive at a position of running a corporation like Exxon. The process that chooses which human beings will rise to the top of these industrial bureaucracies is far more *narrowly selective* than the one that selects entrepreneurs. Precisely because it is a "bureaucratic" system, there will be greater uniformity in the kinds of people who make it up the promotional ladder. A Steven Jobs (a founder of Apple Computer) would be weeded out long before he ascended to a position of control.

Not only does the system select a particular kind of men—willing to sacrifice a good deal to win—but it also shapes those it selects, socializing them not only in the market's way of keeping score in terms of profits* but also in the culture of the particular corporation.

The corporation thus creates and chooses its human agents. The nature of the choices the people make is governed by a corporate system that perpetuates itself even while human beings are born and die. That which chooses the chooser determines the choice.

But management is not autonomous, is it? The managers must answer to the board of directors, and the board is elected by the stockholders. The stockholders are the *owners* of the company, and in our society founded on the rights of private property, it is the owners who have ultimate power. If the owners have values beyond profit—concerns for the sake of which they are willing to sacrifice a degree of their own enrichment—the corporation, which is their instrument, will behave accordingly. Right? Again, not with the giants that rule our landscape.

Take Exxon. (Please! Don't make me ask a third time.) Who owns Exxon? The answer, in a way, is both nobody and everybody. It is "nobody," in that no single person owns as mush as 5 percent of the company. Exxon, the lineal descendent of Rockefeller's Standard Oil, is nobody's baby. It is "everybody," in that more than a third of the company is owned by institutions like pension funds. There is a good chance, if you are a working American, that you own a little bit of Exxon. The rest of the stock is directly owned by countless individuals all over the country. So it might be said that "we" own Exxon.

The polls show that Americans care deeply about the environment and that they are willing to make economic sacrifices to protect it. Doubtless Exxon's owners are richer than a purely representative sample, but I would wager that the owners

---

*A headline in the *San Francisco Chronicle* (October 13, 1989) reads: "Wells Chairman Rated Top California Banker." What made him the top? Was it his service to the community? the way he dealt with his workers? his sensitivity to a variety of important values? Of course not. "Wells Fargo Chairman Carl Reichardt beat out his California peers, placing second in a nationwide ranking of bank chief executives based on his bank's total returns to shareholders." Money is what we use to keep score.

of Exxon are as concerned about the environment as Americans generally. Maybe even more so, since the environmental movement tends to have proportionally more adherents in our wealthier classes. But whatever the environmental values of Exxon's owners as a group, for practical purposes the owners are essentially impotent to impress upon "their" corporation the imprint of their values.

Stockholders, in the present American corporate system, are relegated to a passive, almost irrelevant role. This has remained true for the more than half century since Berle and Means, in their classic work *The Modern Corporation and Private Property*, described the transformation of corporate ownership in the American industrial system. Though the stockholders theoretically have ultimate control of their company, this power almost never has any practical meaning.

Is the management answerable to the board of directors? Legally, yes—but it is a legal fiction. In a great many of our publicly traded corporations, the stockholder has two futile options. "As his personal vote will count for little or nothing at the meeting unless he has a very large block of stock," Berle and Means have written, "the stockholder is practically reduced to the alternative of not voting at all or else of *handing over his vote to individuals over whom he has no control and in whose selection he did not participate.* In neither case will he be able to exercise any measure of control."[1] Since the two alternatives amount to the same thing, he has no choice. What power fills this vacuum created by the impotence of the putative owners? "[C]ontrol will tend to be in the hands of those who select the proxy committee by whom, in turn, the election of directors for the ensuing period may be made."[2] And whose hands are those? "Since the proxy committee is appointed by the existing management, the latter can virtually dictate their own successors. Where ownership is sufficiently sub-divided, the management can thus become a self-perpetuating body even though its share in the ownership is negligible."[3]

Such a self-perpetuating body is really a system beyond effective human control. The board, more fundamentally than being the power over management, is the creation of management. Or perhaps one might say, management and directors form two hands of a single self-perpetuating body.

The stockholders, rather than being the foundation of power, are cut off from power. The efforts of Exxon stockholders in 1990 to effect a change in corporate policy were predict-ably futile.* Stockholder initiatives virtually never pass. Power once again devolves to that same proxy committee, appointed by management. Only the takeover game—in which someone commanding enormous resources goes over the head of the managers to make the stockholders an offer they cannot refuse—qualifies the impregnability of management. And these takeover efforts are fundamentally different in kind from the efforts to engender greater responsibility to values other than material gain.

The takeover business is conducted in the language of the market, and so it is fueled by money. The motive of those seek-ing the takeover is profit, with the costs of inducing the share-holders to side with the raiders figures into the calculation. For the owners of stock, reduced by the system to mere holders of a financial stake, there is no reason for attachment to "their" management or "their" company. Their money being all they have at stake, all it takes is an offer that is attractive enough. A simple proposition is advanced by a campaign whose costs promise to be more than repaid in kind—this is the formula by which the stockholders become momentarily relevant, albeit in a most narrow and mechanical fashion.

Bringing questions of social responsibility before the stockholders is an entirely different matter. Should the corpo-ration forgo some profits to install scrubbers in its smokestack? That question might be more important than whether Gang A should be replaced by Gang B in running the company. But where can the millions be obtained to wage the proxy fight when the benefits are spread across society rather than accru-ing to the few who spend their money? And if the money were raised and the mailings sent out, how could the campaign arouse enough stockholders from their stupor, raising as it does a question far more complex—and easier to ignore—than whether seventy dollars a share is preferable to fifty dollars a share. With its access to corporate funds, management can drown out almost any altruistic shareholder initiative. With glib words of reassurance, management can play on the share-holders' ignorance and their latent desire not to be disturbed

---

*Indeed, I did predict it in an opinion piece in the *Baltimore Sun*, published a week before the meeting. "Who's in Charge Here?" (April 17, 1990).

by concerns other than their own.* With its proxies, management can easily prevail.

The shareholders sleep. The juggernaut rolls on. That's the way the system is structured.

The stockholder is, of course, still honored. Just as McDonald's used to sing out, in its commercials, "We do it all for you!" so also does management sing to the shareholders in its annual reports. Management routinely reports its abiding sense of responsibility to the shareholders. Perhaps it is entirely sincere. Whether sincere or not, however, this responsibility is understood in the narrowest terms of profit maximization. Here's just one example that arrived in my mailbox this week. "Our responsibility as managers of CSGI is to provide a superior return to our shareholders."[4] To say that management's job is solely to make shareholders richer is the equivalent of saying that the corporation will attend only to the values of the market. This means, in turn, that it is the market system and not the shareholders that really controls the corporation.

The shareholders are reduced to the two-dimensionality of Economic Man. The corporation can be the owner's instrument for one purpose only—their enrichment. As human beings, the stockholders may have other concerns as well. Given a choice, they might be willing to give up a dollar in earnings to make all of Exxon's tankers double hulled. But these concerns and that willingness have no way of expressing themselves. As the stockholders are reduced to their pecuniary interests, the "bottom line" is reduced to the bottom line.

If management and ownership are separated as they are in our present system, the corporation is like a vehicle set on automatic pilot. Power is placed in the hands of a few people, but these people are chosen and shaped for the congruence of their purposes with the design of the machine. More than being an instrumentality of flesh-and-blood human beings, these corporate machines are elements in the still-larger machine around them: the inexorable machine of the market economy.[†]

---

*I recall my purchase of the teak furniture in 1981. (See p. 103)
†Not all corporations are alike. People rightly speak of "corporate cultures," designating the significant differences that obtain in the spirit and approach of different corporate organizations. Some corporations show much greater

A FALSE SOLUTION:
THE ETHIC OF GESTURE

Stockholders have not all been resigned to a passive, irrelevant role. Many have not accepted that to invest in the market is necessarily to abet the destructive conduct of these power systems, modern corporations. People have sought ways of combining investment with social responsibility.

One hears much about "socially responsible investment" these days. There are now a number of mutual funds that claim to offer investors a vehicle for socially responsible investing. What this means is that the fund does not purchase shares in "dirty" companies, by whatever criteria of cleanliness are employed. If you buy shares in one of these funds, you will be assured that none of "your" companies does business in South Africa, or is on some environmental "dirty dozen" list, or traffics in tobacco and liquor, or whatever. Whatever issue is particularly important to you, it may be possible to find a fund that buys only into "clean" companies.

When I first began to have some contact with the stock market in the early 1970s, this was my approach also. Like many others of my generation and subculture, I had a sense of the destructiveness of much of our industrial system and a desire to maintain a degree of ethical purity despite having to live in such a world. At the supermarket, I avoided lettuce and table grapes when the exploited farm workers were seeking to organize. My car got more than thirty miles per gallon. And when it came time to invest a few thousand dollars of savings, I told the broker there were industries and companies I would not touch regardless of the way the stock was expected to perform. The chemical companies for example, because of their environmental record; and the drug companies, because I

---

degree of concern for nonpecuniary values than do others: there are publicly traded companies, for example, with a deserved reputation for being good to the people who work for them.

While there are important differences among these corporations, however, there are powerful tendencies at work that tend to shape them in certain ways. It is to this "ideal type" of the publicly traded company that the present critique is directed. Despite the differences among specific "corporate cultures," we are nonetheless imperiled by the "corporate culture" that our present industrial property system creates in our society.

didn't like the approach to health and sickness that they push on the public and on the medical profession.

After a time, however, I came to realize that this approach to the ethics of investment was fundamentally misguided. The strategy of avoiding dirty companies is not ethically superior, at least if you believe, as I do, that ethics is about acting so as to make the world a better place. Given such an ethical premise, the issue then focuses on what are and are not the effects of one's purchase of stocks.

I had imagined that if I bought shares in some evil company—like Johns Mansville, which for years exposed its workers to deadly asbestos while withholding from them what the company knew about the dangers—I was somehow *supporting* the company. But this is true only when the shares are first issued. At that time, the money used to buy shares becomes capital for the corporation. Your money becomes the company's, and it helps the company develop the business. After that first issuance, when shares are traded on the stock exchange, the corporation is not party to the transaction. All that happens is that someone with stock and someone with cash trade places. The corporation remains unaffected. The price paid by the purchaser of stock, say Berle and Means, "does not add to capital or assets of the corporations whose shares he buys."[5]

If I buy a stock in a company and the price doubles and then I sell it, what were the consequences of my purchase?

One's decision to buy shares in a given company does help to support or increase the price of the company's stock, since any increment in demand in a market will help keep up the price of whatever commodity is involved. And one might argue that, the price of the stock being one way corporate managers might gauge their success, supporting the price provides encouragement to the management. But this aspect of the situation seems of negligible importance.

The only significant consequence, I would suggest, of my buying shares that double in price is that I become richer. If this is so, it does not really matter, in terms of the fate of the world, whether the company whose shares I owned was dirty or clean.

My assessment of the ethics of the purchase is premised on an *ethic of consequences:* our choice of actions should be based on our judgment about what the results of those actions will be. My original concern with the purity of companies whose shares I might own derived from a misunderstanding of the effects on the world of the purchasing of stock.

But one might approach the question on a different ethical premise: a paramount concern with *purity of soul*. In such an ethic, my choice of what I deal with might derive from my desire not to touch evil, lest I be contaminated with it. Hence, I might decide to avoid owning a piece of an entity whose conduct I found morally repugnant.

Certainly, what happens to our souls is important. "Consequences" are not just "out there." Moreover, owning a stock in a company that is doing bad things in the world *could* have a contaminating effect on one's soul. It can be confusing for one's financial interests to be on one side and one's moral values on another. To watch the unfolding of the drama of the Bhopal disaster—in which a chemical leak killed and maimed thousands in India in 1984 and in which the victims and their families waited long to receive little in compensation—is painful for anyone. But if you have a good part of your savings tied up in the stock of the responsible company, Union Carbide, surely it will be more difficult wholeheartedly to want justice to be done.

More difficult, yes—but not impossible. To challenge one's soul is not necessarily to contaminate it. To be connected with things impure is not necessarily to sully oneself.

An ethic that focuses on one's own purity is frequently a manifestation of both self-indulgence and self-delusion. It is self-indulgent to think that keeping oneself pure is a higher calling than making the world whole. It is self-delusion to think that one can really keep oneself pure by refraining from contact with the impure. Who is more pure, he who is "above" fighting when tyranny descends on his land or he who is willing to overcome his repugnance for conflict in order to rescue his endangered community? There are sins of omission as well as of commission.

Those who enter polluted domains—such as politics, war, the competitive market of industrial production—place themselves in moral jeopardy because of the temptations that are built into the systems. But by entering these difficult arenas, people also gain access to important levers by which the world can be moved closer to the right path.

The fact is that all of us are tied to the fortunes of systems that are far from pure. Pacificists and militarists alike have been protected by our national defense apparatus. Whether or not we own stock in Union Carbide or Johns Mansville, we would all feel severely the impact of a nationwide depression.

What matters for our ethical status is not so much what we are in contact with but what we do with that contact. Buying shares, on a stock exchange, in a company that cleans up toxic wastes may feel better than owning stock in a company that creates toxic wastes. But if one understands that simply buying and selling those shares will not have any different effect on the world in one case than in the other, one's moral purity may well be unaffected by which one chooses to buy, or by whether one chooses to buy stock at all.

The ethic of moral purity, when expressed in the form of "socially responsible investing," might be regarded as the *ethic of gesture*. By investing in funds that buy shares only in good companies, we can show by our gesture our concern with the morality of business, we can demonstrate that we do not desire profit without honor. But such gestures leave the world unaffected.

If we wish to affect the world in our role as stockholders, our concern should be less with the goodness of the companies we are connected with than with our ability to affect the goodness of their corporate policies.

In fact, if we could exercise such power, it might even be better to be stockholders in miscreant corporations than in companies that are already virtuous.

But as things now stand, as we have seen, stockholders are substantially denied such power. In the next section, I will present a proposal on how stockholder powers could be restructured to allow our values to enter meaningfully into our role as investors. More important, the adoption of such a proposal would, I believe, make our entire corporate system less a machine on automatic pilot and more a vehicle guided by the whole spectrum of our human concerns.

TOWARD A
DIFFERENT APPROACH

Preamble

In meetings with CEOs in the American midwest, I was told that a difference was visible in the conduct of privately owned versus publicly traded companies in the communities in which they operate. The privately owned corporations—where the owners either were themselves the managers or were directly in charge of them—often really sacrificed some of their profit for the good of the surrounding community. If the community had a problem, there was a network of wealthy owners that could be counted on to rally to help solve the problem. The big publicly traded companies were also visibly involved in the community, but, I was told, the involvement had a different character. With these companies, their philanthropic activities had a bigger ratio of visibility to substance, because the underlying motive, my informants said, was public relations—not so much to help as to be seen helping.

Perhaps part of this difference derives from the greater likelihood that the privately owned companies would be headquartered in the communities in question, to have grown in those communities. The publicly traded companies, on the other hand, were often national organizations, with operations in many places with which they had no organic, human relationship.

But from meeting CEOs of both kinds, I am persuaded that the most important reason for the contrast lies in the difference in the structure of ownership between the two kinds of companies. Where owners have real power, the company can have as human a character as the people themselves. Where the owners are a diffuse group of mute and impotent stockholders, the corporation is as unidimensional as a scoreboard.

The challenge, then, is to make it possible for publicly traded companies to be as human as their owners.

Enhancing the Right of Property

Two central ideals in American culture are that people should be free to shape their world according to their own values and that people have a right to own their own property. In many people's minds, these two ideals are inseparable: the right of property allows people to control their lives.

As individuals, most of us own property in the form of a home, a car, and the various items that furnish our lives. As proprietors of our own homesteads, we can create a private space according to our own tastes and values. Taking to the open road in our own vehicles, we are at liberty to explore the world.

But the question of our liberty and autonomy concerns more than just these individual domains of ownership and activity. The shape of our world is determined in good measure in the realm of productive property and commerce, and in this realm individual ownership has become less and less significant. In the industrial system, a few hundred giant, publicly held corporations control the great majority of commercial operations. Even in agriculture, the family farm has been giving way to agribusiness. Private property in this extraordinarily potent part of our society has become a collective affair.

This collectivization of ownership would not in itself impair our capacity to be masters of our fate. It is foolish to imagine that we could, in any event, each be islands, entire unto ourselves; we are joined together in a great many ways, our destinies are inevitably collective. In our present system, however, as we have seen, our collective ownership of these great enterprises amounts not to collective power but to collective impotence. We are not only all in the same boat, but it turns out to be a boat without an effective rudder.

The myth nonetheless persists that our system is the embodiment of liberty. The intrusions of government are still resented as the infringements of a dangerous power upon our personal liberty, even though our democratic polity is more accountable to its collectivity than the modern corporation now is to its.

Many have sought a remedy to the problems of capitalism through the direct regulation of commerce by the state. Better that a democratic political power rather than a private economic power should determine our destiny. In some areas, as I argued in part 1, government action is indeed needed to correct deficiencies in the market.

But the ideologues of the market are right that governmentally imposed solutions have their danger. We should not be eager to strengthen the leviathan of state power, putting all our eggs into the basket of that one collectivity. Moreover, there is a kind of justice in allowing owners to control their property rather than letting all people, including those whose stake is lesser, to dictate to them. Even in the most democratic polity imaginable, the collectivity of owners should have some protection again the collectivity of all citizens.

How useful it would be, therefore, if to the problem of the "automatic pilot" of our great corporations a solution were possible that did not entail having the government exercise vast new powers. How good it would be if the problem of the disempowerment of property owners in publicly traded companies admitted a solution that, rather than diminishing property rights, enhances and strengthens them.

Such a solution is possible. There is a way, as I will show shortly, to use law not to control but to enable, not to supersede private autonomy but to fortify the rights of ownership.

Despite Reservations

In the present situation, no one in the system appears to be free to bring values significantly opposed to profit maximization into play in corporate decision making. The corporate managers say they feel duty bound to represent the interest of the shareholders. Since the stockholders are rendered effectively mute, the managers are compelled to regard those interests in narrowly financial terms, and the stockholders are incapable of communicating a more complete picture of their concerns.

Though this characterization of the present system is largely accurate, the reality is a bit more complex: the stockholders are not completely mute, and the managers probably have their own reasons for construing their responsibilities in more narrow, less human terms.

Stockholders do try to speak. In addition to the kind of "socially responsible investing" discussed earlier, there is another kind of investor that has sought a way of expressing ethical concerns through the role of stockholder. These admirable efforts bring social values right into the annual meetings of America's most important companies. As reported, for example, by the Interfaith Center on Corporate Responsibility in its regular publication, *The Corporate Examiner*, a diversity of groups file resolutions expressing a variety of social concerns for consideration and voting at the meetings of different companies.

To give just one example: the Sisters of the Sorrowful Mother (and several other groups) filed a resolution for the corporate meeting at Figgie International asking the company "to report their actions to insure just and non-exploitative policies toward the international operations of their companies"—specifically in Haiti—including descriptions of "training programs the companies have implemented for employee skills development."[6] Other resolutions described in the spring 1988 report dealt with apartheid, Star Wars, energy, the environment, and so forth.

How the two hundred or so resolutions described in that report fared, I don't know. But it can probably be presumed that the overwhelming majority of them met the same fate as the environmental initiatives submitted to the Exxon meeting in 1990, and for essentially the same reason. Those proposing the resolutions control a small fraction of the stock of the companies involved, the holders of a majority of shares are asleep, and the management has the power to speak in the presumed interests of the "silent majority."

Here arises the question as to how sincere are the declarations by management that their responsibility is to provide a "superior return" to the shareholders. As suggested earlier, management may prefer keeping score on the single-dimensional axis of profits. Americans have brought out of their business culture a penchant for conceiving all endeavors as competitive games with winners and losers and with a clear-cut means of keeping score. It is not only in business that we tend to reduce all information to numbers so we can keep our eye on who is ahead. This is true not only of our sports, with their standings and record keeping, but also of our politics, where every four years the substantive issues get buried beneath the horse race of our poll figures and delegate counts. Businessmen, rising to the top of a great competitive game, have been taught to gauge their performance by measurable quantities. Earnings per share is such a measure; how much better able the people of Haiti are to extricate themselves from poverty and oppression does not fit so well on the scoreboard.

So the managers are probably quite content to construe their responsibilities in terms of maximizing a quantifiable measure—return on equity, earnings per share, market share, and so on. They would probably not welcome being better informed about the three-dimensional human desires of the "owners" of their company, as is evinced by the unfriendly reception most socially responsible shareholder initiatives receive from management. I would guess the managers would regard the company as more *theirs* than the stockholders'—not altogether unreasonably, since the executives may devote the best of their energies of their entire adult lives to the company, while the putative owners these days may hold their shares for a few months or a few years before moving on to the next recommended investment vehicle and are, in any event, passive and invisible and irrelevant.

But while managers may be inclined by more than their sense of responsibility to give a "superior return," it may indeed be true that the managers would not feel free—even if by conviction they wished to—to reduce a superior return to an average or inferior return in order to provide some wonderful service to the wider world. To some meaningful degree, management may feel its hands tied in this system, with its peculiar distribution of responsibilities and its blocked channels of communication.

Just as the managers may be glad to have their hands tied, so may the stockholders not mind that their lips are sealed. In their pure passivity, the shareholders enjoy the benefits of the maximized profits without having to concern themselves about the ethical implications of how they are obtained. It is with good reason that responsibility is often described in terms of burden; thus the shareholder's separation from real power allows him to deposit his dividend check free of care. Responsibility requires us to look at what we are doing. So we are often glad to have a screen placed between us and our impact on the world, such as the way we in modern society can sit down to a juicy steak without having to think about, much less look into the brown eyes of the creature of whose body the steak was days ago an integral part. When at the time of the Vietnam war, television pictures brought into everyone's living room the fearsome human costs of maintaining the American empire in Indochina, public support for the effort proved hard to sustain. Not everyone is glad to have the closer look.

A proposal that would give real power and responsibility to shareholders, therefore, might not be completely welcome either to the shareholders, who would be compelled to assume the burden of making ethical choices, or to the managers, who would be deprived of the ability to play the market game unrestrainedly, as if corporate profits were an adequate measure of the value of the corporation's impact on the world.

But even if such a change in roles evokes an ambivalent response, this transformation is in everyone's enlightened best interests. In the present system, huge organizations of power, attending to a highly selective perception of value, are creating a distorted society for us all. Even if I am pleased to have the corporations in which I own stock enrich me more, so long as I don't have to look too closely at how they do it, I don't want to raise my family in a world where hundreds of such ethically myopic giants are running amok. I will be glad to take on a bit of the ethical burden of operating a profitable enterprise if I understand that all the other owners of shares in all the other big companies are doing likewise.

"LET THE OWNERS DECIDE": A PROPOSAL, WITH EXEGESIS

A quick summary of my proposal is this. *A law should be passed that requires large corporations to submit to their shareholders those decisions in which corporate profits and societal impact do or may conflict in a significant way, with the decision to be made by a majority of shareholders actually voting.*

This proposal can be called "Let the owners decide."

Certainly, to make such a law workable, a number of aspects of such a proposal require clarification. This is not easy, but neither is it impossible. The law labors with such problems—of definition, of clarifying distinctions, of making ideas operational—all the time. Here are some preliminary steps toward clarification.

A Law

The law should be nationwide in scope, just as the Securities and Exchange Commission presently oversees compliance with a number of regulations concerning the communication by corporations to their shareholders. (How to deal with corporations whose shares are not traded in the U.S. but which have significant operations here is another question.)

Large Companies

Many of our current laws apply only to companies above a certain size, the thought being, appropriately, that the proportion of a company's total operations that should be taken up with compliance with regulations cannot be allowed to become too great. Often, the size is defined in terms of numbers of workers. In this instance, size should perhaps be defined in terms of total revenues, which might be a loose measure of how big an actor a company is on our social stage.

How big is big? Certainly all the Fortune 500 companies and probably all the companies traded on the New York Stock Exchange are "big." I would venture that annual revenues over $100 million per year are big, and under $1 million per year are not big. In between, somewhere, the line could be drawn.

Submit

Just what should the shareholders receive? The presentation to the shareholders should present the issue at hand fairly and objectively, in a form that is concise and intelligible and that assesses as clearly as possible the costs and benefits—both corporate and social—of the different courses of action.

How is fairness to be assured? Can management be trusted to present both (or all) sides of the issue? One can hope that this new way of doing business will create a different mindset in corporate managers; but still, can management be trusted to be objective? If management is assigned the task of presenting all the arguments but performs its task in a biased way, who will be monitoring management and what recourse would there be? On the other hand, if management is assigned to present only the argument on the side of profits, that will tend to reinforce in management the idea that high-scoring is still *their* game and while other values represent the adversary.

Some system, I expect, could be devised in which the corporation is charged with representing the competing values objectively and in which the SEC and the shareholders can monitor the corporation's achievement of fairness. It would be a useful exercise for the managers to think in terms of results in more dimension than the "results," measured solely in terms of the corporation's enrichment, that are found in today's corporate reports. This would be preferable to finding some "responsible spokesman for opposing points of view," the way television stations give equal time to those who disagree with their editorials.

The presentations would presumably be in writing, with a concise summary followed by a lengthier discussion. In addition to these written statements, mailed to stockholders the way corporate reports are mailed, it is conceivable there could be a cable TV channel dedicated to discussions of these corporate issues.

198 ◆ Out of Control

Societal Impact

What kinds of issues fall within the universe of this proposal? Defining the outer boundaries of this universe may prove a challenge, but a great many important issues clearly lie within it.

Should we close this factory in Youngstown, Ohio, despite the impact of such a closing on X families whose breadwinners have worked for the company for Y years, and on the city as a whole? Or should we keep the factory open, even though that would cost us $Z each year we keep it open? Or is there some middle course in which we spend less than $Z but mitigate the harm to the community in some substantial way?

Should we invest $P extra so our tankers will be double hulled, even though this is not required by law, in order to diminish the probability of oil spills by an estimated Q percent?

Are we, as owners of this company, willing to give up thirty-five cents per share in earnings, in each of the next three years, to install scrubbers in our smokestacks, so that the area around our plants will have less sulphur dioxide, with an estimated reduction of such-and-such in respiratory illness and so-and-so in acid rain?

Should we make profits from the sale in Third World countries of chemicals deemed too dangerous for use in this country? If we open a factory in a country whose workers customarily earn extremely low wages and work in poor conditions (e.g., Haiti), should we pay workers what the market will bear or do better than we have to, and if so by how much?

Do we want our company to use its lobbyists to try to weaken the clean air laws or to reduce fuel efficiency standards? What would be the benefits to us as stockholders if such laws are weakened and what the benefits to society of the stronger laws?

If our company is part of an industry association that does political lobbying, our involvement in our company's political conduct should extend to how it uses its influence in shaping the industry association's political agenda. If, for example, our company is a manufacturer of tobacco products, we should decide whether or not our company should try to get the Tobacco Institute to alter its decades-old posture of sophistry and deception on the issue of smoking's relation to health.

Should our company, a manufacturer of infant formula, try to persuade poor women in Third World countries to give up breastfeeding? If our company manufacturers cigarettes, how do we want to promote our products—both in the U.S. and abroad—given what is known about the addictive nature of the product and the deadly effects of long-term use?

When our company advertises its cars, how much do we want to use imagery that teaches that a car is the route to being sexy, or worthy of respect? What should our beer ads imply about the relationship between alcohol consumption and the good life with friends? How pornographic should be our ads for our jeans?

There are a great many choices faced by corporations where the conflict between maximum possible profits and social benefit (in human and environmental terms) is clear. I imagine that questions like these arise all the time in corporate boardrooms. If they don't, they certainly should. "Let the owners decide" would bring them also into American living rooms.*

Do or May

While in some instance the question of social costs and benefits may be relatively uncontroversial, in other cases they may be a subject for legitimate dispute.

Some people, for example, regard government expenditures for the Star Wars defense system as a dangerous mistake, while others think it would make a valuable contribution to our national security. In such a case, profits and other values may be in conflict, maybe not. We as stockholders should consider whether we want our company to participate in such a venture if the political system decides to embark on it; and we should decide as a separate issue whether we want our company to

---

*If these questions are to be decided by the stockholders, it suggests a diminished role for the board of directors in setting corporate policy. But a role for the board would nonetheless remain, since the company must still face basic questions of corporate strategy, must make business decisions for which the shareholders lack the expertise. (Questions of values, priorities, and social responsibility are not, however, matters of expertise.) The problem of the symbiosis between management and the directors can still remain. Consider how in recent years the executives of American automobile companies have been given ever-higher salaries, bonuses, pensions, golden parachutes, and other goodies, even while their failures are reducing their companies' market share and profits. My proposal does not provide any protection against such incestuous corruption.

use its lobbying influence to persuade the government to go forward with such a project.

On a question like disinvestment in South Africa, even those who agree on the evil of the apartheid system could disagree on whether the presence of American companies in South Africa was part of the problem or part of the solution. Stockholders should hear the arguments and vote on the issue of disinvestment on the basis of a judgment on what would serve the cause of justice, as well as whether profit should be foregone for the sake of justice.

Scientific knowledge is never complete, and the gaps often leave a considerable range of uncertainty for policymakers. The problem of global warming is one prominent recent example. How much will additional atmospheric carbon dioxide alter the earth's climate? In what ways will this happen and with what effects on rainfall, crop production, ocean levels, forestation, and so forth? It is hardly prudent to wait until our information is complete before taking a possible problem into account. Corporate decisions are always being made in the face of uncertainty—what will be the demand for this product? what will be the rate of inflation? and so on—and it should be sufficient that there is a *meaningful possibility* that our company's policies may effect important social values for the decision to be brought before the stockholders. For example, in view of the *possible* dangers of global warming, should our company alter its practice of burning off the natural gas at its oil wellheads?

Significant

Doubtless, corporate managers must daily make decisions with some kind of societal impact. I know I do: Should I buy colored toilet paper, which looks good in the bathroom though it has dyes that leach into the water, or should I get boring white? Should I pick up that bottle some jerk left in the grass in the park and carry it three hundred yards to the nearest trash can? Should I indulge my desire for a chunk of beef today, despite all I know about the effects of raising cattle on the environment, both terrestrial and atmospheric? Corporate managers, deciding every day on hiring and firing, on materials and marketing, and on countless other matters, wrestle all the time with important decisions that have ethical consequences. These managers can't have the stockholders look-ing over their shoulders every second. The "owners" surely have no proper place in the "micromanagement" of the corpo-ration (just as American presidents often describe what they regard as excessive intrusion of Congress into the conduct of American foreign policy). The stockholders should deal only with the significant decisions. But what are the criteria of "significance"?

No simple rule presents itself, but a few points can per-haps be made.

As making decisions through stockholder voting is a time-consuming process, it can be used only for matters that afford a long interval (at best a few months, but probably more) be-tween when the question arises and when a decision must be rendered. Perhaps the stockholders should be consulted on the order of once a year. (Maybe twice.) That limit in itself would help eliminate much of the danger of micromanagement.

It would take time and money for corporations to prepare their presentations of the issues, and for shareholders to deliberate and vote on them. The values at stake in many small issues would be less than the cost of consulting the stockhold-ers. So a reasonable rule would be that no issue for which less is at stake than justifies the trouble should be brought to the shareholders.

The role of the owners should be to make decisions where a measurable impact on earnings might be sacrificed for other values. "Measurable" might be defined in terms of the equiv-alent of 1 percent of one year's net earnings, or more. It should also be up to the stockholders to determine the *overall policy guidelines* on ethical issues the corporation habitually faces. The stockholders should not be involved in the decision on whether to fire a particular employee, but they might indicate how they want "whistleblowers" dealt with. Once the manage-ment knows what the stockholders feel is their responsibility to communities where their plants are located, for example, from a previous decision on a possible plant closing, the managers' day-to-day decisions might also be influenced by that knowl-edge. Similarly, if the stockholders indicate that they don't want the company lobbying to persuade the government to build particular weapons but only to seek contracts to build weapons that are offered for bid, the managers might align many of their other lobbying practices accordingly.

Management is unlikely to err in the direction of bringing too many, too trivial issues before the shareholders. And there will be some shareholders who will be aware of important omissions, if the management withholds questions that should be submitted to the company's owners. Perhaps some suitable forum can be devised to hear appeals from stockholders who believe that management has failed to consult the owners adequately.

Actually Voting

Judging from Berle and Means's comments on the proxy system (quoted earlier), it would seem that—if the owners and not the managers are to determine how profits are to be weighed relative to other values in the use of their property—management should stay out of the voting (except to the extent that they are also stockholders).

In this new system, the percentage of shareholders actively participating is likely to increase substantially. There is not much reason now for owners of stock to read with care the contents of the notice of the annual meeting, or to weigh their votes. When real power to decide real issues is placed in their hands, more people will take the time to make and vote their choices.

But even if only a fraction of shares are voted, rule by a majority of these shares seems preferable to the present system, in which management benefits from shareholder passivity and reigns virtually unchallenged. In our political system, the leadership of our country is elected by a small minority—even in Reagan's 1984 landslide, he received the votes of fewer than a third of the registered voters (not to mention eligible but unregistered citizens). While the apathy—or whatever it is—of our electorate is to be lamented, the situation would be worse if the power to exercise the franchise in behalf of the apathetic were invested in the hands of incumbents.

In the corporate balloting, as in our political elections, those who choose not to vote will simply render themselves irrelevant. Their abdication of their power will simply magnify the power of those who choose to participate, rather than strengthen any particular interest or party.

There is another complication, however: an enormous amount of stock is held not by individuals but by institutions such as pension funds and mutual funds. How are these shares to be voted?

The managers of these funds need to have some basis for determining how those people whose money they are investing would like their shares to be voted. One way is for the funds to survey the people. Another way is for the funds to recruit investors through an articulation of their own priorities.

The second approach suggests how "Let the owners decide" would create the possibility of socially responsible mutual funds that would be far more potent than mere gestures. Socially responsible mutual funds would be defined not by the purity of the companies whose shares they buy but by their willingness to vote for the social good over maximal profits in whatever companies they hold.

Individuals could choose funds according to the usual criteria—growth, income, risk, and so forth—and also according to the compatibility of the funds' priorities with their own values. Even pension funds could be chosen on this basis, when people are in a large enough system that the organization can offer workers a choice of different investment approaches.

Alternatively, the funds could send out, on a regular basis, some kind of questionnaire in which the owners of shares could indicate some overall guidelines on a computer-readable form. "How much are you willing to forgo profit to protect the environment? (or to oppose apartheid, or to safeguard the health of workers? and so on)"—from zero for not at all willing, to five for extremely willing. Computerized proxy cards are already used to allow voting weighted by shares, and this system could be used to compute the priorities of the shareholders on a similarly weighted basis. The managers of the funds could then vote according to the consensus position of the owners.*

The problem is therefore soluble. An important criterion for evaluating these solutions is the extent to which it involves individual shareholders in a regular process of reviewing his or her priorities. Part of the value of "Let the owners decide," as will be discussed shortly, is its effect in consciousness raising. For an individual to make a one-time choice to participate in a particular mutual or pension fund (for example, one that maximizes profits unreservedly) and then never again have to look at the ethical ramifications of the use to which his resources are

---

*When funds are involved in scores of companies, it would be too cumbersome for the individual shareholder in the funds to involve themselves directly in the affairs of all the companies.

being put, makes the present blindness and passivity too easy to resume. This may be a reason to prefer the "regular survey" approach to the "choice of funds" approach. Or, perhaps, if the "choice of funds" approach is used, the funds should be required in their annual reports to give some accounting of how they voted their shares in the major corporate decisions in which they participated and/or to reinform their shareholders periodically about the priorities and policies that guide their voting choices.

PARAMOUNT VIRTUES

What does "Let the owners decide" have to recommend it?

New Choices

At a minimum, there would at least be a genuine possibility of *choice*. Corporations would no longer be on automatic pilot. The structure of the organization would no longer essentially dictate the hierarchy of values that governs a company's conduct in the world. Each company would become, in a much more meaningful sense than now, the instrument of flesh-and-blood people. These people would confront genuine choices, and the entire range of their values could inform those choices.

Perhaps more genuine possibilities for choice would mean new and better choices would be made. No longer a juggernaut, the corporation, in this scenario, would transform its behavior.

Some might argue that nothing would change. Selfish behavior, they might maintain, is a law of human nature, not dependent on the structure of corporate decision-making.

Which scenario is more realistic? What *would* people choose? The ideologues of the market often seem to dislike the idea of altruism. Not much good, Adam Smith declared, is done by people who say that is their purpose; appeal not to the benevolence of the butcher or the baker if you want to get fed, but to their self-interest. Latter-day disciples of Smith sneer at the idea of public-interest groups, as if the lobbying efforts of Environmental Action against water pollution were identical in nature to the lobbying of the steel industry against pollution controls. Everybody has "interests," and there are no important distinctions to be made among them. The alarm about global warming, I have been told by a corporate executive, has been sounded by organizations and individuals whose own fortunes—how much business and attention they get—are improved the more worried the public is about the future of the environment.

In some cultural environments, it is the powerful element of selfishness that people deny. Capitalism seems to have created the mirror image of that self-misrepresentation, a denial that produces an equal but opposite distortion.* Because this image of Economic Man as inherently and inevitably selfish appears to be immune from the wishful thinking that characterizes so many of our lies to ourselves about ourselves—our rationalization and justifications—this capitalist ideology regards itself as realism. But this "realism" may grow out of wishes of another kind. For the denial of the natural capacity for—and impulse toward—altruistic behavior serves a purpose for a system that not only harnesses selfishness but also effectively thwarts people's need to serve the larger whole.

Would the stockholders of America, given a choice, be any more altruistic in their decisions than management now is?

It is doubtful that the shareholders would cut their corporate throats on the sacrificial altar of public service. Nor should they. Anyone and anything that would serve the world is obliged to maintain its own health as well. Our great corporations need to preserve their own profitability, regardless of what else they do. The stockholder, however, would still face options within the considerable latitude that remains for our successful corporate giants.

I would wager that the stockholders, confronting the choices their companies face, would change the posture of their companies is significant ways. It is not that self-interest would be swallowed up by altruism. As individuals, virtually all of us—except for a Mother Theresa—indulge ourselves every day. Though we know that there are people in the world who are dying for lack of necessities, we choose to devote considerable amount of our resources to our enjoyment of luxuries

---

*This reminds me of an observation, made in the 1960s by the anthropologist Weston LeBarre, that the domain of modesty had changed location in our modern culture—moving from the pubic area to the face, which increasingly has become a mask that hides true feeling.

and superfluities. As investors, also, our altruism is bound to have its limits. But as individuals, we Americans have also shown ourselves to be a philanthropic people. We care about many things besides ourselves and our own enrichment, and we back up our caring with resources voluntarily given. With "Let the owners decide," our corporate system would come to embody a considerably wider range of our human concerns than it does now.

New Understanding

Even if the stockholders were inclined toward exactly the same decisions as present-day management, the process being proposed here could make a valuable contribution to our national culture. The very act of confronting these problems would change people's consciousness.

Part of the reason our world is not whole is that we do not see it whole. The encounters "Let the owners decide" would bring to American investors would help us see important connections.

Part of the fragmentation of understanding is due to the segmentation of our lives into discreet roles. As a citizen I care about the negligence of Exxon up in Valdez; as a consumer, I care about the price of my gasoline, and if Exxon's gas is cheaper than the brand sold across the street from it I am unlikely to think about the oilspill in Valdez when I'm deciding where to buy. On Sunday mornings, I take to heart the teachings about our responsibility to the less fortunate among us; as an investor, I listen approvingly to the broker praise a company's achievement in "keeping labor costs down," by which he means its effectiveness in keeping the workers in its North Carolina factory from organizing for higher wages and for equipment to reduce the occurrence of brown lung disease.

In the current upsurgence of environmental awareness, people are beginning to see some of the connections between their daily lives as *consumers* and the fate of the larger world. Americans are making best-sellers out of books that inform them about how, in their lives as private consumers, they can either continue contributing to the deterioration of the planet or, by changing their ways, help turn things around. Manufacturers of food products, in response to growing consumer interest, are developing whole lines of goods to appeal to the environmentally concerned consumer. People are increasingly cognizant of the network of connections between their patterns of consumption—whether they let the water run while they are brushing their teeth, whether their detergent has phosphates, whether their aerosol has CFCs—and their larger concerns.

"Let the owners decide" can extend that awareness, that educational process, that empowerment, into another important economic role that people play: the role of *investors*.

The unrestrained expansion of the market economy has long been served by an atomism in our thinking, by a failure to see the connections between the various elements of our social reality. In my search for enrichment, it is made easy for me to be unconcerned with my fellow citizens. As I put my dividend check in the bank for my daughter's education, I don't have any reason to think about whether the leukemia of someone else's daughter was induced by chemicals my company didn't think it worth the expense to dispose of properly. When I use my investment income to buy the ring for my true love's finger, I don't give a thought to the worker's fingers that were severed in the service of my meat-packing company, because safety devices were thought too expensive to install (and because the law did not require them, or could be skirted with impunity, or imposed fines less costly than the cost of obeying). When I complain about the corruption of our political process, I don't think about the way my proxy card has just been used to confirm the people in power in a company that uses its lobbying power and campaign contributions to make sure the congressional committee that oversees its industry understands "oversight" to mean "failure to notice."

If we, as stockholders, come to confront the important ramifications of the economic activities of specific companies for the well-being of the whole—the society, humankind, the biosphere—the interconnectedness of the world will become more visible to us.

Connections are not just a minor aspect of the world or of our understanding of it. The meaning of things can be discerned only by seeing how they relate to the context in which they are embedded. The word *holy* derives from the idea of "wholeness." So too does the word *health*. It is only if we see how things fit together that we become sensitive to the holiness in them. A civilization that sees only the pieces will find its achievements devoid of meaning, its values shallow and profane, its fragmented social order beset by sickness.

A procedure that renders our connections visible performs a valuable educational and spiritual service.

Then there is management.

Little in the present situation encourages wholeness of vision in these people, whose actions so powerfully shape our world. The lack of effective two-way communication between the managers and the people whose agents they legally are mitigates against broad human concerns. The unidimensional scorekeeping of the profit system fosters a disregard for the health of the social context as a whole. Ambition, atomism, and alienation make a toxic mix for human consciousness.

Merely having to identify those decisions in which important values of the whole are at stake would be a powerful tool for reorienting the awareness of management. Going then beyond that, the process of weighing objectively the competing costs and benefits of alternative policy paths is bound to lead to a greater depth of understanding of what it means to be a large actor in a delicate and interconnected world. And to follow the guidance of shareholders—of a public now become active—would lead to a transformation of the managers' image of themselves, from big-league game players to trustworthy stewards.

The world will look different to everyone because of the redefinition of their responsibilities. And then the world will become different.

Salability

"Let the owners decide" has one more salient virtue: it should not provoke ideological antibodies in the body politic of our liberal and individualistic society. The involvement of the coercive arm of the law is minimal. Though it is a law that would redefine the rights of stockholders, the redefinition is in the direction of strengthening not the collective power of the state but the rights of property owners.

In our political culture, efforts by the state to infringe on our individual liberties are resented. Thus, even regulations to correct obvious defects in the market provoke political antibodies—not only in the monied interests that profit directly from preserving their powers unchecked, but also in the political mainstream of our society. So powerful is this "Live Free or Die" impulse in the American consciousness that many Americans will regard government attempts to prevent pollution by U.S. Steel as a case of *them* trying to tell *us* what to do.

With "Let the owners decide," all "they" tell "us" to do is to make up our own minds. Rather than having our property employed in ways that escape our knowledge and control, we who are the owners should set the priorities. Who should choose? Not these "faceless bureaucrats" who rise to the top of these industrial bureaucracies, but whom the owners of the corporations never chose in any meaningful sense. But the owners themselves, those whose property the company is.

The conservative ideology that normally protects the market's status quo is defenseless against this revolution. For a century, that ideology has been leaning against state power in the name of the sanctity of the right of private property. Pushing so hard for the rights of property, when confronted with "Let the owners decide" the ideology must either rush forward to embrace it or fall on its face.

"Let the owners decide" offers revolution by aikido.

12

The Cult of Growth

Is the economy our servant? Or have we been fashioned into instruments for the purposes of our economic system? Of course the answer is—both. But it matters a great deal just what the proportions are.

In discussing the problem of the "automatic pilot" on which our giant modern corporations are operating, I argued for the importance of allowing our "full range of human concerns" to weigh appropriately in the determination of corporate policy. Companies that unreservedly seek only their own economic enrichment—that pursue the strategy best rewarded by the market system—do not create a healthy world. A way was proposed to make our corporations as human in their values as the people who own them.

If we look at the overall thrust of our present political system, however, what we find is rather sobering. A great diversity of values and concerns, it is true, contend in the arena of our national polity. Pecuniary values do not drown out all others in our political life to the extent they do in our corporate economy. But even here, where our democratic system would appear to give us the genuine capacity to choose, the drive for a material "more" still seems overwhelming. Free to vote the full spectrum of our humanity, the body part that seems preponderant in the urges we bring to the voting booth seems to be the pocketbook.

Over the generations, the land and the people of this country have been wrought into a productive system of ever-increasing material productivity. With all this magnification of our productive power, our dominant mainstream ambition for the future remains "more of the same." More growth. Harnessing ever more resources ever more efficiently to yield ever more production. This value—what might be called the "cult of growth"—dominates our national aspirations.

So great is the consensus on economic growth as the measure of value that alternative points of view do not seriously enter our political discussions. On abortion, some candidates may label themselves pro-life and other pro-choice. Some favor gun control, others militantly defend the rights of citizens to bear semiautomatic assault rifles. But hardly anyone challenges the notion that maintaining maximum sustainable economic growth indefinitely into the future—as far as foresight can see— is the proper goal of social policy.

When economic issues are discussed, the issues are overwhelmingly technical, not substantive, in nature. Some may think the Fed should tighten money supply, while others call for loosening it up. Some may think that government spending should be slowed to keep the economy from overheating, while others disagree. But no one disputes that the aim is to keep the economy growing (while preventing inflation from getting out of control). The overriding value of steady economic growth is the foundation of the American political ideology.

If there is anything approaching dogma in our national belief system, it is the idea that economic growth is the key to solving all our problems, the sine qua non of our individual and national well-being. E. J. Mishan describes growth as "not merely one of the economic goals of social policy. Like Aaron's rod, when transformed into a serpent, it was seen to swallow all its rivals—or almost all."[1] And the anthropologist Marshall Sahlins describes modern Western civilization as not only obsessed with economic growth but also intolerant and destructive of any other form of human cultural life with other "codes of existence."[2]

At one level, this cult of growth in our society as a whole might call into question whether or not the problem in our destiny is indeed an issue of our freedom of choice, as the discussion of "Automatic Pilot" would suggest. Maybe even if we were fully captains of our ship we would chart the same course. But the image of the iron fillings and the magnet (presented in Chapter 10) suggests that the problem of choice may remain alive at a still more fundamental level. In the presence of the magnet of the fable, the filings "chose" to fly toward the magnet and cling to it fast. If the American people, as a whole, appear as devotees of a cult of economic growth, we cannot infer from this alone that this priority of values is truly freely chosen.

The question of which is the master—the human or the machine—thus occurs again at the larger scale of our national life as well as on the smaller scale of the corporation. In our fixation on economic growth without limit, is our economy serving as an instrument of our human purposes? Or has our sense of purpose been pulled into alignment with the logic of an economy predicated on expansion?

Something is out of control. Is it human wants that, as we are told, have no limit? Or is it the lack of limit in the logic of our economic system?

THE MEASURE OF VALUE

The clear assumption in our national discourse is that economic growth can roughly be equated with an increase in human welfare. With minor caveats, this is the presumption of mainstream economics.[3] In this assumption, the economists reflect that impulse in our body politic, mentioned early, to vote our pocketbooks, to reward and punish our leaders more according to their ability to keep the economy growing at a satisfactory rate than for any other aspect of their performance. Woe to the president if, in an election year, this year's economy is no bigger than last year's.* Several decades ago, John Kenneth Galbraith wrote:

Some years ago, the Republicans, currently in office and defending their stewardship under heavy opposition at-

---

*A current example of this, as this passage is being written in July 1990, is the recurrent remark on the weekend talk shows that if there is a recession in 1992, President Bush's reelection chances will be in trouble.

tack, were moved to protest that the current year was the second best in history. It was not, in all respects, a happy defense. Many promptly said that second best was not good enough—certainly not for Americans. But no person in either party showed the slightest disposition to challenge the standard by which it was decided that one year was better than another. Nor was it felt that any explanation was required. No one would be so eccentric as to suppose that second best meant that second best in the progress of the arts and sciences. No one would assume that it referred to health, education or the battle against juvenile delinquency. . . Second best could mean only one thing—that the production of goods was the second highest in history.[4]

The enshrinement of GNP is irrational in some fairly obvious ways. Some of these concern the adequacy of GNP as a measure of economic wealth.

For example, the system values only what is transacted. If I pay you to clean my house and you pay me to clean your house, our present system of accounting declares that we have both become richer and, therefore, better off. Of course, we don't make exchanges that so transparently would cancel each other out in a more rational calculus. But what we have done amounts to much the same thing. Women who used to take care of their own children and to tend their own houses have now joined the "workforce," that is, have channeled their labor into the marketplace where human effort is bought and sold. By the millions, women are earning money at their jobs and spending much of it to pay other people to watch their children, clean their houses, cook their food. When something like 60 percent of women with children under five years of age work outside the home, there may well be profound hidden costs in terms of the human health and well-being of our society. But in the calculus embedded in the concept of GNP, all this proliferation of transactions registers as a large and unqualified leap forward in our economic welfare.*

---

*While our skewed accounting registers our enrichment, the children must spend their days in the care often of comparative strangers whose feelings toward the children are not as full-bodied as those of family members and who, in many places, are caring for so many children that "maintenance" is

Another irrationality is the way that "the defensive expenditures incurred to protect ourselves from the *unwanted* side effects of production" are added to GNP rather than subtracted from it.[5] In other words, if pollution is a hidden cost in the market system, and spending resources on cleaning up the mess serves to make those costs visible, our present system of accounting simply adds both the original production and the subsequent clean-up to arrive at an inflated measure of the creation of wealth. Making steel is a plus, and cleaning the curtains soiled by steel-factory smokestack soot is another plus. It is as though trampling a garden and then replanting it made us better off than we were before.

Such a system of accounting corresponds quite imperfectly with the realities of human welfare, but rather well with the logic of a system that is dedicated to the maximization of economic activity for its own sake.

In his 1980 book *Free to Choose*, in a passage lamenting the rise of what he describes as "antigrowth" movements such as the ecology movement, Milton Friedman chooses as an illustration of the "problems" that movement creates the example of the regulatory burden on the nuclear power industry. Friedman quotes, approvingly, the sarcastic remark of "the great nuclear physicist" Edward Teller: "It took us eighteen months to build the first nuclear power generator; it now takes twelve years; that's progress."[6] The question of nuclear power is complex, but in the aftermath of Chernobyl and in the absence of

---

all they can reasonably aspire to. Because our present system *values* only labor that is sold and not labor that is given outside the marketplace, the magnet of the market draws women out of traditional roles into the workforce.

The market's selective valuation of human activities, has contributed to women's experience of oppression in American society. Because, traditionally, it was men who entered the marketplace, while women's contribution was made outside the realm of financial exchange, the market's prejudice in favor of transactions amounted also to a devaluation of the roles and values traditionally represented by women. In our time, women increasingly have responded to this discrimination by abandoning their traditional realm and entering the domain of the market where work is more respected.

But this solution leaves unaddressed a fundamental problem, for it was not only women but whole domains of value that the magnet of the market has led us to disparage. The entry of women into the market leaves essential life-serving values in the shadows like neglected step-children.

Human values are molded into an image of the values of the marketplace. Society becomes "richer," while becoming impoverished in its understanding of what is of value.

any adequate solution to the problem of the disposal of nuclear waste, one may rightly wonder what would constitute real "progress" in the area of the construction of nuclear power plants. ("Progress" might mean their dismantlement.) But such uncertainty does not afflict the minds of those whose calculus mirrors that of the market system, in which the more activity the better, regardless of the direction of the movement.

The thinking of the cultists of growth recalls a story from an ancient Chinese classic. A man named Chi-liang tells this story to his ruler in an effort to dissuade him from his plans for war:

> I came across a man at Taihang Mountain, who was riding northwards. He told me he was going to the state of Chu.
> "In that case, why are you heading north?" I asked him.
> "That's all right," he replied. "I have good horses."
> "Your horses may be good, but you're taking the wrong direction."
> "Well, I have plenty of money."
> "You may have plenty of money, but this is the wrong direction."
> "Well, I have an excellent charioteer."
> "The better your horses," I told him, "the more money you have and the more skilled your charioteer, the further you will get from the state of Chu."[7]

This fable also helps illuminate a much more profound problem in the dogma of the cult of growth. The inadequacy of GNP as a system of accounting for our real increases in material wealth is not a trivial matter. But much more important is the larger question of how well suited for the maximization of human fulfillment is a strategy that seeks to maximize wealth. Even if our attention were not on such gross measures as output or throughput in the system of production and exchange, and even if our measures truly captured changes in our wealth, the question would still remain: does economic growth without limit promise us the richness of life we desire?

THE WEALTH-HAPPINESS CONNECTION

In a country in the grip of the cult of growth, the idea that greater wealth—whether it be for an individual or for an entire country—implies a greater sense of happiness or well-being is so obvious that it requires no demonstration or explanation.

Sure, our mythology includes the image of the "poor little rich girl," one whose great wealth is insufficient to overcome the burden of loneliness or neurosis. One need only go through the grocery store check-out line, reading the headlines of the various tabloids, to see how hungry we are for evidence that even the rich and famous are not immune to the heartaches, ills, and personal tragedies to which lesser people are prone. We all understand that wealth does not *guarantee* well-being, that money cannot *ipso facto* buy happiness.

But even without such a guarantee, we still buy into the market's materialistic bias. It remains an article of faith that the product (i.e., wealth) generally works. While we watch with pleasure the marital triangle of a Donald Trump, the less pleasurable side of envy's emotional constellation predominates in our view of wealth. We watch the "Lifestyles of the Rich and Famous," believing that if only we possessed all that sumptuous and beautiful property, we would feel wonderful. It is difficult to overestimate the extent to which life in America—the decisions made by individuals in their own lives, and the course that we take as a nation—is predicated on the assumption that "having more" fairly reliably means "feeling better."

Dogma needs no proof, but unfortunately for the cult of growth, social scientists have examined the empirical foundations of this cornerstone of our national creed. What they have found is hardly solid support.

LIMITED UTILITY

An important study on this subject is that conducted by R. A. Easterlin in the early 1970s. Easterlin explored the level of happiness reported by people living in various countries around the world and at sharply different levels of economic development. Within each country, Easterlin found, the evidence seemed to support our national dogma on the value of wealth. The richer people in each country were, in general, more satisfied with their lives than the poorer. But before we conclude that material wealth is a major contributor to people's happiness, we must confront another aspect of Easterlin's findings. Easterlin went beyond studying the correlation between wealth and happiness *within* countries to look at how that correspondence held up *between* countries.

If each country's per capita GNP is charted on one axis of a graph, and the reported happiness of that country's people is charted on the other, a striking finding emerges. There is no clearcut relationship. Among the countries whose people are relatively happy, poor countries are represented as well as rich. And likewise in the nations that are relatively unhappy, the rich are represented as well as the poor. This finding has been dubbed the "Easterlin paradox."[8]

Judging from the Easterlin paradox, one could double the wealth of everyone on the planet without necessarily increasing the level of human happiness. Yet the overriding premise of our vision of *improvement*—both in our domestic society and in the global system—has been to strive ceaselessly in that very direction. This fixation on putting our economic pedal to the metal seems like harnessing our fine horses to our well-driven chariot to charge headlong down a road that does not lead to the Kingdom of Chu.

Another more recent study substantially bears out Easterlin's discovery. Poll data in the late 1970s found some correlation between the wealth of a country and the happiness of its people.[9] But the correlation was apparently due entirely to the very poorest countries, where the level of deprivation seems to have a depressive effect. Above that level of impoverishment—a level that this country may be assumed to have passed a number of generations ago—wealth and happiness were again uncorrelated between countries.

The question of why being richer than one's neighbors is important to one's happiness, while being richer than people in other countries is not, is an important one. The value of being richer than those in one's immediate proximity would seem to bear out a famous observation made by John Stuart Mill in the nineteenth century, that what people desire is not so much to be rich as to be richer than their fellows. Wealth would appear to be an arena of interpersonal competition for status (and also for power). This competitive dimension, which includes the good feeling people apparently derive from feeling superior as well as the pain of envy people can experience when they see themselves scoring lower than their competitors in the language of their contest,* raises significant psychological questions.

The pertinent issue raised by these international findings concerns the value of increases of wealth for a national system as a whole. These findings suggest quite clearly the irrelevance (at least beyond a certain point) of the *absolute level* of wealth to people's happiness. This, in turn, calls into question the wisdom of a wealthy country, like ours, making sustained and indefinite economic growth the overriding, or even a central, goal of social policy.

Some interpreters, such as Wolfe and Kassiola, have stressed the importance of class interest in maintaining the cult of growth. The most affluent classes, according to this argument, can use a growing economy to ward off discontent that might threaten their ascendancy. The cult of growth, "by steadily raising everyone's standard of living in absolute terms, would for an indefinite period stifle socially disruptive demands for a change in distributional shares."[11] This analysis probably has considerable validity at one level. But such "reasons" can in no way resolve our suspicion that the whole fixation on growth is irrational. If wealth, beyond a certain point, is of little marginal utility, why should people who are extremely rich be so profoundly movitated to resist redistributional pressures? And if what is at stake is not abundant wealth per se but scarce status, how rational can it be for the society as a whole to stage its competition in this profligate form?

If the economic chase is really about the struggle for higher *relative* standing, economic growth is a wasteful way to conduct the contest.

In a discussion of the high cost of unrestrained contests for status, Robert H. Frank uses the example of Ivy League football. Compared to "big time" college football, Frank says, the Ivy League has adopted some stringent limits on the conduct of the competition. "Ivy League rules require, among other things, that spring practice be limited to one day, that athletic scholarships not be given, and that athletes be admit-

---

*Quoth Thomas Hobbes
    Continually to be outgone is *misery*.
    Continually to out-go the next before, is *felicity*.
    And to forsake the course, is to *die*.
    (Quoted in Bellah et al., p. 294)

ted according to the same academic standards applied to other students."[10] While fans accustomed to watching Big Eight football games may find the Ivy League contest amusing,

> if they remain in this environment for long, they usually come to appreciate the contests for the spirited, hard-fought encounters they really are. In Ivy League games, half the teams win each autumn Saturday, and half of them lose—the same as in other football conferences. *Yet the scale of what is sacrificed in the process is in many ways much lower here than in other conferences.*[12]

Similarly, if wealth is just—or principally—a way of determining, within a given community, who are the winners and who are the losers, then it is intolerably profligate to despoil the planet in order to achieve on an extravagant scale an outcome that could be accomplished just as well with the game scaled down.

All competition is subject to the waste and futility that characterize an arms race. Since each actor is striving to get more of something that has been construed as intrinsically scarce—power, security, status—the net effect of the frenetic agitation, for all the actors taken together, is necessarily nil. When competition escalates, the costs to the system as a whole go up, but the system, as a whole, cannot benefit.

This is the curse of the zero-sum nature of much competition, where the "goods" sought are in fixed supply. But economic growth, we in modern liberal society have always thought, is not about such unyielding scarcity but about abundance. We can all have more, our political economy has reasonably claimed, by expanding the pie. Comparison with others is irrelevant, even irrational, in the proper pursuit of happiness.* What matters to Economic Man, with his calculating reasonableness, is not his *relative* standing but the absolute amount of resources at his disposal. The growth economy has delivered to us an ever-expanding absolute level of resources

---

*The premise of one central economic concept—Pareto optimality—is that so long as you will compensate others for whatever harm you do them in bettering your condition, rationality dictates that they will allow you to proceed. If the pollution you cause in making yourself $1 million richer does me $100 worth of damage, I will be glad to take $101 plus the pollution in exchange for the status quo ante.

with the promise, and on the premise, that our fulfillment would expand accordingly. But if the premise is false, the promise is empty.

A rising tide, it is often said by the proponents of growth over redistribution, lifts all boats. But that metaphor can work for the other side of the argument as well—if the utility of wealth is primarily a matter of comparison and not of absolute level. A rising tide still leaves the big yachts bigger than the little skiffs.

How well has the rising tide of the expanding economy of the post-war era succeeded in lifting our spirits?

When I was a boy in the 1950s, I sensed an excitement and a sense of well-being as the economy expanded after the years of economic dislocation in the Depression and economic sacrifice during world war. People seemed to feel rich and optimistic. (It didn't hurt that we also compared so favorably with the still-recovering, war-ravaged economies of Europe and Japan.) In the media, one often heard that we were the richest nation in the history of the world. In the decades since then, even correcting for inflation, we have become considerably richer. A man employed full time earned, in constant dollars, more than twice as much in the mid-eighties as his counterpart in the mid-fifties.[13] Yet the feeling of wealth and well-being that characterized the 1950s seems to have eroded substantially over the intervening decades. It is not just our present worries about the future—worries that may be warranted in view of our national irresponsibility in consistently living beyond our means. Beyond that, despite their present high level of wealth—and even before the onset of the current recession— the American people have seemed to suffer from feelings of deprivation and discontent.

This informal observation has been borne out by poll data. Among others, Paul Wachtel, in his book *The Poverty of Affluence*, has described the evidence of declining economic satisfaction among Americans. Our sense of national well-being peaked in the late 1950s and then went downhill for many years—even as the economy continued to grow. Our feeling of malaise is not as low as it reached in the 1970s, but neither have we achieved again the feeling of well-being we had over three decades ago, when our per capita GNP was less than half its present level. As Robert Frank observes on the basis of public opinion polls, "Although people know their incomes are larger than those of their parents, this does not seem to count for much."[14]

Perhaps the data (from Easterlin and the other sources) understate the utility of wealth. Happiness is not such an easy variable to measure. People's reports on their own state of satisfaction may be unreliable. Cross-cultural comparisons are fraught with uncertainties. Different generations express themselves differently. I get real pleasure out of my microwave and my VCR, and it is difficult for me to believe that increments of wealth do not at least make *some* contribution to our happiness.

But even if all that is granted, a remarkable fact remains for us to confront. Even if, contrary to some empirical evidence, wealth is worth something, it is shocking that so central a postulate of our entire cultural calculus has been shown to be a good deal less than self-evident.*

Seismic convulsions should ripple through our cultural landscape in the face of such findings as the Easterlin paradox. Even if it turns out that the richer the better, but not by much, the fact that the contribution of economic growth to human happiness is evidently underwhelming should be enough to challenge our worldview and to induce a crisis in our sense of national purpose.

Yet our nation's devotion to growth remains substantially undiminished. What can account for this perseveration of belief?

Is it perhaps because the disconfirming data remain largely unknown? That cannot be it. The Easterlin paradox, far

---

*There is another, more recent indication of how insubstantial our relation to our material wealth really is. It is found in what might be called the mystery of the vanishing prosperity of the 1980s. Until the onset of recession in 1990, our public discourse was full of talk about "the longest peacetime expansion in American history." For most of a decade, it seems, the American people were persuaded that they were enjoying an era of growing prosperity. Now, all of a sudden, figures are surfacing that show that for the great majority of American families, the 1980s were a decade of barely holding even in terms of real income. My point is not the class issue, of why Americans applauded policies that concentrated our much-vaunted expansion on the richest stratum of our society. It is, rather, the rather remarkable—though wholly unremarked—psychological phenomenon that middle class Americans were apparently happy in the belief they were prospering throughout a decade in which their level of wealth stayed virtually flat. The mystery of this vanishing prosperity can be solved by postulating that what we need is not the wealth itself so much as the placebo effect of *thinking* ourselves rich.

from being a secret, can be found discussed throughout the (admittedly small) body of literature where serious consideration is being given to the question of human economic welfare.[15] If it is true that however far we drive our horses of economic growth we will not get appreciably closer to our goal of fulfillment, that is as important a discovery for the world we now live in as a cure for cancer. But it cannot be doubted that if a cure for cancer were presented in any reputable medical journal, it would not remain obscure a decade or two later.

Are we to say that it is simply difficult to change old habits of belief and behavior, the way the theory of evolution still is opposed by creationism more than a century after Darwin, or the way our bodies still respond to stresses with the biochemistry of fight or flight, though we live in a world that demands of us less physical ways of expressing either our anger or our fear? Robert Heilbroner has suggested that we have been conditioned by ages of poverty to have an appetite that won't readily shut off.[16] Are we, who now live in conditions of unaccustomed abundance, like some sheep that will eat themselves sick when surrounded with more readily accessible food than is found in natural pastures?

There may be an element of this, but I doubt it is the heart of the matter. Even back in those bygone ages of poverty, the teachers that human cultures adopted as their principal guides—teachers like Buddha, or Jesus, or Chuang Tzu, or Rabbi Hillel—all taught that the pursuit of material riches was not the key to fulfillment. It is not just that what was a good and sufficient guide in one circumstance has recently become inadequate with a momentous change of circumstances, the way Newtonian principles are adequate for the speeds of the objects we encounter in normal human activities but must yield to Einsteinian physics at speeds approaching that of light. Even when we were poor, the craving for wealth was not the basis for wisdom in the pursuit of fulfillment.

If we are looking in the psychological realm for an explanation of this perseveration of belief in the efficacy of wealth, we might note how much our behavior in relation to the craving for economic growth is like that of a person in the grip of an addition. The addict typically looks to the "stuff" to which he is addicted as the key to "getting right." The repeated failure of the next fix or next drink—or next doubling of income—to lead to real satisfaction does not, however, lead to a change of belief or of strategy. Even if the addiction produces more problems than solutions, the belief in the efficacy of the "stuff" can endure.

The question of belief is, to be sure, not the only issue. Philip Slater, in his work *Wealth Addiction,* concluded from his study of the lives of some of the most famous wealth addicts in American history that they often "know *when* to stop, they just don't know *how.*"[17]

> "I shall never use what I have" [Slater quotes Henry Ford as saying]. "Money doesn't do me any good. I can't spend it on myself." John W. McKay and H. L. Hunt both said that someone with $200,000 was as well off personally as they were with their many millions.

Knowledge, or right belief, is not sufficient to guarantee enlightened behavior. Even when explicit conviction falls away, the craving and the obsessive drive can remain the driving force in a person's life.

Nonetheless, for us Americans now, the question of belief is an appropriate starting place in the quest for a wiser and more balanced society. It is not at all clear that, in American society generally, the dogmas of economic growth have collapsed. We remain firmly in the grip of our addictive thought patterns. Consider this. We are already many times richer than our grandparents. E. J. Mishan has calculated that if our per capita income were to increase at 3 percent per year for five hundred years, it would be *one million times higher than it is now.* But never, in our national discussions, to we hear the question even broached, *what would be enough?* Enough? But the word "enough" doesn't seem to be part of our vocabulary. Even if we were not compelled to confront the urgent matter of the ecological unsustainability of our growth-addicted industrial economy, it would be important for us to ask this question.

In this, is not our society as a whole—as an economic entity—OUT OF CONTROL?

The God may have failed, but the religion of Economic Growth still brooks no heresies. It seems radical, in the context of the current orthodoxy or our political economy, to suggest even that there may be physical limits imposed on our growth machine by the facts of the finitude of the earth. But it is hardly even whispered in mainstream circles that even if growth *could* go on forever, there may be no sound reason for us to *want* it to.

The Spreading Conflagaration

In much of America a degree of balance remains—between the natural world and the human economy, between the values of the marketplace and the deep currents of other values. Those readers of these pages who live in such parts of this country may think overblown the concern expressed here about the implications of unlimited growth. Perhaps the homogenization of commercial strips in very small towns in the United States is regrettable. Perhaps industrial excesses during the recent period of our history have left the land scarred, as with the toxic waste dumps strewn across our countryside. But the overall thrust of economic growth, from a small-town perspective, might look quite benign.

As I sit and write in Maryland, inside the Washington Beltway, on the southern stretches of the great American Eastern megalopolis, I feel like saying to those with such a sanguine view, "I have seen the future and it is problematic." The pace of "development" is so rapid in this area that the speed of change confers on the observer the benefits of time-elapse photography: one can discern the overall momentum and trajectory of the evolving system. The city is extended into the remote suburbs, as woods are bulldozed down to make room for new office buildings and industrial plants. In Frederick, Maryland, which is increasingly being absorbed into the Washington Metropolitan area, the last hold-out has been overcome, and the lovely green acres where horses grazed by a stream, two blocks behind the strip where Burger King and K-Mart and all the others are found, a bucolic scene that recalled the town's historical charming and rural character, are now at last transformed into grist for the developers. (Did the old man who owned the land finally die? Did they make him an offer he could not refuse?)

Read the history of virtually any urban area in the country, and you will see the pattern repeated. Today's wilderness is tomorrow's farmfield. A rural landscape will the next day become a suburban development. And what is suburban one day is soon absorbed into the city. Expanding human numbers are part of the dynamic, but the limitless logic of economic growth drives much of the transformation as well.

Do we not need to ask, how much development is enough? And what do we need to do to control the dynamo of growth, lest it run over us and obliterate the world we cherish?

People comfortable with the way the world looks from their front porch might look to see what is coming their way. The future cannot always be foretold by extrapolation, but neither do things stand still. The reign of the cult of growth has many parts of our country already choking on its fumes, the landscape defaced and congested and incoherent. Those who live in unruined places cannot afford the luxury of complacency.

Machiavelli described how the ancient Romans managed to bring the whole of the Mediterranean world under their dominion. While the "potent prince" is making war upon one of the areas adjacent to his domain, Machiavelli said, the "other powers that are more distant and have no immediate intercourse with him will look upon this as a matter too remote for them to be concerned about, and will continue in this error until the conflagration spreads to their door, when they will have no means for extinguishing it except their own forces, which will no longer suffice when the fire has once gained the upper hand" (*Discourses*, 2.1).

The dynamo of economic growth is our advancing Roman Empire. A writer in the Washington metropolitan area can see the imperial expansion near at hand, but the story is unfolding similarly all over the country.

The voters of Fairfax County, Virginia, in the late 1980s, pulled off a major upset—rejecting entrenched political officials who had presided over the excessive development of the county. But by the time these Virginians had acted, the conflagration had largely consumed their county. In the fall of 1990, the voters of Montgomery County, Maryland, similarly astounded political observers by turning out the agents of overdevelopment. But here, too, the "potent prince" of economic growth had already done his imperial work.

Our complacency about the present will allow the empire of productivity for its own sake to continue its momentum into the future—a future we would not have chosen.

The dogmas of economic growth remain strong and intact, and we are unlikely to make real progress toward a more balanced social policy and way of life until we take the first step of recognizing that, however difficult it may be for us to do so, we need to turn our chariots around.

UNSHAKABLE BELIEF

The dogmas are founded upon illusion, but we as a people resist our disillusionment.

The perseveration of belief, even in the face of disconfirming evidence, was the subject of Leon Festinger's famous study, *When Prophecy Fails*. Festinger's immediate focus was a cult that believed the end of the world was at hand, at a particular time announced by the movement's prophet. When that time came and went and the world was still around, the members of that cult were confronted with the "dissonance" between belief and reality. For some, the solution was to abandon the belief. But, Festinger found with this and other historical cults, sometimes people's commitment to a "belief system is so strong that almost any other course of action is preferable" to "discard[ing] the belief and admit[ting] one had been wrong."[18] For such people, Festinger discovered, the solution was to "effectively blind themselves to the fact that the prediction had not been fulfilled."*

What is it, we may wonder, that would make the dogmas of the cult of economic growth so difficult for Americans to abandon, even in the face of disconfirming evidence?

Any addiction can serve to cover over feelings of emptiness and despair. One clings even to a false god in order to escape a confrontation with the void within.

In the case of the god of economic growth, the underlying sense of despair is suggested with particular clarity by the fervent emphasis the system places on hope. People will make the promise of "more tomorrow" the core of their lives only if they feel intensely the inadequacy of what they have today.

---

*Festinger notes that one of the ways that people can shore up the endangered foundations of their belief is through proselytizing. "*If more and more people can be persuaded that the system of beliefs is correct, then clearly it must, after all, be correct*" (p. 28, in original). This emphasis may bear upon the observable American tendency to prosyletize our economic system and the holy grail of economic growth.

The craving for bettering one's condition can be fueled only by profound dissatisfaction with one's present condition.*
We are accustomed to thinking of hope as an unmixed blessing. But hope has its pathological forms also. Our cult of economic growth is a tool our culture has contrived to prevent our having an indispensable confrontation with a hollowness that our enculturation places at the core of our being and our experience. This is evident not only at the macro scale of our economics, where the horse-race of GNP statistics provides us as a nation with the hope that the future will be one of progress, of getting ahead. A pathology of hope is exhibited also in the micro scale of our individual consumerist behavior. Insightful students of consumption have observed a cycle of hope and disillusionment in consumer behavior.[20] At the foundation of the cycle is a feeling of longing, of unfulfilled yearning. In this cycle, each new not-yet-purchased object becomes involved with fantasies of one's future happiness, of psychological transformation and redemption. When, after the purchase, these fantasies remain unfulfilled, rather than abandoning the fantasies the consumer transfers them to some new, not-yet-attained commodity that becomes the repository of hope.

These may be some of the psychological elements contributing to the persistence of belief in economic promises that prove false. But perhaps the real force behind the cult of economic growth does not lie in the psychological realm, with its beliefs and hopes and dissatisfactions. Perhaps it is the

---

*In making his case for the indispensability of economic growth, Michael Novak presents the following shaky logic: "A democratic system depends for its legitimacy . . . not upon equal results but upon a sense of equal opportunity. Such legitimacy flows from the belief of all individuals that they can better their condition. This belief can be realized only under conditions of economic growth" (*The Spirit of Democratic Capitalism*, p. 15). Surely, there is a non sequitur here. By the same logic, the National Football League could only offer its member teams hope of bettering their condition if the system promised that the time would come when all teams would have winning seasons. Subsequently, Novak goes on to say that "in the trap of a zero-sum economy, the Hobbesean 'war of all against all' makes democracy come to seem unworkable" (p. 16). The possibility of change in one's relative standing would be insufficient to preserve the viability of a democratic social order. In assuming inevitable dissatisfaction with actual absolute levels of wealth, the free-marketeer Novak is inadvertently giving testimony to the element of discontent and despair at the core of the cult of economic growth.

economic system itself that dictates and shapes our commitment to an ever-expanding economy. Perhaps, in our holding
to these dogmas of belief, we are again like the iron fillings in
the presence of a magnet.

Of course, the psychological dimension will always be an
essential part of the picture. Magnets cannot attract rose petals.
The iron filings "decide" to fly toward the magnet because
their own internal electrical alignment makes them susceptible
to the magnet's field. Similarly, we will not become efficient
conductors of the market's forces except as our own structure
makes us responsive to the systemic forces around us. Yet, as
we saw in part 2, "We Are Driven," the market has the power
to mold our internal structure, over the course of generations,
into a form that serves its purposes.

So is it perhaps the case that what is out of control in this
limitless quest for growth is ultimately not so much the limitlessness of human needs or even of the needs of humanity as
rendered in our particular modern market culture as the un-
quenchable demands of the system itself? Is the root cause of
the cult of growth to be found not so much in the psychological nature of the people within the system as in the logical
thrust inherent in the market economy?

MACHINES HAVE NEEDS, TOO

At one level, the matter of the "needs" of the system
might be explored in terms of the question, can there be a
healthy economy that is not constantly growing? Is the economy like a bicycle that, by its nature, must move forward in order not to fall over? Are we faced with a situation in which,
even if we were to have what we all felt was enough, we would
be compelled to scramble for "more" in order to avoid our system's collapse into "less"?

It was mentioned earlier that in the system of our political
economy, the discussion is overwhelmingly devoted to technical questions rather than to questions of value or purpose, to
the "how" rather than to the "what" or "why" of our economic
life. As important as it is to call attention to the vital substantive questions that we so completely neglect, it would be a mistake to deny the importance of the purely technical challenge.
A modern economy is an enormously complex mechanism, a

balance of countless forces geared to meet a multiplicity of important needs. Keeping the economy functioning smoothly, without excessive swings and dislocations, is a task both important and difficult.

As imperfect as our system is, sometimes it seems a miracle that the system works as well as it does. We need only look at countries whose economies have been mismanaged—the experience of Argentina over the past half century comes to mind as one example—to appreciate the economic technicians working to keep the national and the global economic systems running.

The question of whether the economy is capable of being healthy without simultaneously being expansionary is a technical question. A detailed examination of such a technical issue may lie outside the proper scope of this inquiry. But we might touch upon some grounds for skepticism about this "argument from necessity."

A point worth making is that if an economy both stable and healthy is impossible, then eventual disaster would appear to be an inevitability. Unless one believes that the rest of the universe will become significantly available as grist for our economic mill, the finitude of the earth suggests that it will not be possible for hundreds of millions of people (talking only about the G7 countries, that is, the principal industrial democracies) to increase their consumption of the earth's resources one millionfold every five hundred years. (The quantity of natural resources consumed for every unit of what we call "consumption" can certainly decrease with changing technology, but there is certainly a strong relationship between "consumption" and our impact on the earth.) If this argument from necessity is valid, we are charging toward a cliff's edge and the only question is, how far away is the abyss?*

Must we assume it an impossibility to create an economy that can work well without continually getting bigger? More than a decade ago, Herman Daly wrote a book entitled *Steady-State Economics*. Daly makes a case, in this work, for an economy predicated not on expansion but on stability. "Steady-state" is not synonymous with stagnant. "If we use

---

*This same kind of reasoning needs urgently to be applied to that other runaway form of contemporary growth—the still unrestrained growth of human numbers on this planet.

'growth' to mean quantitative change, and 'development' to mean qualitative change, then we may say that a steady-state economy develops but does not grow, just as the planet earth, of which the human economy is a subsystem, develops but does not grow."[21] To those who argue that an economy without growth must collapse, it can be countered that the dislocations caused by the cessation of growth in present-day, growth-oriented economies constitute no proof. Daly says that a steady-state economy is not just a growth economy that is failing to grow.

> The fact that an airplane falls to the ground if it tries to remain stationary in the air reflects the fact that airplanes are designed for forward motion. It certainly does not imply that a helicopter cannot remain stationary. A growth economy and a SSE [steady-state economy] are as different as an airplane and a helicopter.[22] *

How has the mainstream of economic thinkers responded to the case Daly has made for a viable alternative to the growth economy? Have the economists refuted it? According to Daly, in a personal conversation, his argument has not been countered. It has not been accepted. It has only been ignored.

Over the years, I have had conversations with religious fundamentalists of various hues—Christian, Jewish, Muslim. What always strikes me about the thinking of fundamentalists is that the search, in the process of intellectual inquiry, is never the search for an answer, for the answers are given. All the intellectual energy goes into finding the means to arrive at a conclusion that was predetermined at the outset.

In that perspective, it is hardly surprising if the fundamentalists of economic growth—the high priests of American society—are unwilling to employ their intellectual ingenuity to find alternatives to destructive growth. "Full speed ahead" is the foregone conclusion; the task of devising a more viable approach to economic life is not seriously undertaken. Thus our

---

*Daly points out that for "over 99 percent of its tenure on earth," our species has lived under conditions "approximating" a steady-state economy. "Only in the last 200 years has growth become sufficiently rapid to be felt within the span of a single lifetime," Daly wrote in 1977, "and only in the last forty years has it assumed top priority and become truly explosive. In the long run, stability is the norm and growth the aberration. It could not be otherwise" (ibid, p. 18).

famous Yankee ingenuity seems to desert us when the need for economic transformation is argued.

We see this dearth of imagination, what might be called "selective unresourcefulness," not just with respect to the question of growth as a whole but wherever restraint of economic forces might be contemplated. Can we save the old-growth forests of the northwest? No, we are told, we shouldn't sacrifice people for trees (as if those were the only two conceivable options). Again and again, we are told that people must continue to be paid for work that we, as a society, would be better off were it left altogether undone. Jobs must be protected. Options are foreclosed; necessity reigns.

But in a society where so much needs to be done, must the fear of people losing their jobs really inhibit us from making constructive economic transformation? Of course, the market itself is always affecting transformations that dislocate people, eliminating jobs in some sectors while creating new jobs in others, drying up economic activity in some geographical areas while intensifying it in others. But the same people who say we can't make a collective political decision to save virgin redwoods—for jobs must be preserved—are often just as adamant that companies must be free to close down their inefficient factories despite the economic dislocation it will entail for whole communities. The common denominator is not solicitude for any human needs but rather an insistence on submission to the will of the market, letting the system decide what it will chew up and what it will spit out.

If we had the will, I expect, we could devise a more balanced, more whole economy. Our national abundance of ingenuity could find ways to make the necessary transitions, to provide people who are dislocated by change with temporary roles that make a constructive contribution. (A half century after they were erected, one traveling across American still discovers wonderful constructions on the landscape wrought by the Civilian Conservation Corps.) Our great national wealth would surely enable us, if we had the will, to compensate those who bear the brunt of decisions we make, as a whole society, about the shape of the future we want.

But for now, our fundamentalist mentality is continually constructing "necessities" to constrain the path of our thought, to compel us toward conclusions in the service of the expansion of our economy's empire. Thy Will, oh Growth-Machine, not mine. Philip Slater has observed the circular logic that supports an economy running out of control. According to this logic, says Slater, "we need unnecessary jobs so that people will have unnecessary money to buy unnecessary things. And we need to buy unnecessary things in order to create unnecessary jobs so people will have unnecessary money."[23] It does not take extraordinary sagacity to conceive an alternative to this economy of insatiability. The anthropologist Marshall Sahlins once wrote that one can be affluent "either by producing much or desiring little."[24] One can be content with what one already has, or one may be constantly driven by the craving for more. Sahlins was writing in *Stone Age Economics* about what he called "the original affluent society," that of hunting-gathering peoples. Despite their low level of material consumption, Sahlins and others have found, hunter-gatherers apparently felt they had enough. They seemed more content with their wealth than we are with ours.*

We are in the grip of a system that drives us relentlessly toward more and more. The system itself gets fatter and fatter as it takes into its maw more and more of the earth—as well as ever more of our humanity—while we still feel lean and hungry.

It is, one suspects, less the system's functional "need" for growth than its unbridled appetite that demands this compulsion, this sense of necessity, from the market's human agents. The fundamentalism of our cult of growth derives not from an objective requirement of a healthy economy to serve human purposes but from the unfolding of an economic system that at once exercises power over people and has in its body no nervous system capable of saying "enough."

One means by which it exercises its power is to reward, to empower, those people who will make themselves into its image. As creatures we, unlike the market, do have a nervous system that can say we have eaten enough. As Joseph Hirshhorn said of the superfluity of money beyond a cer-

---

*Even our progressive economists—those who might one day advise a progressive, Democratic president—are well within the bounds of orthodoxy. Consider Lester Thurow's argument for the necessity of economic growth, which claims that an economy without growth "does not jibe with human nature. Man is an acquisitive animal whose wants cannot be satisfied" (Quoted in Wachtel, p. 40). Economists look to economic theory, not to anthroplogy, for their concept of human nature. Don't confuse me with facts, my mind is made up.

tain point, "You can't wear more than two shirts a day, or eat more than three meals."[25] But if those people tend to rise in power whom the system can persuade to buy into its logic—the logic that says, do work that is unneeded by society to buy products that you don't need so people will continue to be employed to make such superfluities—that logic, too, will gain power in society. The insatiability of the mechanical system gains ascendance over the sense of proportion inherent in organic process.

CONSUMER AS COG

Human needs or the needs of the machine? That is theme of the present inquiry.

The rise of consumer culture in America gives some clues about whose needs are running the show. Toward the end of the nineteenth century, Simon Patten, the "social theorist of abundance" (as Stuart Ewen calls him), reflected on the meaning of the rising standard of living. "The standard of life is determined, not so much by what a man has to enjoy, as by the rapidity with which he tires of the pleasure."[26] Patten, it must be understood, was not challenging but extolling the use of such a standard to measure human lives. Clearly, it is not human satisfaction that is being maximized by this approach but the empire of the productive system.

Several decades later, in the interwar years, advertisers understood themselves to be the tools by which demand could be stretched to meet the potential supply. "Advertising has stimulated more work," the Ayer advertising agency said, since people proved willing to work harder to get the goods so enticingly dangled before them in the ads.[27] Marchand quotes other advertisers expressing satisfaction at the way the fostering of style consciousness created "progressive obsolescence," so that "even our extravagance turns more wheels." The more wheels get turned, obviously, the better.[28] By increasing our dissatisfaction with what we have, by making the goods that had given us pleasure seem obsolete, "We lift ourselves by our bootstraps."[29] This sounds elevating. But in a different perspective, the advertiser has fashioned us into more willing components of a perpetual motion machine of maximal production.

After World War II, the work of producing consumers re sumed. "The major problem [confronting us]," said the industrial designer Gordon Lippincott in 1947, "is one of stimulating the urge to buy!"[30] What this requires, he said, is generating "a mass-buying psychosis." The principal job that "advertising, research, and the industrial designer are doing in common is . . . [the] job of convincing the consumer that he needs a new product before his old one is worn out."[31]

The system has empowered those who have thought like this, who have seen in the manipulability of human wants a natural resource for the productive apparatus to exploit.

Where do human needs fit into this picture? Surely, they are part of it. Not every kind of product catches on, however well it is promoted. Even the need to be stylish was not created out of whole cloth, as it were, by market forces. But massive resources have been devoted in the course of an entire century to the creation of the consumerist mentality. As the above passages suggest, the question is not always, How do we best organize economic resources to satisfy human needs? It is often, rather, How can we best restructure human wants to foster the maximal consumption of economic resources?

The whole situation is filled with paradox. "Lifting ourselves by the bootstraps" is a benign way of describing a situation in which we have become manifestly ungrounded. We discover the tool wielding the man. The circular logic of unnecessary labor straining after superfluous goods suggests that we are not the masters but rather the servants of our own creations. The economy grows but the human spirit, seduced into losing its way, is diminished. In the phrase of Ralph Waldo Emerson, a century and a half ago, "Things are in the saddle, And ride mankind."[32]

The cult of economic growth is a part of our servitude. The system runs on human energies, but its expansion is not to be understood as a human victory.

POVERTY AND THE WEALTH OF NATIONS

But what about the poor? Those who challenge the cult of growth are often accused of being elitists, people who have already made it up the economic ladder and who are selfishly proposing to pull the ladder up after them, leaving the impoverished to their misery. Should not the engines of economic growth be stoked at least until even those living under conditions of clear deprivation also participate in our material abundance?

Poverty certainly remains. There are millions of people in this country and hundreds and hundreds of millions elsewhere on the planet whose material conditions of life stand in need of improvement. Doubtless also the workings of the market system have helped to raise regions and nations out of poverty and into affluence. Some kind of economic development will clearly be needed in the future. (Even the wealthiest countries will need "development" in some senses, if only to restore balances upset by the excesses of our present headlong rush toward "growth.")

I am not arguing for stagnation. I am not even saying that all of what is conventionally regarded as growth is deleterious. My argument, rather, is with the cult of growth, with a single-minded and disconnected fixation on numbers, with the disembodied hunger for production for its own sake. My plea is for us to take control of the machine.

The defense of growth in the name of poverty warrants, however, a closer look. Whether the market is the most effective means of addressing the problem of genuine poverty is open to question. It is arguable that the continued growth of the wealthy on this finite planet absorbs scarce resources necessary for significant improvement in the lot of the poor. This, of course, leads back into that question of the nature of "resources," and of the reality of "scarcity."

Beyond such questions, it seems quite unlikely that the concern for the poor is really what animates the cultists of growth. Those who call environmentalists elitists are hardly the Mother Theresas of the world. In the United States in the 1980s, for example, when especially devout proponents of growth held sway, concern for the poor seemed strictly confined to those occasions when the question of constraints on the market or on unbridled growth was raised. The best way to help the poor, it was said, was not to stand in the way of the economic activity of the rich. This decade was marked, however, by a pronounced widening of the gap between the richest and the poorest—both in the United States and in the world generally.*

---

*The New Republic reports, "the proportion of all national income earned by the richest 1 percent of all families went from 8.7 percent in 1977 to 13.2 per-

The historical perspective, it is worth noting, reveals that in its origins the ideology of economic growth was not founded on a concern for the fate of the least fortunate. Indeed, in the early nineteenth century, the "Iron Law of Wages" had persuaded liberal thinkers that it was futile to hope for much material improvement for the working class in general. Jeremy Bentham, the utilitarian philosopher of the late eighteenth and early nineteenth centuries, wrote that "in the highest stage of social prosperity, the great mass of the citizens will most probably possess few other resources than their daily labor, and consequently will always be near to indigence."[32]

The poor, they thought, we will always have with us. But this dismal assumption in no way impaired their commitment to growth. As in its origins, so, it seems, in its contemporary manifestations: the impulse behind the cult of growth is not fundamentally a charitable one.

There are people lacking necessities, but this is not the necessity that drives the headlong rush toward economic growth.

Is there, then, no human necessity underlying this limitless expansionary drive? Is it only the insatiability of the machine itself?

There is one more necessity we must look at. To discover it, we may recall that the foundational book of the market's ideology was not entitled *The Prosperity of the People*, but rather *The Wealth of Nations*. Not only individuals but also nations need to survive. We may understand the "necessities" of people in terms of such material elements as food, shelter, and clothing. But the material needs of nations relate to their requirement for security in a very dangerous intersocietal system.

It is in this context that nations have felt a genuine compulsion to develop and grow economically. Material wealth has been understood as an indispensable component of the power on which national survival depends. Perhaps it is in this context that the cult of economic growth gains its unchallengeable

---

cent in 1990. For the bottom 40 percent, it dropped from 15.5 percent to 12.8 percent. Those in the middle fifth dropped from 16.2 percent to 14.8 percent" ("Lip-Flop," editorial, July 23, 1990).

When budget director Richard Darman declared in 1990 that "the needy of the world will not be helped by, and will not settle for, a neo-Luddite attack on technological advance" (Darman, *Keeping America First*, p. 5), it was not in the context of a program that, in other contexts, displayed particular concern with the plight of the world's needy.

legitimacy. These days, in the United States, amid concerns about our nation's declining economic dominance, one frequently hears exhortations from experts of various stripes telling us that losing ground to our economic competitors will have dire consequences for our future. To avoid such a fate, we are told, we *must* do this and we *must* do that. Perhaps it is in the perspective of the necessities of national security that such a sense of compulsion finds its validation. If our economic necessities must be understood in *relation* to the economic power of other countries, it cannot be sufficient to look solely at the absolute level of our wealth. Perhaps it is in view of this competitive dynamic that the *limitlessness* of the growth imperative finds its justification.

Maybe the national unit is "out of control" because it is embedded in a world system beset—now, as it has been for millennia—by an uncontrolled struggle for power.

This problem of power will be the subject of the next chapter.

13

Power Struggle

I. Driven to Excel

Freedom or Necessity

Does the existence of our fellow human beings extend or restrict the range of our economic options?

At the foundation of classical economic theory is the notion that the presence of our fellow human beings greatly enhances both our welfare and our range of options. From the very first sentence of book 1, chapter 1, Adam Smith's *The Wealth of Nations* is a paean to the beneficial consequences of the division of labor. "The greatest improvement in the productive powers of labour, and the greater part of the skill, dexterity, and judgment with which it is any where directed, or applied, seem to have been the effects of the division of labor." And the division of labor, in turn, is possible to the extent that we are able to widen the network of contact and exchange among peoples.

It is the division of labor that gives us the wealth of economic choices available to us in the modern marketplace. If each person or household had to be entire unto itself, such a solitary life would indeed be nasty and poor. The inefficiency of unspecialized labor would condemn us to work hard for meager results. But we are able to improve our lot, Smith argued, by virtue of our natural tendency to barter and trade. This allows each to specialize in what he does best. This division of labor, by magnifying labor's productivity, enables everyone, after exchange is made in the marketplace, to enjoy more of everything. We are thus raised from the state of poverty, which is ruled by necessity, to a condition whereby we enjoy an abundance of choice.

The logic of this encourages us to extend our network of synergistic exchange without limit, to embrace the whole of humanity. Smith captures this with the title of his third chapter, "That the Division of Labour is Limited by the Extent of the Market." The larger the better. Even the day-laborer in Great Britain of Smith's time, the founder of liberal economics declared (in a passage similar to Milton Friedman's panegyric about the manufacture of a pencil, quoted earlier), is the beneficiary of the labor of countless specialists who contribute to clothing, feeding and furnishing him.

> Compared, indeed, with the more extravagant luxury of the great, his accommodation must no doubt appear extremely simple and easy; and yet it may be true, perhaps, the accommodation of an European prince does not always so much exceed that of an industrious and frugal peasant, as the accommodation of the latter exceeds that of many an African king, the absolute master of the lives and liberties of ten thousand naked savages.[1]

The famous argument concerning *comparative advantage,* repeated in every economics text, extends to nations the same rule as that applied to individuals: don't draw a boundary around yourself, for the more people out there with whom you exchange freely, the better off you are. Thus to every beginning student of economics it is proved that, between any two countries with different ratios of efficiency in the production of different goods, trade can give both countries more of everything.

The liberal dream of a whole world woven together by trade, of all humankind benefitting from unfettered voluntary exchange, would seem to be a wonderful extension of our species' ancient adaptive strategy. From the beginning, from before we were human, we have adopted the strategy of living in social groups. Finding more security in association with our fellows than we could in solitary life, we developed as social animals. Cooperation and sharing emerged, over the ages of our life in small bands, as salient tendencies of our human nature. The market would appear to elaborate and formalize that ancient pattern of cooperation, to fortify still further our security and to broaden the range of our options.

But the question of our freedom is not so simple as that. The most fundamental question concerning freedom is, *How do we want to live our lives, and are we free to live that way?* Only to a mind that has been completely taken over by the propaganda of consumerism would the question, How do we want to live our lives? be seen as equivalent to, What do we wish to obtain in the marketplace? The division of labor fostered by the market system truly gives us an abundance of options as consumers wishing to enjoy the fruits of others' labors. But when we are embedded in this economic system, what impact does the presence of other actors have on our range of choices about how we—as individuals, as societies—want our lives to be *as a whole?* If other people, or other nations, disappeared from the face of the earth, would we suddenly enjoy options, previously foreclosed, more desirable than those we can contemplate today?

In the first place, it should be observed that the questions, "How do we—as a nation—wish to live?" or, "What do we want our society to become over the coming generations?" are questions that are almost never asked in our public discourse. As utterly vital as they would appear to be, they are almost completely neglected. Is it because the answers seem self-evident? Is it because the questions seem unanswerable? Or is it because, deep down, we do not feel free to choose?

The sense that we are governed by necessity, with free choice foreclosed, seems certainly to be implied by a whole chorus of voices prominent today on the public stage. There people are telling us that we *must* transform ourselves in certain ways, which they proceed to prescribe. And the reason? Because of the challenge posed to us by our competitors. The Japanese are overtaking us—we must change to become more competitive. The Germans are assuming a dominant position in an increasingly united Europe—we must realign our industrial organization and our traditional patterns of culture to meet the threat.

The existence of other actors, it appears, constrains us under the yoke of necessity. The workings of the market, these arguments imply, rather than simply proliferating our options, are dictating what our society must become.

How well founded are these arguments about necessity? Does the presence of our economic competitors indeed compel us to transform ourselves in ways we would otherwise reject, and foreclose ways of living we would most desire?

Let us examine these necessities.

SPURIOUS NECESSITIES

What if we felt we had *enough?* What if, having reached a level of material wealth barely imaginable even to our grandparents earlier in this century, we felt satisfied with what we have. As with the Faustian *Verweile doch*, we might say that we feel no need for further striving, if the prosperity of the present moment could but be extended indefinitely into the future.* But what if, at the same time, there are other nations still striving, other countries whose ambitions would lead them to surpass us in wealth if we were to stand still? Are we free to choose to stay content with our sufficiency?

Maybe we are not free. But before we can come to grips with any genuine constraints upon our range of choices and and with the problem of how we might become more truly free, it is essential that we peel away some of the false claims, the spurious necessities, with which some apparent experts are trying to drive us into a competition in which there can be no such thing as enough.

Michael Dertzouzos, a professor at MIT, appears on the MacNeil/Lehrer News Hour in June, 1989, to warn us. If we don't change our economic practices, he says, "our standard of living will become *worse.*" Then he adds, as if in fine print and parentheses, "relative to other countries." An alarming fall in our standard of living—that is the message of warning that

---

*Saying "Enough" would not necessarily mean rejecting all material increase or technological improvement. The essence of the point is not an insistence on stasis but a satisfaction with what one has in material terms and a refusal to sacrifice much of value to get more.

comes through. "In relative terms," he continues, then placing the emphasis on the last word, *"impoverished."*[2] The specter of poverty dances over our heads, unless we get our act together and transform ourselves into a more competitive form. In fact, we could become continually richer in absolute terms while our relative standing fell. If we are getting richer, does it make sense to talk in terms of declining "standard of living" and impoverishment?

A vice president for a large regional brokerage firm, Piper, Jaffray and Hopwood, writes a piece that is the headline article in the March 1990 newsletter sent out to all the firm's clients. The article is entitled "U.S. Faces Challenge to Maintain Its Standard of Living." He, too, is concerned about the adverse trend, the fact that the economic performance of the United States has not been improving as fast as its competitors. "To lose our economic leadership role in the free world," writes Ronald Reuss, "would reduce us to a second class nation, and substantially decrease our standard of living."[3]

In this single sentence, Reuss conflates two different issues—first or second class status as a nation and standard of living—and it seems that confusion is the result. In the late nineteenth century, Great Britain was indubitably a Great Power, a nation of the first rank. Now it is certainly, in this somewhat dubious parlance, a second-rate power. Britain's share of world product has fallen from about 25 percent to a mere 3 percent during the past century or so.[4] Does this mean that its standard of living has fallen substantially? Far from it. "Britain today has far greater wealth . . . than in its mid-Victorian prime."[5]

This kind of confusion can hobble our national effort to find our way. What kind of country are we if our national goal is simply to be richer than everyone else? Among other things, it would mean that it is not *we* who are choosing our destiny, but the world around us. If getting richer slower is equated with falling into poverty, how could we or anyone else *ever* talk about what might be "enough"?

Some things, admittedly, are scarce: some games are zero-sum. Not every nation can be first class. Not every nation can claim a position of leadership in the world economy. Underlying these scare tactics about our supposedly impending impoverishment appears to be a better-founded concern about our national status in the world. The real imperative seems to be,

"We must remain Number One." Truly, in a dynamic and competitive world economy, preeminence can be maintained only by continual striving. There is no *Verweile doch* possible, for what is sufficient for supremacy today will not be enough tomorrow. But is it really *necessary* to be Number One? Does the struggle for economic preeminence really deserve to rule our social destiny? Does the outcome of that struggle truly affect our legitimate concerns?

Again, we will shortly see that, in some ways, it may. But it is worthwhile, once again, to point out some spurious dimensions to this supposed necessity.

In our society, and in particular among men, and still more particularly among the men who form our political, economic, and intellectual elites, winning—getting to the top—is so central a value in life that it may be impossible for many of them to make rational judgments distinguishing where winning is important objectively from where it is not. For people whose own sense of worth is so tied up with demonstration of their superiority, trying to weigh reasonably what might be the value of alternative approaches to life is like trying to see electromagnetic waves that lie beyond the visible spectrum. *Of course* it is necessary to be the superior nation!

Otherwise . . . what are we? how can we be worth anything? how could we stand not being the object of the admiration and envy of others? (Who could stand hearing foreigners saying derisively, as an advisor to French President Mitterand, Jacques Attali, has said, that "America has become Japan's granary, like Poland was for Flanders in the 17th century."[6]) In his May 1990, talk "Keeping America First," Richard Darman, director of the Office of Management and Budget, sees "the real and symbolic power of the American example" as inseparable from "American primacy." This leads him to declare the essential question to be, *"How can we keep American Number One?"*[6.5]

"To forsake the course," said Hobbes, "is *to die*."

In my study of the ethic of the warrior in *Out of Weakness*, I entitled a section "In other men's eyes." This dealt with the tendency for warrior men to be controlled by their concern with how much they are esteemed by other warriors. In many of the western movies of the postwar era, the hero wanted to lay down his guns, but the reluctant gunman would be "compelled" to re-enter the fight by shaming insults: What are ya, yella? Afraid to fight it out like a man?

There are now voices that call us back into the street of world economic competition with similar references to how we look in other men's eyes. "America's difficulties . . . look to the Asians like failures of character," James Fallows says in his book *More Like Us*, trying to rouse us from our complacency.[7] And in a *Washington Post* piece on the same theme, Fallows reports, "After two years of listening to Japanese and Koreans, I've grown accustomed to hearing 'lazy' used before 'Americans' as if the two words form a natural compound, like 'brazen hussy' or 'fellow traveler.' "[8]

At this point, I should clarify just what values I am, and what values I am not, intending to defend in this discussion of necessities, real and spurious. I believe it would be desirable for us *to be free to choose* a way of being that is different from the course that brings maximal economic productivity and power. I am not, however, interested in arguing the desirability of the course of mediocrity, failure, and folly in themselves.

Many of the factors that have contributed to the relative decline of American international economic competitiveness in the past two decades probably *do* reflect "failures of character." One thinks, for example, of the complacency of our automobile industry; the dishonesty of our political leadership, rewarded by the voters, that spoke to us about amending the Constitution to require a balanced budget while mortgaging the future by tripling the national debt; and the multiplicity of cultural factors that have lowered the performance of our educational system according to *its own criteria*. A system that is trying to achieve something but is doing it badly is not worthy of justification. It is not as though America gave up economic performance in the name of other worthy values.*

But it is possible for people to have *other purposes*. A people's idea of success may have little relationship with its rate of economic growth. An educational system can be devoted to criteria other than those measured by the SATs or by

---

*Jacques Attali, a Frenchman, explains the "American malady" in terms of "a fundamental cultural ethos" he describes as "the cult of the immediate." (Quoted in Kennedy, *New York Review*, p. 39). Whether this "cult" represents an alternative system of values, or simply what remains after a deterioration of values, is an interesting question.

international tests. An Amish farmer is not a mediocre or a failed John D. Rockefeller.

From some perspectives, "winning" may be a form of losing. But to people whose only value is winning, those who live in the service of other values may well look like losers.

In the eyes of those who are fully caught up in the competition, any other way of being may look like failure or mediocrity. A society that decides that it has enough of wealth and chooses to preserve a way of life that serves other values may be derided as "backward." Fallows writes of the "fall" of Great Britain from a first-rate to a second-rate power that "England's diminished estate meant narrower, meaner lives for Englishmen."[9] When I was in England a couple of decades ago, at a time when England's estate was presumably quite diminished, the lives of Englishmen did not impress me as "mean." Indeed, what most impressed me was that even the meanest of the homes I saw there—the little houses whose tiny backyards abutted the railroad tracks—had lovely and well-tended gardens. The time that went into those gardens did not, presumably, contribute to the recovery of Britain's "sick" economy. But the gardens did speak about the dignity of the English men and women who lived there.

As I was appreciating the ubiquitous gardens visible from my train windows, there were a variety of British industrialists and journalists decrying the "English disease" that was threatening to leave Britain "bypassed by the twentieth century."[10] In writing about this growing concern, E. J. Mishan lamented the narrowness of the calculus of value underlying this litany of decline.

> By then, of course, every facet of our national life, other than the economic, had faded from the horizon. The British contribution to science and literature, to drama and ballet; Britain's unparalleled institutions, her broadcasting services, her police, her law courts, her university system; the political genius of the British people, the humaneness of their society; the prevailing climate of moderation and good sense—the inestimable assets, all the products of a complex historical process, were just not agenda for this new economic assessment of the worth of a nation.[11]

In the decade of the 1980s, Great Britain managed, under the leadership of Margaret Thatcher, to recover somewhat from the "English disease." But which England was the meaner place— the England of the 1960s or that of the 1980s—is less than crystal clear.

Evaluating our lives by any form of external score keeping is always dangerous. What is objectively measurable will never correspond perfectly with what really makes a life worth living. In the case of maximizing economic output, the correspondence is not only imperfect, it can be profoundly askew. At one stage of social evolution, the most productive societies were those with hordes of slaves. Paul Kennedy writes of the "horror and awe" with which continental Europeans beheld a more recent ratcheting up of the terms of economic competitiveness, that British innovation, the oppressive factory system of the early industrial revolution. Those for whom winning is, in Vince Lombardi's phrase, "the only thing" have to blind themselves to much that is vitally important in human life.

As the United States now wrestles with the "American disease," we should certainly hesitate before leaping to the conclusion that seems self-evident to those for whom preeminence is life's paramount goal. Lester Thurow compares the message we are getting from our economic competitors, such as the Japanese, to the message we got in the Olympics from the East Germans, which was, we have to approach international competition as they do or we won't win medals.[12] But the question naturally arises whether getting Olympic medals is worth subjecting our youth to a sports factory system. Surely, the United States has to change. Its present course— piling up debt, selling off our assets—cannot be continued indefinitely. But do we need to change, as so many argue, to become more like the Japanese so that we can maintain our preeminence in the Olympics of economic competition?

For the past decade, there have been a series of books that call on Americans to emulate the Japanese. The counterpart of the "lazy American" is the hardworking Japanese. In contrast with our "Thank God It's Friday" culture, the Japanese take only 60 percent of their allotted vacation time.[13] If our concern is with the freedom to choose how we will live, it should be noted that the exuberant team spirit of the Japanese worker, who willingly devotes his life to the company, is not the whole story. Closer investigation reveals that these Japanese companies have their ways of subtly coercing their workers to put in their sixteen-hour days and six-day weeks.* An issue in Japan today is whether the companies can be held responsible for a not infrequent phenomenon, the worker who literally works himself to death, who drops dead from sheer exhaustion. The modern workplace hardly looks like the ancient civilizations, where thousands of slaves would labor under the whip to build monuments to their masters. But the dramatic differences in appearance may obscure some important, underlying continuities in the human reality. In his book *Why Has Japan 'Succeeded'?* Michio Morishima writes that "the elite of the Japanese industrial world—the employees of the large enterprises—had, and have, no freedom of choice of employment. In just the same way as their fathers had worked for the domain lord (*daimyo*), they dedicate their whole lives to the new domain lord, the enterprise."[14]

If the payoff in terms of national preeminence is simply the narcissistic pleasure of being Number One, the best, the guy on top, is it worth the cost? Would it not be better to devote some resources to getting a more grounded, more life-serving apprehension of what life is about?

We "lazy Americans" may be sluggards by the standards of the workaholic Japanese, but people from many countries around the world continue to be struck by how hard working Americans are. We are still very much the descendants of those of whom Henry David Thoreau said, "The better part of the man is soon ploughed into the soil for compost." ("It is hard," said Thoreau, "to have a southern overseer; it is worse to have a northern one; but worst of all when you are the slave-driver of yourself."[15]) It is clear to me that a great many

---

*In a society like Japan, Morishima writes: "each individual must strive to demonstrate his loyalty to the society to which he belongs. The extent of his loyalty is measured in terms of the degree to which he is prepared to sacrifice himself. Therefore if he participates in the athletics meeting, abandoning any plans he may have had to enjoy the weekend with his family, this is regarded as a certain proof of his feelings of loyalty. Even if the company lets it be known that attendance at the meeting is up to each individual to decide, it does not make any difference. . . . So when most people do attend, the small number of "libertarians" who do not are frowned upon by the others as disturbing the "harmony" of society. In this sort of society the freedom of the individual is often regarded as treachery or as a challenge to society or to the majority, and anyone who dares to assert his freedom will probably become completely isolated" (Morishima, *Why Has Japan 'Succeeded'?* p. 117).

children growing up in America—even in our present "decadent" condition—suffer from insufficient contact with their fathers. Our men are trained to take care of their families through making money away from home, and many men have difficulty limiting their time at the office in order to assure that they will be a major presence in the lives of their young children in their most formative years. But the average Japanese father, placed on a treadmill spinning even faster than that of his American counterpart, spends only one-sixth as much time with his children as the average American father.[16] As score is kept in the realm of economic competition, the Japanese are winning.

Too often, those who say we must regain our position of economic supremacy are reflecting not an objective necessity but their own—largely unconscious—emotional needs. Among the voices that dominate our public discourse, a disproportionate number are those of people who have sacrificed a great deal to rise to the top. The narcissistic needs that have driven their own ambitions are projected onto the larger "We" with which they identify. But the course on which they would lead us would entail great human sacrifices for the society as a whole.

Big Eight football teams can certainly beat the teams of the Ivy League. But the costs of this "pursuit of excellence" are high.

Must we become like the Japanese? The quality of the Japanese workforce has been much described, as has the intensity of the educational process that produces it. Frequently one hears how many more days a year the Japanese child spends in school than the American and how many more hours they spend each day doing homework. Our children, it is often said, must work harder. (Especially in those areas like science and mathematics and engineering, which are especially useful to the productive system, we must catch up.) But what are the human costs of imitating the successful Japanese? In his book on the "success" of the Japanese, Morishima writes that

> since Japanese teenagers are compelled to study for 6 hours in regular school, 3–4 hours at the private crammers and another 4–5 hours in their own homes, i.e. some 13–15 hours in all per day, *this degree of 'exploitation' is little different from that of child workers in Victorian Britain.* Some Japanese economists say that it is as a result of hav-

ing had in childhood this kind of hard work and discipline that the quality of Japanese workers is so high. But it must not be forgotten that it has also resulted in the annihilation of their own selves.[17]*

Of course, matching the performance of our competitors does not mean we have to become completely identical to them, and surpassing them does not automatically mean doing the same thing, only more so. The thrust of Fallows's book is not that we should become just like the Japanese, but should become *More Like Us*. His idea is that we should enhance our economic performance by realizing more fully some of those qualities in our own national character and social structure that have historically generated American economic dynamism. And Lester Thurow, despite his comment about the East Germans' Olympic message to us, does not really urge us to achieve greater competitiveness by strictly imitating the Japanese. We Americans, Thurow says, are not going to be as meticulous in the first grade as the Japanese, so we will have to find some other way, consistent with American culture, of making automobiles of the same high quality.

What is mandated, as it were, is that the edifice we construct be of a certain height, while the architecture can reflect the cultural heritage of the builders. Either a pagoda or the courthouse on an American main street might rise forty feet off the ground.

But one must not overestimate the range of options available to him who would be sure that no one builds an edifice higher than his. This is more and more true as the mandated height gets higher and higher. A teepee and a log cabin may be the same height, but when one needs a structure that rises a thousand feet, one is compelled to employ the technology of the skyscraper. Similarly, the range of choices in technological and social organizations is extremely restricted, for those who determine that it is necessary that they attain to the highest level of economic productivity.

---

*Maybe our kids don't have to be enslaved as intensely as the children of Japan. One hopeful sign: it is said that the automobiles built in America by Americans working for Japanese companies are as well-built as those built in Japan. The implication of this would seem to be that the source of our manufacturing difficulties lies in our corporate system and not in the human resources of our workforce.

We are not, therefore, free to become simply "more like us." American culture contains a great wealth of values, a multiplicity of ways that we might choose to nurture the human potentiality of our children to become "more like us." But if we establish competitiveness in the global economy as the governing criterion of our socialization process, not many of those paths of nurturance remain open. (Thoreau is out; Thurow is in.) As Morishima likens the education of children in Japan today to the exploitation of child laborers in Victorian England—England in its prime, when it was a "first-rate nation"—so also does Paul Kennedy make his reference to the "awe and horror" with which the continental European powers beheld the potency of the early English factories to illuminate the nature of the threat the Japanese pose to American society. In both cases, Kennedy writes, "what is clearly a more effective arrangement of workers, and of society, in terms of *output* (and thus wealth creation) involves a disturbing challenge to traditional norms and individualist ways of behavior."[18] What is worrisome is not just that we are challenged but that meeting the challenge will likely compel us to choose options that are not entirely agreeable. We might find ourselves compelled to become more like them, less like ourselves, in some ways we consider important. "[T]he emulation of the Japanese industrial miracle would involve not merely the copying of this or that piece of technology or management but the imitation of much of the Japanese industrial system."[19]

We have been through something like this before—in the cold war struggle against the Soviet Union. There also we felt compelled to maintain competitiveness, whatever it cost. And there also the costs were great in terms of the sacrifice of our national values. When I worked in foreign policy circles in Washington during the reintensification of the cold war during the early 1980s, I frequently heard our cold warriors lament some of the competitive advantages enjoyed by the Soviet leaders. The Soviets could play the contest unfettered by the considerable restraints imposed by our democratic system. They could act in secrecy; they could impose their will in foreign lands without fearing exposes in *Pravda* or protests in the streets of Moscow; they could make alliances with evil without being annoyed by congressional inquiries or refusals of funding; etc. It is not coincidental that in all three of the major

threats to our constitutional system in the postwar era—
McCarthyism, Watergate, and Iran-Contra—underlying the
usurpation or abuse of power were the alleged requirements of
our *national security*. In order to maintain our competitive
power, this country did indeed become more like the tyrannical
and opportunistic power that threatened us.

At least in the cold war, the nature of the necessity compelling us to maintain our competitiveness was starkly clear.
The cold war was about life and death. It was a modern, ther-
monuclear version of the ancient struggle among nations for
survival. In the arena of war and peace, the weak have often
been annihilated by the mighty, or, when not destroyed, they
have often been subjugated and enslaved. Whatever room
there is for dispute among us about our national aims and interests, about what quantity and quality of armaments might
have sufficed to protect those interests, and about alternative
diplomatic strategies, there is no room to doubt that real necessities weighed upon us, as they have on all sovereign societies throughout the history of civilization. No doubt, our
national narcissism and lust for supremacy played a role in our
conduct in the cold war. Objectively, however, our choices
were circumscribed by inescapable circumstances.

Are the necessities that would compel us to remain economically competitive similarly real and inescapable? Clearly
some of the talk about our necessities shows muddled thinking; we are not going to be poorer just because someone else is
richer. Some of these ostensibly economic arguments seem to
be a smokescreen for narcissistic strivings that remain unac-
knowledged. Nonetheless, after a decade of hearing exhortations about how we must not permit ourselves to be overtaken,
the American people are apparently persuaded that we confront necessities no less imperative than those of the cold war.
As the 1980s came to a close, opinion polls revealed that Americans regarded Japanese economic power as having become a
greater threat to our "national security" than the military
power of the Soviet Union.

National security? Would the preeminence of Japan in the
world economy really threaten the security of the United
States the way superior military power has historically threatened the security of nations? Does being relatively poorer place
one in some kind of jeopardy? Is it necessary to strive for more,

simply to keep what one has? Is it therefore impossible, in a world of contending economic powers, for anyone ever to have *enough?*

It is arguable that the answer to those questions is, Yes! that economic competition is indeed a matter of national security and survival. It may be that in our competition with the Japanese and the Germans in the world economy we are no freer simply to opt out than we were in the arms race with the Soviets.

Let us examine the arguments for this proposition. For if it is true, it is vital that we understand just why and how it is. If the world economy is an arena that circumscribes our options as brutally as an arms race, understanding this should profoundly affect how we relate to the competitive dynamics that drive our destiny.

II. IMPERATIVES OF SURVIVAL

NATIONAL ECONOMIES IN THE STRUGGLE FOR SURVIVAL

For ten thousand years, the world has not been a safe place to be weak. This problem of power, and its far-reaching social-evolutionary implications, were discussed earlier in chapter 8. Because of the anarchy that obtains among sovereign societies, a struggle for power has been inescapable for humankind. Consequently, of all the many cultural possibilities apparently opened to the civilized animal, only those are really viable that confer on a society sufficient power to withstand threats from other societies around it. Since the beginnings of history, ways of organizing human life that generated insufficient power—however beautiful and humane those cultural forms may have been—have been swept aside and eliminated. This is the perspective on the evolution of civilization I call "the parable of the tribes."

The question then arises, what aspects of a society determine its level of competitive power? In our earlier discussion of the parable of the tribes, our focus was on technology: to survive, a society needs to harness the power of nature on a scale comparable to what its competitors are doing. Millennia ago, for example, this principle mandated the spread of metallurgy for the fashioning of bronze and then of iron weapons, and it helped disseminate the domestication of horses as mounts for warriors. In our time, we have witnessed a desperate competition in the construction of weapons of mass destruction and in the development of mechanisms to deliver them over long distances.

But technology is far from being the only determinant of competitive power. Power has been a function of political structures, favoring those that are best able to harness and direct the latent capacities of society; thus kingships long ago displaced less centralized structures; more recently the nation-state model of political organization developed in Europe proved overpowering to more archaic polities around the globe. A society's power is determined also by the psychological structure of its members; neither the meek nor the content have inherited the earth.

More pertinent to the present discussion is a determinant that is closely associated with several of the others: a society's power in intersocietal competition is closely tied to its *level of economic productivity*. This has been especially true of the modern world of the last several centuries. The importance of the economic dimension was magnified with the coming of the modern world because of the Industrial Revolution, which unleashed an unceasing stream of economic and technological developments that has continually revolutionized production and thereby opened a vast chasm of potential difference between the productive power of those societies that are at the cutting edge and those that lag behind. It was because they understood the potentially catastrophic implications of falling behind that the European powers looked upon the British innovations in industrial organization with that "horror and awe."

ECONOMICS AS ARMS RACE

The bitter lessons of history have taught nations to regard the issue of economic competitiveness, of relative economic standing, of comparative rates of economic growth, in terms of the grimmest necessities. *Economic competition between nations, in other words, has been but a form of arms race.* George Dalton, for example, describes the great conflicts of this century as "GNP wars." These wars, Dalton says, were "won by the side which was able to supply its millions of soldiers, sailors and armies with sufficient food and clothing, and the most military equipment—ships, planes, tanks—over a four- to five-year period."[20]

In this perspective, it appears that economics as an arena of human action is about something different from—or at least, in addition to—the abundance of choice that the market ideology presents it as being. Economics, it appears, functions as a component system in the overarching system of inter-societal conflict; economic activity is part of a society's arsenal in the competitive struggle from which no one is free to choose to withdraw.

In part 2, we explored how the unleashing of the market system in America irresistibly drove our society to develop in ways that Americans might not have freely chosen. But in the larger perspective of the parable of the tribes, one can wonder how free Americans (or others) have been to choose a more humane and balanced path anyway. Thomas Jefferson, the apostle of the vision of a nation of yeoman farmers, eventually came to believe that the dictates of national power required that the nation develop economically along lines whose potentially corrupting effects he had earlier so eloquently deplored. And in his study of the life of John D. Rockefeller, Allen Nevins mused on the necessity—apparent in retrospect—of America's headlong rush into modern industrial power a century ago:

> Down to 1910 it could be said with great apparent force that even if the transformation of our [American] economy was inevitable, it had proceeded too fast. Why such reckless speed? Why not more time, more caution, more moderation? Today this view appears dubious. Had our pace been slower and our achievement weaker, had we not created so swiftly our powerful industrial units in steel, oil, textiles, chemicals, electricity, and the automotive vehicles, the free world might have lost the First World War, and most certainly would have lost the Second.[21]

While the United States was laying the economic foundations of its victories in future wars, the situation in Russia was different. The insistence of Czar Nicholas on the "sacredness of serfdom," writes Marshall Berman, prevented the modernization of the Russian labor force and "ensured that Russian economic development would be held back, just at the moment when the economies of Western Europe and the United States were taking off."[22] But, eventually, through the Crimean War, the intersocietal system delivered to the Russians its message about the mandatory nature of power and thus of economic development. "It took a major military defeat to shake the government's monumental complacency. It was only after the disaster at Sevastopol, a political and military as well as an economic disaster, that Russia's official celebration of its backwardness came to an end."[23]

The Russians were not the only ones learning the lesson that economic backwardness is an impermissibly dangerous course. The Japanese, pried open by American gunships, "realized the need for change and thought seriously how to construct a national economy which could compete with the West."[24] Morishima thus ascribes the rise of capitalism in Japan quite directly to the Japanese determination "to do away with the military and scientific-technological disparities which existed between Japan and the West."[25]

As economic development becomes an integral part of the arms race, the distinction between the state of war and the state of peace grows blurry. With these GNP wars, the outcome of the conflict is largely determined by the activities of the combatants during perhaps may decades of "peace" preceding the outbreak of active hostilities. These activities include more than the specifically military preparations that we ordinarily associate with a military buildup, such as the building of weapons and the training of forces. The outcome in the arena of war is also governed by which powers, with differential success in stoking the engines of economic growth, have developed the most productive and advanced economies.

The Japanese, with their extraordinarily cohesive and single-minded drive to develop the bases of national power, outstripped the Russians, and in the early years of this century, inflicted on the Russians yet another military disaster. Japan continued its drive to be a "powerful country comparable to the West"—in the historic Japanese phrase translated by Morishima[26]—until its attack on Pearl Harbor, when it bit off more than it could chew.

The Russians, meanwhile, pressed ruthlessly toward economic growth and industrial development under Stalin, finally emerged from the Second World War victorious and as one of the two great powers in the world. The Stalinist-style command economy has proved incapable, however, of sustaining sufficient dynamism to maintain the long-term foundations of Soviet power. Partly as a result of the recurring fear of the consequences of economic backwardness in a world of intersocietal competition, the Soviets once again launched a drive for economic transformation and modernization. Commenting on the need for perestroika in the late 1980s, a Soviet economist, Nikolai Shmelev, declared in *Novy Mir*, "If radical changes in the economy are not carried out successfully, we will find ourselves left on the sidelines of history . . . and our revolution will ultimately be stifled."[27]

These grim necessities of national economics form the core of Paul Kennedy's vision in his recent book, *The Rise and Fall of the Great Powers*. Looking over the history of the international system "since the advance of Europe in the sixteenth century," Kennedy observes that the pattern of rise and fall of powers "shows a very significant correlation *over the longer term* between productive and revenue-raising capacities on the one hand and military strength on the other."[28] In the context of this historical analysis of great power politics, Kennedy affirms that wealth, like power, is "always *relative* and should be seen as such."[29]

Kennedy's book—appearing just as the cold war with the Soviet Union was winding down—became a best-seller. Its success was due, one may presume, not to its lucid style and its excellent scholarship (sustained for more than five hundred dense pages of text), for these have never been the recipe for success on the commercial book market. Rather, its message about American decline would seem to have touched upon a sensitive nerve in this country.

The imperatives of the race in strategic weapons may be melting away, but, one learned from Kennedy's book, the grip of necessity never releases us. Even "the coming of peace does not stop this process of continual change" in the standing of great powers, Kennedy said.[30] It is specifically the differentiated pace of economic growth among the great powers that ensures that some will rise while others will fall. Eventually, history suggests, a contest of force readjusts the world scene, taking away from those who have lagged behind and giving to those who have surged ahead in the economic race: "The new territorial order established at the end of each war [the history of 1500–1945 shows] thus reflects the redistribution of power that has been taking place within the territorial system."[31]

Does it matter if the American economy is not growing as vigorously as those of other powers? Do we lose anything if the Japanese economy overtakes ours? Kennedy approvingly quotes David Halberstam's comment that in the challenge posed by Japan, the U.S. faces "a much harder and more intense competition than . . . the political-military competition with the Soviet Union."[32] (The decline in the respect with which the outside world, especially Asians, regard Americans, says James Fallows, "can be useful in getting our attention, like a nonviolent Pearl Harbor."[33])

The relativity of wealth, in the light of the competitive dynamics of international relations, suggests that economic growth may ultimately not be about abundance and freedom after all. It is about power, which by its nature is inherently scarce. And it is about necessity, for we are no more free to choose to live modestly than we are to be pacifists if we would survive as a society that is master of its fate.

Machiavelli believed that states that have lost their appetite for power are doomed to be destroyed by their more vigorous neighbors.[34] The same, according to this view of the role of economics in the struggle for power, can be said of the appetite for economic growth. In a world where economic competition, like our recent perilous arms race, is out of control, no one is free to say, I have enough. As in *Faust:* to hell with whomever, from contentment, would say *Verweile doch.*"

MOURNING LOST CHOICES

We began this chapter with the question, Does the existence of our fellow human beings extend or restrict the range of our economic options?

When it comes to our visits to the supermarket, in our role as consumers, the web of trade that increasingly interconnects all the world's peoples enormously extends our choices. But freedom is not to be measured by the length of the menu of goods from which we can order. How we live consists of far more than what we consume.

If it is taken as a given that we as a nation must remain preeminent in the competitive world economy—if it is judged that being surpassed by our competitors would entail unacceptable costs to our national welfare—then the existence of those competitors does significantly narrow our freedom to choose our way of life.

The foregoing discussion suggests that it may indeed be necessary to maintain economic preeminence. The consequence would seem to be, therefore, that the global market system, rather than making us freer, becomes one of the chains that bind us to an unchosen fate.

This is not the way it was supposed to be. The market system, enshrining as it does the *voluntary exchange* as the quintessential form of human interaction, was not supposed to dictate to all within its grasp how fundamental aspects of their lives will be shaped. But *the problem* we have uncovered *is not a defect in the market system itself*. The problem, rather, arises from the fact that our economic life is inescapably embedded in a much larger system that is clearly not benign: the system of intersocietal interaction where anarchy and its partner, violence, hold ultimate power.

Does the existence of our fellows make us freer? Clearly not in systems where coercion rules. If all our interactions with others were voluntary, this would be a very different kind of world. But the people of ancient Israel were not free to choose to have nothing to do with the Romans and to worship God in peace in their own country. The Native American societies of this continent were given no choice about whether European societies would be allowed to intrude into their continent, eventually sweeping aside and shattering the cultures of the aboriginal peoples. And the Dalai Lama's vision of his native country being made a demilitarized preserve for the reverence of all life is not one the people of Tibet are free to realize, given the determination their Chinese oppressors to maintain their brutal dominance and to turn the land into an extension of the Chinese empire.

For millennia, the existence of societies that are strong has foreclosed for others the option of being weak. The market's role in the arsenal of power has evidently turned it into an instrument of our bondage.

The costs of the loss of freedom should not be underestimated. Looking back across history, it may be easy for us to appreciate how, at many junctures, the selection for the ways of power entailed profound human tragedies. We may be sensitive to the loss of humanity imposed, over the centuries, on peace-loving peoples compelled to become as fierce as their warlike neighbors, lest they be cut down by them. When, millennia ago, cultures of small, loosely-connected villages of free people were destroyed by centralized empires, in which a few could crack the whip over the backs of a hundred thousand slaves, we can grieve over the way power has sifted through the spectrum of human possibilities. That the Dalai Lama was granted the Nobel Prize is testimony to an awareness, in our civilization, of how wrong it is for a country imbued with the spirit of the Buddha to be recast in the image of a totalitarian oppressor.

Our capacity to grasp and to mourn the loss entailed by the necessities of modern economic competitiveness, however, may be stunted. Every society tends to make a virtue of its necessities. In earlier times, when a society's power was more directly dependent on the warrior spirit, the worldview of a culture often blinded the people to how much the humanity of their young males needed to be sacrificed to prepare them for their warrior roles. Young males would be brutalized and desensitized in order to produce the highly valued warrior virtues of obliviousness to pain, contempt for weakness, ferocity in battle, and unswerving loyalty to the commanding authority. In our market society—a society that, in two centuries, has emerged from little colonial outpost to world superpower—we are trained to regard as virtues all those characteristics of individuals and social systems that are conducive to a nation's rising to economic preeminence. We admire the discipline, technical proficiency, ambition, and organizational efficiency that the market rewards.

Surely, many Americans will think, it is a false analogy to liken the bloody traits of a successful gladiator with the characteristics of individuals and societies that lead to success in the marketplace. Even if it is true that the requirements of power compel us to strive to assure that our economic growth keeps pace with that of our competitors', are we not simply having to do what we would want to do anyway? From my point of view, the answer is no.

Consider but two crucial questions every culture must answer: how do we want to treat our children? and how do we want to relate to the natural world around us? These, indeed, are the world's two great gifts to us. In what spirit do we want to receive those gifts?

What if the terms of economic competitiveness escalated to the point that to be of the "first rate," a society had to goad its children, from a very early age, into being anxious and driven? Early industrial countries exploited the natural resource represented by their children by turning them into drones for the factories and the mines. What if getting a competitive edge among postindustrial economies depended on how well we honed our children, how tempered they were by the consuming fire of ambition, how thoroughly beaten by fear about displeasing the judging eyes of the world? Indeed, this is not so far from what the competitive world economy presently seems to favor. Morishima, it will be recalled, spoke of the costs to Japanese children of the intensely competitive educational ratrace into which they are thrown from the age of two—"the annihilation of their own selves." In the late 1960s, R. Lynn discovered a strong positive correlation between a society's rate of economic growth, on the one hand and, on the other, the level of anxiety among its people.[35]

A happy people is very different in its psychological dynamics from a maximally productive people. We might well wish to be free to raise our children to feel secure, having no need to fortify themselves behind imposing structures to feel safe; to feel confident of their worth as human beings, without being incessantly driven to prove it; to feel joy and contentment in being alive, not aching with an inner void they desperately try to fill with material things. This is what I want for my children. If we as a society all achieved it, I do not doubt that we would create a wonderful culture, that we could live in harmony and nourish each other, and that the flower of human creativity would bloom in diverse and marvelous and unexpected ways. But I strongly doubt that, living this way, we would long continue to be a "first-rate" economic power, at the cutting edge of productive dynamism.

To the market system, the human being is a resource whose great potentiality can be realized only by a motivational and affective configuration which, from an internal human perspective, is far less than optimal. As masters of our own destiny, we might well choose to refuse the demands of the market and to allow our children to bloom quite differently. But then, to the system of societies struggling for power, the market system has itself been a resource to generate the materiel of war.

Similarly, free to choose our way of life, we might choose to live in harmony with nature, tending our gardens like Zen monks and, like those pious disciples of the Buddha, being content to take back from nature just enough to keep our rice bowls full. We might choose to live in relation to our natural surroundings in the spirit of the native peoples of this continent, who knew that they belonged to the earth and were mystified by the white settlers who regarded the earth as belonging to them.* The market sees no value in treating the Black Hills as sacred, particularly if there's gold to be blasted out of them. When the market beholds a thousand-year-old redwood tree, what it sees is picnic tables, house siding, and mulch. In the land of the Zen monk, meanwhile, the air is choked with pollution, and enterprising companies send agents around the world to assist in the despoliation of the tropical forests, to conduct "research" on declining whale populations, and to make money from the tusks of the disappearing elephant. And whatever nation best enriches itself off the impoverishment of the biosphere drives its competitors even

---

*Said Chief Seattle to the president of the United States in response to a request to buy the Indians' land:

> We know the sap which courses through the trees as we know the blood that courses through our veins. We are part of the earth and it is part of us. The perfumed flowers are our sisters . . . All things are connected like the blood that unites us all. Man did not weave the web of life, he is merely a strand in it. Whatever he does to the web, he does to himself . . . So, if we sell you our land, love it as we have loved it. Care for it as we have cared for it. Hold in your mind the memory of the land as it is when you receive it.

Now Seattle is again in the news, this time as a city expanding so rapidly the natives are distressed. The picture, taken from the air, shows how the developers, in their rush to make a profit from the current boom in Seattle real estate, have simply gone in with their bulldozers, shorn the beautiful pine forests from the hills, and flattened the hilltops, treating them as mere obstacles to the imposition of their grid of houses onto the land.

further away from a vision of a life lived in reverence for the whole web of life.

In *The Iliad*, there is a vision of the beauties of a life in a world at peace. But the vision is not of a life actually lived, or available to be lived, within the framework of that epic. It is, rather, a scene emblazoned upon the shield of the warrior, Achilles. This is the life that Achilles, the warrior driven to battle and to glory and, finally, to his fated death, will never live. Likewise, it may be, we may have our vision of how we would live in a world at harmony—in alignment with the needs of human nature and with the flows of the living earth—but, so long as we are compelled by the struggle for power, we may be driven to a life sharply divergent from the one we would choose.

The course of maximizing our economic growth cannot, therefore, be assumed to be the path we would freely choose to take. But the question still remains: must we be resigned to the necessity of pursuing economic growth as a form of arms race?

III. SEEKING TO FREE OURSELVES
FROM THE TRAP OF NECESSITY

There are several possible reasons for hoping that the imperatives of intersocietal competition may be escapable and that we may be—or soon become—freer to choose our way of life than the foregoing discussion would suggest. One has to do with the possibly changing nature of war, while two others concern possible changes in the nature of the global order.

WAR ON THE CHEAP

It may be that the great wars of the early part of this century were GNP wars, but it does not inevitably follow from this that high levels of economic productivity will continue to be necessary for military security. World War II, until its final cataclysm over Hiroshima and Nagasaki, was fought with basic industrial technology—tanks and battleships, engines and steel and bombs. With the coming of the nuclear age, however, a nation can threaten any attacker with mass destruction from weapons that cost but a small fraction of GNP to produce. Perhaps the changed nature of warfare enables societies to choose a path that would make them relatively poorer, but no less secure for that.

Even if, however, these advanced weapons give one "more bang for the buck," in John Foster Dulles's expression, they cannot simply be purchased. In the absence of an open market for weapons of mass destruction, a nation must have technical knowledge and facilities of very great sophistication to be able to produce such devices as nuclear explosives and the vehicles to deliver them. Such requirements in themselves imply limits on the range of cultural possibilities open to a society that would possess such deterrent power.

The limits entailed by the need that *some* of a society be technologically sophisticated are quite minor, however, compared with the great range of cultural options foreclosed for a society that feels compelled to keep its entire national economy unsurpassed in its overall productive power. Mishan, for example, argues against the notion that economic growth must remain the foundation of military security, saying that, because technological innovation is "increasingly the outcome of highly organized R & D [research and development]," Western governments "could in principle, maintain an up-to-date war technology in virtual independence of the rest of the economy."[36] In this view, the demands of military security need not dictate so much of our way of life as earlier in the development of modern warfare.

While these arguments have a degree of plausibility, it is certainly understandable if a nation would feel reluctant to bet its survival their validity. Almost half a century into the nuclear age, it remains uncertain just what role nuclear weapons can play in protecting a nation's security. Particularly if one's potential adversary also possesses them, the credibility of one's threat to use them in response to an attack with conventional weapons may be questionable. Our nuclear weapons may inhibit others from infringing on our vital interests, but they may also be irrelevant.

In the world in which we still live—a world where force, rather than law, still rules and where a reckless adversary may gamble that one is only bluffing—it seems prudent to assume that a society's security continues to depend on the conventional forces at one's command. This, in turn, suggests the continued relevance of economic productivity to national security.

THE DISPLACEMENT OF WAR
BY WORLD ORDER

It is the customary assumption of conservatives that evils that have been chronic through history will persist for as long as people do. In most circumstances, this presumption has been considerably more prudent than the contrary belief, that a new day is dawning. Nonetheless, it would be foolish to assume that a "new day" is inherently impossible. And the belief that the flawed old day must of necessity continue for ever can be self-fulfilling. We have little chance of ever living the kinds of lives we want if we never even envision how we might cast off the chains that historically have bound us to an unwanted fate.

Paramount among these chains has been the chronic syndrome of war and insecurity among civilized nations. According to the parable of the tribes, it has been the ceaseless struggle for power among sovereign societies that has driven the entire edifice of human civilization to develop in directions we would not have chosen but have been powerless to stop. In the perspective of the parable of the tribes, the rise of this struggle for power and the consequent warped social evolutionary trajectory were inevitable. But from this analysis, it does *not* follow that the reign of power must go on forever. A new day can dawn. Indeed, there are glimmers on the horizon.

What made the chronic problem of war inevitable was not any ingrained feature of human nature but an inevitable characteristic of the system of civilization from its emergence: its fragmentation. It was inescapable that civilization would emerge with a multiplicity of autonomous entities compelled to interact with each other outside any order that would protect the harmony and well-being of the whole system. Under the resulting conditions of anarchy, power would inevitably act as a contaminant. Because the system lacked the wholeness, the cohesion, to respond to an aggressor in a coordinated fashion, some of the worst of our cultural possibilities could be magnified into laws of our social existence. Because any *one* could impose upon *all* the necessity for power, the ways of power could spread irresistibly across the globe.

But the peoples of the world are becoming interconnected. While the international system of sovereign societies persists, the inevitability of fragmentation is disappearing. It is now possible for all the nations of the earth to sit down together to confront problems of a global nature. The depletion of the ozone layer is being addressed on a global basis; the possibility of global warming is the subject of international conferences. Need we assume that humankind cannot move forward to create a world order capable of preventing the aggression of one group of people against another?

There were hopeful visions of such a world order in the wake of this century's two catastrophic conflagrations. The establishment both of The League of Nations after World War I and of the United Nations following the Second World War represented attempts to move toward a world order ruled by something other than the free play of power. In both cases, the hopes that inspired the founding of these global institutions were badly disappointed. Certainly salient among the obstacles impeding the creation of a more benign world order after 1945 was the outbreak of a new, and different kind of world war—the protracted cold war, in which the entire planet became a chessboard on which two great powers vied for supremacy.

We should not be surprised that the first result of the global interconnection of peoples has been not world order but world wars. Disorder always comes first. But it does not always last.

With the apparent end of the cold war, after almost half a century without a major global shooting war to create psychological scars and geopolitical disruptions, the prospects for significant progress in the development of world order are far better than they have ever been in human history. As I write this passage, in early August 1990, the reaction of the world community to the Iraqi invasion of Kuwait suggests the hope that a new day may be, if not at hand, at least achievable within the next few generations. The strong actions adopted by the Security Council, with unanimous support from the major powers, the virtually universal compliance with an economic embargo against the aggressor, the rapid formation of a multinational force to block Iraq on land and sea—all these show what a unified world community can do to change the old law of power's reign enunciated more than two thousand years ago. The ancient historian Thucydides put into the mouths of the Athenians, about to slaughter their weaker neighbors who had opposed them, this grim but accurate characterization of the intersocietal system: "the strong do what they can and the weak suffer what they must."

Even if the world community proves adequate in this instance, however, to the task of creating an ad hoc system of *collective security*, even if Kuwait's autonomy is restored and Iraq properly chastened for its blatantly unjust use of raw force, this instance will be very far from demonstrating that the world has become a safe place to be weak. Characteristics of both the aggressor and the victim make the present example a good deal less than a limiting case.

Iraq, though it commands a formidable force, is still a minor power. As the world is presently organized, there are several nations with sufficient destructive power at their command that the rest of the world, even if every other nation were united against it, would be afraid to stand in its way to save one of their number. (Even in the present case, as some have noted, had Saddam Hussein waited a few more years until he possessed nuclear weapons, the world might have opposed his aggression with nothing more than words.) Collective security arrangements are of questionable use when there exist actors whose power is even roughly comparable to that of the whole.

Then there are the special characteristics of Kuwait and of the alleged next target, Saudi Arabia. They sit on the oil the rich countries of the world need. Iraqi conquest of that entire region would not only represent an injustice, which the rest of the world would condemn, it would jeopardize vital interests of great powers. The world's response to the Iraqi's swallowing of little Kuwait and menacing of Saudi Arabia can offer little assurance to many other small nations—an Ecuador, say, or a Ghana—that the world would act to rescue them if a neighbor of theirs should arise with great military might and a lust to devour them.

If we did conclude that the new day was almost upon us, we might well decide that the United States has such a huge reservoir of power that we could afford to moderate our allegiance to power's mandate.* We might judge ourselves to be

---

*For all our fear about losing our primacy in the economic realm, the dynamic economy of Japan remains only half the size of the American economy. Japan is demilitarized. The militarized Soviet Union, meanwhile, is an economic basket case.

sufficiently secure to be able to ask ourselves how we *want* our society to evolve, rather than be ruled by how it *must* develop. The choice, after all, is not between protecting our values and endangering them. It is, rather, between two different kinds of threat to the values we wish to embody in our lives.

But if we were to conclude both that power will remain the arbiter of the destiny of nations and that economic productivity will remain a principal determinant of national power, does it follow from this that we—and our global economic competitors as well—must be resigned to having our way of living dictated by the market system's logic of economic growth?

Not necessarily. The postulated continuing need for power makes free choice considerably more difficult, but still not impossible.

CHOOSING TOGETHER

Ideally—and perhaps someday—global cooperation would take the form of a world order that completely restrains the use of force among the world's peoples and subordinates power to justice. Eventually, one may hope, a people's capacity for violence will be no more essential for its security than is an individual's or a community's in a well-ordered polity. But even in the absence of such a thorough interweaving of humankind into a single order, the dangerous fragmentation of our species can be overcome in other, more piecemeal ways.

Even competitors can perceive their common interests. Even in the midst of a zero-sum game, the participants can agree to ameliorate the most pernicious effects of their struggle. To the extent that our economic competition is like—is indeed a form of—an arms race, we can deal with it as an arms race.

Even during the cold war, the competition in armaments was not completely uncontrolled. Even as the two superpowers were building the mechanisms to annihilate each other, they also worked together intermittently to control the conditions of their lethal competition.

If the nuclear arms race could be limited to some degree, how much more readily should it be possible to rein in the unwanted and compulsive aspects of our economic competition.

If the arms control process was, in many ways, disappointing in its harvest, it must be recalled how intense were the suspicions and animosities that divided the competing powers. By contrast, the United States and Japan and the Western Europeans have been allies for two generations. The most advanced economic powers have gathered in annual summit meetings for years, coordinating policies to serve their common interests. Problems that arise from there being a multiplicity of sovereignties persist. But the bases could exist—if there were the will—for international cooperation to reduce the compulsion that nations feel to become what they do not wish to become so that they do not fall behind.

Do we wish to be free to allow our children to have a childhood, and not be driven—like some East German athletic *Wunderkinder* of recent decades—to transform themselves into instruments for the glory of the nation? Do we wish to avoid feeling compelled to send our children to school all year and make them work fifteen-hour days? Perhaps we can make a treaty among the industrial nations, or at least with a major competitor like Japan, to limit school time.

Are we afraid of pouring less of our life's energy into our economically productive work because we are afraid of falling behind rivals who might work harder? Is there a consensus possible among the richer nations that we could have "enough" with a workweek that really does not exceed forty hours, or still fewer? If the Americans and the Russians could agree to limit the number of missile launchers, maybe our economic competitors will agree to limit the workweek.*

Do we want to reform our industrial system so that our air and our rivers can regain and retain their purity? But we're afraid of the competitive disadvantage it would impose on us to be the only ones taking care of our natural environment? Why not see if we and our competitors can negotiate a set of environmental laws that all would adopt and obey.

Rather than submit our fate to a system that rewards, among other things, certain forms of ruthlessness and irresponsibility, we can band together to impose our will upon the system, to manage a kinder and gentler global economy.

---

*Indeed, in the bilateral talks in early 1989 between the US and Japan, one of the mutually agreed points was that the Japanese should work less.

The existence of other players does make our free choice more difficult. In isolation, we could simply choose our own path. In the struggle for power, a single actor—if it is mighty enough—can impose upon all the others the necessity for power. In the process of international treaty-making, the refusal of a major competitor to agree to limits might foreclose for others the desired, more life-serving option. But we do not require consensus among all the nations of the world. Just as containing the dangerous escalation of the strategic arms race required that we come to terms with only the one power that could threaten our security, so in the realm of economic competition the concurrence of but a few nations is all that is necessary to set us free.

TREAT A PROBLEM AS A PROBLEM

The idea here is rather straightforward. The first step is to identify how we *want* to be able to live. If we believe that the world, as it is presently ordered, *requires* us to organize our lives differently, we should recognize that requirement as an affliction in our world and set our ingenuity to curing it.

If the necessities of competition warp our lives, it is such necessities—not particular other societies—that are truly our adversaries. Often it seems as though our leaders, so attached to the task of remaining preeminent over our rivals, are in love with the necessities that rob us of the freedom to make the most meaningful choices about how we will live our lives. When they succeed, in their own terms, these leaders do indeed keep us free from the dominion of other human powers. But succeeding only on those terms does not leave our humanity free. For we remain under the boot of the compulsions of the competitive struggle for power. To these necessities, too often, our leaders offer no resistance. To this adversary, they surrender without a shot. Of this foe, our power-loving leaders too often are loyal servants.

"We must do this; we must do that!" If that is what we want to do—fine! Let's do it. But if it is not, the necessity that requires it is a problem. We should adhere to a simple principle: *let's treat a problem as a problem.*

The arms race was virtually universally decried as a problem. Aside from the terror to which they subjected the world, if our expensive swords could have been beaten into plow-shares we would all have been better off. And we treated it as a problem, trying to find ways out of the costly and dangerous, ever-escalating competition for security.

If the arena of economic competition is mandating that our society assume a form other than what we would choose, then it, too, is a problem. The pernicious effects of global competition should be addressed through global cooperation. The arms-control process should be matched by a corresponding process of "economic competition control."

There were some in America, admittedly, who were opposed even to arms control negotiations and treaties. They gave reasons: the Soviets could not be trusted to comply; major violations could be concealed and would endanger us; the American people could not be relied upon to maintain vigilance (i.e., support an adequate defense budget) at the same time they saw their government cooperating with the adversary. But one suspects that for some of our cold warriors, these reasons were rationalizations. For some, the unbridled contest—the race for supremacy—was viscerally more attractive than the more staid game of cooperation, parity, and mutual security.

Similarly, those who have absorbed into the marrow of their bones the demands of economic competition are unlikely to lead us onto the path of international cooperation to mitigate competition's deleterious dimensions. Those who have aligned their own apprehension of value and meaning with "necessity's" dominion will tell us what we *must* do rather than how we might work to escape necessity's grasp. In my conversations with corporate and political leaders, I have sensed this. Many of them have been eager to use the pressure of international competition as the reason why we as a country *cannot* adopt socially responsible policies. But when the talk turns to the possibility of cooperating with other countries to implement mutually beneficial changes in the rules of the competition, the eagerness vanishes. There is not so much a conviction that such treaties were impossible; the process simply seems to lack visceral appeal.

Those who rise in our system tend to be those for whom the march of economic development represents unadulterated progress; for whom every canyon inundated by a dam is a symbol of our indomitable national spirit; for whom every farm field turned into a factory makes us more advanced. Every granite mountain should be blasted into building blocks, every sleepy little town should be roused from its slumber. America is a professional football team, and it is coached by Vince Lombardi.

To the extent that we as a people are like these leaders and only the narcissistic enterprise of winning can make our blood move—"to foresake the course is *to die*"—then we will not solve the "problem" of these competitive necessities. But to the extent that we can commit our hearts to a vision of a world where other values and other choices are viable, we can find solutions.

We can be free, but only if we recognize and treat our bondage as a problem.

IV. POWER IN A WORLD FREE OF FORCE

We have been exploring, throughout this work, "the illusion of choice." Implied in this idea is the notion that there could be a reality of choice. Underlying this discussion is a vision of a world in which how we live is governed solely by the free expression of the human spirit.

If a community lived in complete isolation, it might be entirely free to choose its way of life constrained only by those necessities imposed by nature that it must secure for itself enough of food and of the other necessities of life. Eons of evolution have shaped our bodies so that our nature is aligned with the necessities of survival in the surrounding system of the natural world: we have evolved with a desire to eat the food that will sustain us, with an immune system to resist intruding microbes bearing disease, with a homeostatic system to deal with fluctuations in the temperatures around us, and so forth. Beyond the limits dictated by such natural necessities, a solitary community is free to organize its life into any cultural form—within its capacity to create—that the people find most fulfilling to the nature within them. So long as it can survive the demands of nature, an isolated community is free to be weak.

Since the beginnings of civilization ten thousand years ago, isolation has become increasingly impossible until today, in the latter part of the twentieth century, even the last retreats of protective solitude are being absorbed by the encroaching power of more advanced societies. The Eskimos of the arctic survive now at the sufferance of Canadian and American authorities, while the Indians of the Amazon continue to be dispossessed and exterminated by the expanding Brazilian civilization. Isolation is no longer a protective cloak for "backward" cultural ways anywhere on the planet.

But the development that has eliminated isolation is the very same as the one that might also, ultimately, abolish the rule of force. The same growth of civilization that has brought everyone into contact can now lead to a world order that would transform that international system where the strong have been free to do what they can while the weak suffer what they must. This prospect, however distant or improbable we may judge it to be, brings us to a thought experiment that will culminate our search for *real choice* in a world where the market system is in operation.

Imagine a world in which war of all kinds has effectively been forever banished. Imagine further that the peoples of this world are knit together by a global market. *In such a world, would we then be free to choose to live in whatever way we wish?* Would our freedom include even ways of life that are economically backward in comparison with others? Or, even in a world without GNP wars, would being less rich than others still make one vulnerable? Even in a world liberated from the patterns of predation, would the peaceful competitive process inherent in the market system itself continue to compel people to become something other than what they would freely choose to be?

The world we are postulating would, in effect, make of the whole of civilization a single domestic society: one interconnected market, with peace maintained by an overarching political order. We might rephrase our hypothetical circumstance: imagine that the United States were the only country in the world. How free would any or all of us be to choose how to live? Would the problem of power continue to arise, in other forms, to limit our options?

In his book *The Political Theory of Possessive Individualism*, C. B. Macpherson characterizes "the possessive market society" as one in which the Hobbsean "war of all against all" persists even in the absence of violence. The market society, Macpherson says,

> is a society in which men who want more may, and do, continually seek to transfer to themselves some of the powers of others, in such a way as to compel everyone to compete for more power, and all this by peaceable and legal methods which do not destroy the society by open force.[37]

The abolition of war, in this view, would free us from bloodshed but not from bondage. The problem of power persists, and with it the compulsion to match the power of our competitors, lest we . . . Lest we what? Does there remain a problem of power so important as to govern our destiny? And, if so, has it a solution?

THE IMPERATIVES OF THE MARKET

War or no war, the market imposes its own necessities on those who would sell their products.

The market inevitably changes the ecology of our interrelationships, and as new niches are created, old ones disappear. My grandfather may have been a wheelwright, my father may have been a wheelwright. But if the rest of the world now travels on rubber tires placed around metal hubs, I won't be able to make a living following my family tradition.

If innovations developed by others render my product unappealing, I cannot go on as before, prospering while making the old product. However much I may like my old business of making old-fashioned adding machines, the development of the silicon chip and, through that, of the ten-dollar pocket calculator that can do far more than my machine ever could, means that my business will have to change.

If others have found a way to produce a given product more efficiently, other less-efficient means of producing the same thing are rendered impractical. If my more efficient neighbor can make a profit at a price that would be a loss for me, I must either match his efficiency or go out of business.

This is directly analogous with the parable of the tribes. There, a powerful and aggressive actor can impose on each of his neighbors the unhappy choice: match my power or I will devour you. A crucial difference, it might be argued, is that what anarchy rewards is often the worst of our vices—the ruthless ambition of the warlord, for example—whereas what the market rewards is a virtue, the ability to give people something better at a lower cost. While that distinction is valid, some important qualifications are required.

One qualification was discussed at some length earlier, in chapter 2: the market's tunnel vision fosters a dangerously distorted idea of what constitutes efficiency. The farmer who protects his soil, and who conserves water rather than wantonly pumping out the aquifer under his land, may be condemned by the market as "inefficient." The steelmaker who can price his ingots low because he never installed scrubbers in his chimneys will be rewarded by the market for his efficiency.

In our earlier discussion of the market's tunnel vision, this problem of the market's skewed model of costs and benefits established the need for a deeper involvement of political decisions in adjusting market mechanisms. With taxes and subsidies, government can assure that neglected costs and benefits are incorporated into market prices. In some cases, laws should ban outright certain practices (the use of DDT or chloroflorocarbons, for example) and mandate others (such as restoration of strip-mined lands and proper disposal of hazardous wastes).

The issue of the use of laws to correct the market again raises the question of the scope of the political system that makes and enforces the regulations.

In our national debates over such laws, an argument frequently raised by those seeking to protect the market against governmental intervention is that the producers in our country would be placed at a competitive disadvantage relative to foreign producers. Surely, this is a legitimate concern. But what the fragmentation of the world into a diversity of polities calls for is not a retreat, within our own polity, into the anarchy of the uncorrected market. We are called, rather, to move forward to eliminate the anarchy in the global system.

Treat a problem as a problem.

Freedom requires order. Otherwise, the necessities of unrestrained competition force everyone down an unchosen path. Global economy necessitates global regulation.

Some people have welcomed the rise of multinational corporations with their ability to be free of politics because they transcend political boundaries. The multinationals, some think, should replace nation-states as the principal organizations molding our world. Look at the mess that nation-states have made of history, the argument goes.

A more misguided prescription for a future we would want would be difficult to conceive. Not only are multinational corporations less accountable to any real public than are the democratic polities of the Western world. Not only are the values to which these corporations tend to be devoted only a part of the spectrum of our concerns. But the system—the world market—in which they are embedded does not make even the corporation really free.

Only collective decisions, democratically arrived at, can create an economic order that makes us free. The scope of the decisions must correspond with the scope of the market they seek to regulate.

In the early nineteenth century in America, the economy consisted mainly of small enterprises operating in local communities. Before the end of the nineteenth century, as the market developed according to its own powerful inner dynamic, a national economy emerged. Huge railroads and steel empires and other great corporate networks bestrode the continent. They were too big for local communities or for states to be able to deal with effectively. With the emergence of a national market, a strong national government became indispensable to the health of the society.* These big corporate empires long sought to block the establishment of any regulatory authority that could encompass their activities. But ultimately the need generated sufficient political will to overcome the resistance (though the battle, of course, still goes on). The scope of the

---

*Lester Milbrath poses the problem thus in his *Envisioning a Sustainable Society:* "If a local or state government forbids the pollution discharge, another market comes into play, the competitive market among states to attract and retain industry. A local manufacturing plant can threaten to move or shut down if local and state governments propose to establish tight controls over pollution emissions. The only way that local and state governments can be freed from being held hostage in this fashion is for the national government to establish uniform pollution emission standards across the country" (p. 24).

order grew to contain (albeit inadequately) the scope of the market.

During the past century, the market has continued knitting its network. More and more, the pattern of exchange is global in range. Some of the actors—the multinational corporations—have revenues greater than those of many entire countries. But once again, the political evolution lags behind the economic. Dangerous chemicals outlawed in this country are still sold abroad to poison some other part of the earth. Sweatshops that would not be tolerated within one country's borders can be opened in another, so that jobs migrate to wherever the political authorities do the least to protect workers from unsafe or unfair working conditions. If environmental regulations are too burdensome here, we'll move our factory over there.

Once again, the corporations resist the necessary political evolution. In the United States, the business community has steadfastly opposed American adoption of international labor laws, for example, so that unbridled competition can still encourage the transplantation of work to the places on earth where the political authorities are most willing to sacrifice workers' welfare. The political authorities in the U.S., meanwhile, have given the business community virtual veto power over American ratification of such international agreements.[38]

The disparity between national borders and global commerce understandably inhibits national governments from unilaterally making those decisions that, in the absence of the cost of competitive disadvantage, might create within their borders the kind of world their people would choose. Unregulated competition robs them of real freedom of choice.

The answer to this problem is global order. As was pointed out in the previous discussion of the economy as arms race, nations can make treaties. They can pass laws and create the enforcement agencies able to make them stick. With only sovereign nations, the Mediterranean will continue to be choked to death, as the more responsible nations must simply watch the poisons from the less responsible wash up on their shores. Those who work to reduce their emissions of CO_2 will find the oceans rising onto their shores just as high as onto the shores of those who recklessly continue their assault on the atmosphere. With international agreements, we can prevent competitive advantage accruing to those who produce wealth by using virtual slave labor. Without creating a political order as vast as our economic order, we cannot be masters of our fate.*

Hanging together, we can avoid hanging separately.

PROTECTION

A proper system of global regulation can go a long way toward allowing humankind to choose its destiny, rather than letting the market choose for us. Do there remain other important ways in which the market would take choices away from us?

The dynamism of the market acts as a powerful solvent, ungluing the structures of cultural traditions. All that is solid melts into air.

Small communities can protect their own way of life; but to do so it seems they must restrict some of the freedoms of individuals to interact with the surrounding world as they please.

The Amish farmers of Lancaster County, Pennsylvania, exemplify one such solution. Economically, the Amish farm seems to be viable, even while eschewing the "advanced" technology of the rest of American agriculture. In part, this may be helped by the fact that they already owned their land before the industrial revolution transformed agriculture, and they can now benefit from the care and hard work invested in that land over the succeeding generations. In part, also, the Amish success reflects the comparative self-sufficiency of the Amish community. Their commerce with the outside world is

---

*On *The Nightly Business Report*, in 1989, Lester Thurow discussed the global nature of the problem of the denuding of the tropical rain forests. The forests are growing in certain countries, especially Brazil and Indonesia, but the whole world has a stake in their preservation. So, said Thurow, the way to solve the problem is for some of the rich countries, like the United States and Japan, to pay the poorer countries to spare their rain forests, and so on. But there was no mention, in this presentation of the problem, of the need for the creation of global institutions. How else can one expect that nations will share the costs of environmental measures whose benefits are global? Will the United States or Japan spontaneously know what their proper share is and unilaterally proceed to pay it? Really understanding the global nature of our problems includes recognizing the need for global agencies to make and to implement policy.

relatively limited. To the extent that a community can live in relation to nature alone, to that extent it is free to be "backward," whatever the dictates of the market.* And the Amish have been protected, in large measure, from the historic penalties of weakness by being contained by the very powerful American industrial state. The Nazi machine that imposed its totalitarian domination on the land from which the Pennsylvania "Dutch" emigrated never even came close to the hills of Pennsylvania. (Even so, the Amish in Pennsylvania are not immune from the encroachments of the powerful society around them. In recent years, there has been the threat of a great highway—deemed necessary to deal with the increasing traffic that is an inevitable outgrowth of the development of the Lancaster area—being cut through the rural landscape, across the heart of the Amish community and a number of its farms.)

But the ability of the Amish to perpetuate their traditional culture is due in no small degree to the community's exercise of broad control over its members. Deviations that threaten the community's traditional values are punished by various forms of exclusion beginning with the kind of internal exile called "shunning," where no one in the community talks to the person who has been declared to be out.

Valuable freedom from the market's dictates can come into conflict with other valuable individual freedoms.

Another interesting example concerns the worry of Canadians about maintaining their national culture in the face of the "threat" from the larger and dominant culture of the United States. In the context of the negotiation and subsequent ratification process for a treaty between the two countries to create a free-trade zone—that is, to make a single open market of the two countries—deep fears surfaced in Canada about the dis-

---

*A somewhat appalling example of the option of isolationist self-sufficiency is the country of Burma. Over the past several decades, it has insulated itself from the outside world, taking a path that is free of the necessities of the market discussed in this work. Alan Berlow comments on this "freedom" and its bleak results. "For a Westerner, it may be pleasant to visit a country where there are no signs advertising Coca Cola, Nike, or anything else, no high-rise condominiums, and relatively few automobiles. But the people who have to live here do not seem grateful for this crackpot brand of socialism." With per capita income of about $200 per year, Burma is, Berlow says, "an economic basket case." (*The New Republic*, June 4, 1990, p. 23).

appearance of a distinctive Canadian culture. Canada has, for some time, interfered with the market by such measures as limiting the proportion of television programming that can be of American origin to a level lower than that would be dictated by price and viewer demand alone. Correspondingly, the stations have been required to devote more time to Canadian-produced television fare than what market forces would have yielded. Truly free trade between the countries would result in a kind of homogenizing of cultures, as the result of the exercise of a kind of power, just as the parable of the tribes does.*

The market system—with the progress it produces and with the economic order it allocates—*inevitably* remains a potent force shaping our world. Much of this power is benign, even wonderful. Much of it is regrettable. Sorting out the forces and their consequences is difficult.

---

*Within each country, meanwhile, similar forces can be at work.

Within Canada, a similar kind of protectionism is operating—with one province guarding its identity against the rest of Canada just as Canada does with respect to the United States. In the province of Quebec also, individual freedoms have been restricted to protect a cultural identity that fears itself endangered. Laws requiring all signs to be in French and forbidding the use of English are expressions of a cultural community's desire to choose to remain itself, to preserve its distinctness; and these laws have had among their effects the departure of English-speaking Canadians from the province for an environment friendlier to their own identity.

Within the United States, it might be said that what the Canadians fear would happen to them in a free-trade situation has in fact already happened to the regions of this country. Different parts of America developed with different values and symbols. But in our free market of culture, these regions are being overwhelmed by the flow of information and ideas and images from the national media centers in New York and Los Angeles. Just as the Canadians have their excellent National Film Board, so might Montana have its own films, or so might Georgia require some of the evening television programming to be of Georgian production. But that is not, for the most part, how it works in our market society—for better and for worse.

Yet even the most liberal nations in the world exercise a form of restriction to protect the integrity of their societies from the transformations that unrestricted "imports" would engender: they restrict immigration. Admittedly, the freedoms limited in this case are not those of the society's own citizens. Moreover, cultural integrity is not the only reason for limits on foreign immigration, although in many instances it is a powerful motivator. The analogy is thus quite relevant: immigration is a form of commerce between countries, and each nation imposes limits on what it will take in, in order to regulate its own cultural development.

WEALTH AND POWER IN
THE ORDERED POLITY

We have just touched again upon some of the ways that the *system*, unless it is checked by political decisions, can exercise power over *people*. It is time to return to the problem of the power of some people over others.

The question that runs like a thread throughout this chapter can be stated; are people truly free to adopt a way of living that is economically less productive than the ways of other people around them? Can a people choose to be (relatively) poor and still maintain control over their destiny?

In a world where money buys guns and one group can use guns against another, the poor clearly are vulnerable. But when a political order eliminates the guns, are we then free of the compulsion to keep up with the wealth of our neighbors? Is it still costly to refuse to allow our choices to be dictated by the demands of economic competition?* The answer depends on the nature of the political order. If the political order in which we are embedded is truly democratic, it might well be safe to be poor. For the premise of democracy is that each person is entitled to an equal voice in the determination of the community's collective destiny.

The concept of 'collective destiny' is crucial to understanding this problem. It is not enough for us all to work together to create and maintain an order that protects our freedom and autonomy. We must broaden our very understanding of freedom. Real freedom requires more than each of us acting as isolated entities cultivating our own separate gardens. We may be protected, in those private gardens, from marauding armies, only to find our garden ruined by the acid rain produced from other people's toxic emissions.† No one is really free unless everyone is bound by laws that are just.

---

*Given that the hypothetical world we are positing is without war, we can imagine the "we" that chooses the path of simplicity to be a family that owns a homestead in some community or a whole society participating in a global order.
†In New York, a great park was created in the Adirondacks to be preserved in its pristine natural beauty. But in our times the fate of this enclave of preservation has been to be contaminated by the toxins wandering above the land through the atmosphere.

The question of our freedom to choose relative poverty comes to rest, therefore, on the question of whether in our political order the wealthy have a greater voice than the poor in the formulation and implementation of the laws.

I saw a television article about the course of some major power lines across New York State. At a few points, the path of the line veered, evidently being diverted from a few fields on one side of the road in order to cross instead the front yards of homes on the other side. The fields that were spared, it turns out, belonged to rich people who used their influence to get public officials to intercede in their behalf. In American legislative bodies, measures drafted to serve some specific company routinely succeed in gaining passage. (Sometimes this is in exchange for campaign contributions, sometimes—as apparently happened in a recent FBI sting operation in the California Assembly—in exchange for outright bribes.)

So long as money can buy political power, we are less than free to choose the way of life we find most meaningful, irrespective of where that life would put us in the spectrum of economic wealth. Even "enough" if it is also "less," exposes us to injustice.

At its most extreme, the incestuous relationship between wealth and political power replaces democracy with tyranny. The company towns in coal country in the late nineteenth and early twentieth centuries illustrate the totalitarian possibilities. The coal companies, though enriching themselves in the wider market, denied the workers the freedoms of the market with their own dollars, in order to assure that the workers and their families could never get free of the company. ("I owe my soul to the company store.") Not only could the companies virtually enslave the workers, but they could count on the support of federal troops to keep the miners in check.

In his discussion of the market in *The Battle for Human Nature*, Barry Schwartz tells how the constitutional system decided against the idea of a company town in a more benign case—the case of Pullman, Illinois. Pullman was built by George Pullman, the railroad man, and run by him "as a property right." "Pullman had clear ideas about how people should live, and he imposed his ideas on the residents of the town." The Supreme Court eventually required Pullman to divest himself of the town. In reaching this decision, Schwartz writes, "the court was in essence enforcing the distinction between different spheres of life. Companies could be owned; towns could not."

But the distinction between spheres is quite imperfectly enforced in this imperfect democracy. If one cannot own a town, can one "own" a Senator?* One is not supposed to be able to, but at least subtle forms of ownership do seem to be possible. On a recent panel discussion of campaign financing, Senator Rudman, a Republican, and Senator Kerry, a Democrat, agreed that, even if big campaign contributions do not buy a senator's vote, they at least buy "access." Either access is worth something or it is not. If it is worth something, it means that having access increases the probability the senator will vote your way. If you can buy that increase in probability, you have bought a piece of the senator.

The protection of our democracy from the corrosive intrusions of plutocracy is again seen (as in the earlier discussion in chapter 4) as an essential element in the institutional reorganization required to liberate ourselves from the compulsions imposed by our economic machine.

BUYING INFLUENCE

The workings of power pose one more knotty problem. Power does not always involve coercion. And inequalities of power do not always lead to injustice. But even without coercion or injustice, power can be a problem. Here is why.

War between societies and corruption within a democratic polity are, fundamentally, two aspects of the same thing. In each case, the group with more power can compel those with less to bend to their will. Even though the battles in the polit-

---

*If one cannot own a town, one can own a shopping mall. And so far, the courts have upheld the idea that the shopping mall is a private establishment rather than a public space. People can be prohibited in these malls, therefore, from giving public expression to their political concerns. The courts have declared this despite the fact that in many communities all across the country, the shopping mall is the closest thing to a main street or a town square. Right now, however, the triumph of the right of property over the protection of equal power in the democratic public arena has this consequence: that when Americans enter these "main streets" and "town squares," they do not bring with them their constitutional rights to freedom of assembly, freedom of petition, and freedom of speech.

ical sphere—over what laws will be passed and how they will be implemented—are fought without force, in the background the guns still lurk. Laws are en*forced*. Even in an order that effectively disarms all those living within, the order itself is maintained ultimately by arms. (The state, as it is said, maintains a monopoly on the use of force.) If one group can buy a greater portion of state power than it is justly entitled to, therefore, it is, in effect, conquering by force of arms those whose voice in the political process is correspondingly and unjustly diminished.

This is most blatantly obvious when federal troops are called in to help break up workers' strikes, as happened in late nineteenth-century America. But it is really true also with any unjust laws that people are compelled to obey.

Imagine we have rid ourselves of the evils of plutocracy. What if we had a world in which not only was war banished, but the democratic process was also scrupulously protected against corruption, while the market process still made some people much wealthier than others? Would we then be altogether free to choose a way of living that left us poorer than our neighbors? Is there any way that relative poverty would still leave us with a lesser voice in determining our collective destiny?

The problem that remains derives from the fact that *cooperation can be bought*.

Here is an illustration. A major developer in northern Virginia said to an acquaintance of mine, "If you want to get something built, it's easy. You buy the land and then you bribe your neighbors until they shut up."

What's wrong with that? Perhaps one may be offended at the implicit premise that, as the saying goes, everyone has his price. But in some ways, that is probably a valid premise in most situations. My wife and I have worked, together with our neighborhood, to block a development that would adversely affect a nearby stretch of woods along Sligo Creek near our home. If someone offered me a million dollars to drop my opposition, would I refuse? Certainly that million dollars would more than make up for the development's adverse effects on me personally. And even if I were wholly devoted to the protection of the earth, in preference to my own welfare, the earth would arguably be better off if I took the million dollars and gave it to the Nature Conservancy or to the Natural Resources

Defense Council than if I stood firm to defend this particular ribbon of woodland. So, in that sense, on this issue, I do have my price.

Isn't it unethical to take bribes? Despite the developer's using the same word—bribe—to describe his compensation of the neighbors as we use to describe the illegal payments made to influence legislators or judges, the two acts are quite different in their ethical nature. If a senator accepts a bribe, he or she is selling something that is *not his*. His power is a trust conferred on him by the public, with the understanding that it will be used on the public's behalf. If he sells his vote as a representative for money that goes to him as an individual, he is guilty of a kind of theft. If I sell by vote as a citizen— say in a referendum on a plan for development—in exchange for what someone is willing to give or to promise me, what I have given was mine to give, or more precisely, to trade. Indeed, whenever we vote for someone because of his or her campaign promises, we have made some such exchange. And if a developer "bribes" us to refrain from objecting to his plans to turn a nearby river area into a chemical plant, our silence was ours to give.

So, one might say, those with enough money can get their way. What's wrong with that? If no force was used and no theft perpetrated, what's the problem?

One problem is that not everyone's cooperation need be bought. Imagine that a community of one hundred people needs to approve the plan to allow the chemical plant to be constructed. Imagine further that the harm of the plant's construction to each person can be quantified as one thousand dollars. If, as with most democratic decisions, a simple majority is all that is required to approve the deal, and if each voter is assumed to be concerned only with self-interest, then the developer needs to pay compensation of little more than fifty thousand dollars to get approval. (Just over one thousand dollars each to just over fifty people.) If the approval is worth, say seventy five thousand dollars to the builder, buying the approval at that price is a good deal. A majority of the people end up happy—the 50 percent plus whose cooperation was purchased and the developer. But *the deal is still bad for the system as a whole*. For the benefits to the system as a whole are seventy-five thousand dollars, while the damages are one hundred thousand dollars. Those hurt are hurt more than the others are benefitted.

This problem, however, is not at all peculiar to situations in which cooperation is purchased. It is a potential danger in all democratic decisions where a majority rules. Just because a decision benefits most of the people, that does not prove that it is beneficial to the society as a whole. The lesson of this is that a democratic society whose citizens consider only their own self-interest when engaged in the public business cannot evolve in a healthy decision.

The undependability of altruism, however, does point out a danger in relative poverty. The only one who is safe in such a system, where the legitimate needs of one party are of no inherent concern to the others, is the one who commands sufficient resources to control the self-interests of the others. Even in a world order liberated from war and operating by democratic principles, we might pay a cost for giving up the "influence" that comes from being rich. Even if we had "enough" in terms of our own desire for wealth, if the Japanese have a good deal more they will be able to get the rest of the world to make collective decisions more to their liking and not necessarily to ours.*

---

*As this analysis intimates, however, not all worlds would be equally vulnerable to the corrupting effects of this kind of influence buying. The hungrier people are for more material wealth, the more readily can one with wealth to dispense purchase the cooperation of others with his designs. But the more people feel a sense of satisfaction, a sense of the sufficiency of what they already possess, the less will the goods the wealthy command serve as inducements to others to abandon other values they care about.

When people really love their way of life, there may indeed not be a price that would lead them to abandon it. The old couple that stands in the way of Faust's grand design refuses Faust's offer of a cash settlement—it is only through violence that the developer can get them out of his way. A Wyoming rancher responded to the idea that the solution to the economic difficulties of the region's ranchers would be to draw more tourism to the area to make a better living, saying: "That looks fine on paper, but what it comes down to is your wife and daughters go to work cooking for tourists and making their beds, and your son is driving a bus for them or whatever. I'm sure that's fine for some people, but I'd rather stay on the land and starve right along with the rest of the cowboys" ("Saving the Plains: The Bison Gambit," *Washington Post*, August 6, 1989, p. 83).

Some people feel rich without material wealth. An Amish farmer has recently published a book that is a journal of appreciations of the wonders of the natural world he encounters in his daily life. The book is called *Great Possessions.* How much do you imagine this farmer, who is already celebrating his great possessions, would have to be paid in turn his land over to a developer to be turned into a shopping center?

But let us eliminate this concern, stipulating that we have prevented this kind of injustice to which a majoritarian democracy is prone. For the plan to go forward, let us propose, *all* the neighbors need to be bribed until they shut up. Not a majoritarian but a unanimous decision. If everyone with a stake in the matter is adequately compensated and willingly agrees, is there any problem? If there is no coercion and no injustice, does it matter that the wealthy can use their money to get us to buy their vision of the future?

I believe it does. Here, once again, we return to the theme whose deep vibration resonates throughout this work: the power of the system to shape our destiny. For if it is the rich who can design the future, and if it is the system that can determine what kind of people become rich, then, in an important way, it is the system that governs how our future will be designed.

To F. Scott Fitzgerald's statement that the very rich "are different from you and me," Hemingway's rejoinder was "Yes, they have more money." But that hardly captures the nonrandomness of the selective process through which some people come to have a great deal more money than others. It is like the Midas muffler commercial in the late 1970s, in which a pennypinching and pinched-faced tycoon brings in his antique luxury car for a free replacement muffler—"guaranteed for the life of your car"—and says, "How d'ya think a man like me got to *be* a man like me?"

Great fortunes are accumulated by a single-minded devotion to accumulating great fortunes, Philip Slater shows in his study of wealth addiction. John D. Rockefeller, Slater says, "had no real friends and, in fact, taught his Sunday School class that they mustn't let 'good fellowship get the least hold' on them."[39] Henry Ford was described by his biographers as "a sort of human dynamo, made to run purposefully along a single track."[40] His obsession with finding ways to save labor, Slater says, was "not so people could enjoy themselves more, but so more energy would be freed to 'do the job.' "[41] Ford also "took a dim view of friendship" and said that "Too much good fellowship may indeed be a very bad thing."[42]

As the fortunes—made from such single-minded pursuit of riches for their own sake—pass along through later generations of Rockefellers and Fords, the spirit governing the use of the resources doubtless changes. The values directing the programs of the Rockefeller Foundation and the Ford Foundation are not identical with those that ruled the lives of John D. and Henry the first. Yet neither can it be assumed that the way these foundations work to shape the world is identical with the role that would have been played by foundations set up by Albert Schweitzer or Mohandas Gandhi, had it been they rather than these industrial entrepreneurs whose work had been rewarded by the world with the command over billions of dollars they could not take with them. But as our world is organized, it is the genius of a Henry Ford and not that of an Albert Schweitzer that brings to a person the rights to direct the use of resources on so large a scale. And, in the meantime, as old money gets put into foundations, more or less benign, new fortunes are made by the Hunts and the Trumps and Frank Lorenzos.

It is not just that inequalities of wealth mean that some people will almost inescapably have greater power than others to shape the world that all will live in. More than that, those with this greater power are a nonrandom sample of humanity: they are not, of course, all like the pinched spirits depicted in Slater's portraits of Rockefeller and Ford; but certain kinds of personalities and values will inevitably be more represented in this group than in the larger population from which they emerged. To the extent, therefore, that greater power tends to go to people with certain value orientations, the world will tend to evolve toward a greater embodiment of those values. And even if this evolution occurs with the acceptance, at each step, of the other people, whose cooperation has been bought, it cannot be said that the reason the world is going that direction is that this is the destiny that the people, collectively, preferred.

Other outcomes, other images of the world-to-be that were conceivable and feasible, might have been more in keeping with the overall values of the community at large. But here comes the developer, with his vision of a project he wants to build—most likely because it will make money ("How d'ya think a man like me got to *be* a man like me?")—and with enough resources, from his previous profitable projects, to get all his neighbors to shut up.

For us—as individuals in the community, as a community in the society, as a society in a world order—to have completely equal say in our collective destiny as the richest players in the group, even in a true democracy, we would have to play the wealth game as successfully as they. The parable of the tribes presented peoples with the unwanted choice: match the power of the mighty or be gobbled up. In either case, the ways of power are spread throughout the system. Here, even without conquest of arms, even with democratic integrity protected, a similar—but much less extreme—choice is imposed on us: match the wealth of the rich or have a smaller voice than they in saying what the future will be. Either way, the ways of wealth are spread throughout the system.

In both cases, it is ultimately not so much the powerful that shape our destiny. The real master, rather, is the structure of the system, which determines what kind of values and ways of living will be empowered. The problem of power remains.

BREAKING FREE

Are we then condemned inevitably to be caught up in a ceaseless competitive struggle for wealth? No, I think not. To say that a choice has costs is quite different from saying that the choice is foreclosed.

The situation with regard to "buying influence" does indeed present parallels with the parable of the tribes. But the weight of necessity in the one case in no way compares with that in the other. For the weak in the anarchic struggle among societies, life and death are at stake. With the buying of cooperation in a well-ordered democratic polity, the penalty for the weakness of relative poverty is only a somewhat smaller voice in determining what the future will be.*

Economists speak of "opportunity costs," referring to the fact that the costs of any course of action include the foreclosure of all alternative courses of action that one had the opportunity to take. If the cost of relative poverty is a smaller voice in collective affairs, this cost must be weighed against the cost of striving to be the richest around. According to some values

---

*For those within the system who choose a way of life that makes them poorer than others in the system, there are some costs, but the greatest costs of the problem of "buying influence" are borne by the system as a whole. What is most at stake with this comparatively benign problem of power is less the fate of individuals than the evolution of the whole community, or society, or world.

that are salient in our inadequately controlled market society, the costs of competing for wealth without limit are negligible or nonexistent. But for people who feel that they have "enough" and who have found a way of living—incompatible with seeking more and more—that gives them "Great Possessions" of a different kind, the costs of seeking wealth simply for the sake of power may be high indeed.

In the just and nonviolent order we have postulated, we would be *free enough* to choose to live the life we found most meaningful, even if this conferred on us some competitive disadvantages. For most of us living in the wealthy industrial countries, such a choice would probably be an enlightened one.

But that is not the world we live in today. Our politics *are* corrupted by wealth; the global order *is* still ruled by force of arms. What is the enlightened course for us in the world not as it should be, but as it is?

Part of the answer must be that it is essential for us to work to remake our present world into the world as it should be. The analysis in this chapter shows that our freedom to live as we truly wish depends on institutional transformation to prevent the unjust use of force. Democracy needs to be protected from corrosive effects of money on the vessels of public power; a world order must be created that makes even the weak safe from invasions and intimidation. It should be clear to us, of course, that such institutional restructuring is vital even if we have no desire to escape the compulsions of economic competition. But it is, at the same time, not surprising that many of those who stand prominently on our national and world stages do not speak of this essential work. For justice is the antidote to power, and the voices we hear tend to be those of the powerful. A just world would give them less of what they value than they are getting now.

In any event, a just world—a world where it is safe to be weak—will be generations in the making. (Once made, such a world will need constantly to be maintained, like a building erected in the midst of hostile elements). Are we in the meanwhile helplessly trapped in the grip of necessity?

For us in the United States, I suggest, the answer is that, even if our freedom from competitive necessity is not complete, it is nonetheless considerably greater than our public discourse would suggest. Our democracy, though imperfect, provides *reasonable* protections for those individuals who are poor but vigilant. For us as a nation, our wealth and our power are already so great that the risks we would incur would not be great if we chose to sacrifice some of our economic supremacy in the service of other values. And in the meanwhile, on the other side of the balance, there are the opportunity costs of asking only, How must we be? and never How would we like to be?

We are freer than we now act, freer to seek a vision of an *intrinsically meaningful* way of life and not just a way imposed on us by the necessities of *external competition*.

Freer, that is, in objective terms. Subjective factors can also enslave. One cannot say, I have enough, if one is in the grip of *insatiable greed*. One cannot say, It is safe to relinquish the position of unquestioned supremacy, if one is compelled by an unrelenting *narcissistic need* to be Number One.

CONCLUSION:
ENVISIONING THE GOOD LIFE

A Meditation
on Past, Present,
and Future

What kind of future do we want? Do we want a world like today's, only more so—more advanced technology, more wealth, for more people? This appears to be the mainstream aspiration for the future, if it can be said that dreams about the future, in our society now, are alive at all. This is the kind of future the market would choose for us. This is the market's idea of "progress."

Such progress might well contribute a good deal of value to our lives and those of our descendants. But is there anything else for us to aspire to? Even if it is granted that the market drives our destiny, we as a country seem to embrace it as the destiny we would want anyway. Even if it is granted that it is within our ability to repossess the power that the market system has taken from us, we might judge that our fate is already in good hands.

Look around us. What reason is there to think there is anything better for us to seek?

ROMANTICIZING THE PAST

We already have it good, in fundamental ways, by any historical standard. A few centuries of economic growth have lifted those of us who live in the rich market societies from conditions of great deprivation. In the preindustrial world, by far the majority of the income of the average person was absorbed in obtaining even a poor diet. This was in good times.[1] When time were bad, famine descended on the land and carried off many of the people. (Even in our own times, the mismanagement of a nonmarket economy—that of China during Mao's infamous "Great Leap Forward"—brought about the death by starvation of many millions of people.)

McKendrick speaks of the prelapsarian myth, the idea that somehow the forces of modernity have swept away "the good old days." But how good were they?

Many of the critics of the world created by capitalism show an unmistakable nostalgia for times gone by, for a world more whole, for a world that held its members in the comforting embrace of a traditional order. (Earlier in these pages—on p. 78—I spoke wistfully of "a world lost.") Traditional society, however, was no utopia.

Does the market system treat our children as resources to exploit—as drudges in the factories and mines of Victorian Liverpool or as driven technicians-in-the-making in contemporary Tokyo? The abuse of children was hardly an innovation of the market. In some traditional African societies, female children are sexually mutilated, leaving them permanently incapable of natural sexual pleasure. Some of their traditional Chinese counterparts had their feet bound, disfiguring them so that natural locomotion, or even comfort, became impossible.

Does the market system fracture community cohesion, grinding it into so many discrete, self-interested social atoms? The community of past forms of cultural organization was no heaven. Michael Novak writes that his early antagonism to the individualism of democratic capitalism stemmed in part from a "nostalgia for the medieval village."[2] He later came to recognize not only the virtues of the modern system but also the structures of domination that characterized the ancien régime.

Even today, we are plagued with some of the destructive by-products of the way people have traditionally formed their community bonds. Their way of creating an "us" was inseparable from a strong, and often hostile sense of a "them." In Sri

Lanka, the Tamils and the Sinhalese are shedding each other's blood; in Northern Ireland, it is Catholics and Protestants; in many African societies, the nation splits violently along the fracture lines created by exclusive tribal identities.

Here in America, the quintessential market society, peoples from all over the world, from all races and religions, live together in comparative peace. The market system, arguably, deserves some of the credit for this significant achievement. A system that is concerned only with "the color of your money," rather than with the color of your skin, is liberating. What holds us together may not be nourishing emotionally and spiritually. But our mechanical system does hold us together and not drive us at each other's throats.

Every form of social organization, as a solution to the problems of human life, inevitably represents trade-offs between different areas of value. Each of us in our own lives, in choosing a path, of necessity gives up other paths that would confer other benefits. Each culture, likewise, embodies such trade-offs.

In an article on the settling of the Bedouins in the Negev Desert, this sense of trade-off is brought into clear relief. "The hills I looked out on as a child had the rounded shapes of tents and camels," says one Bedouin who has become the principal of a secondary school in the Bedouin village of Lagiya. "Now the soft contours have given way to the stark cubes of the block houses. It reflects a new mind-set. Now we're thinking in cubes; we're thinking in frames that are already made."[3] Is this progress? A twenty-year-old Bedouin, about to move from a tent to the village, says, "I'm ambivalent. There's much more comfort, not having to walk two kilometers for water. On the other hand, I'm no longer free. Being a Bedouin is the feeling of freedom."[4]

The defenders of capitalism, not romanticizing the difficulties of the past, seem unambivalent about which side of the trade-off is the more beneficial. Most of us, it seems, concur.*

---

*Another vivid illustration of the problem of trade-offs is found in Philip Slater's *Earthwalk*. Slater quotes from a letter written by a Moroccan graduate student.

> Every single act becomes a very complicated interaction. I live in the old Arab city where there are not many phones. I need a phone to contact the people I am to interview and who happen to

In the Olympics, there are some events that are scored according to the "difficulty factor" of what the contestant is attempting. The score is a product not only of how perfect the execution is, but also of the difficulty of the maneuver. Making a civilized society work is an enterprise of such extraordinary difficulty, it may be argued, that the execution can fall rather short of perfection and still be a resounding winner.

---

be the bourgeois modernized elite who will be shocked if I drop by as we traditionally do. I went to the public phone which is not an automatic one. I gave my list of numbers to the operator who happens to have known me since ages. He wanted to know why I want to call all these people. I explained briefly that I was doing a sort of sociological survey. He wanted more details. I told him that it will take us about an hour, and that by then the post office will have to close. He took it as an insult and asked me to wait until he called me. I did. He called me to say that the numbers were either busy or not answering, and that in any case I should not try to monopolize a public phone by calling so many people. I then told him I was sorry I was so worried about the time, and that I was ready to tell him what I was doing. I did. He wanted to know how can 10 or 20 people, very special and particular, be representative of hundreds and thousands, who have only some things in common with them. So I proceeded to explain *"la theorie de la probabilite."* He then disagreed and rejected the theory as being junk. I told him that it was his right to reject it, that was the normal destiny of a theory—some accept it and some reject it. He did not like my attitude and said that I was avoiding discussing the matter with him, because I think in my head that he is not worth discussing with because he did not have my chance to carry on his studies and ended up doing a stupid job, etc. I tried to convince him of the opposite. It took me two more sessions and three days to get to use the phone.

The famous "anesthesie" which bothered me so much in Cambridge, . . . is in fact what allows you to be efficient there, and its absence leaves you completely immersed in an environment you can't control because you are so emotionally involved and at such a passionate level.

About this, Slater observes:

A traditional culture is full of distractions. One cannot deal impersonally with the environment . . . One is caught in an intricate web of ties that pull one back and demand an examination of how every new act interrelates with everything else. Relationships are primary, taking precedence over the pursuit of knowledge or personal achievement. (Slater, *Earthwalk*, pp. 26–27.)

History shows human beings to be disposed to do quite atrocious things to one another, to themselves, and to the world around them, according to this point of view. Liberal market society channels our dangerous energies in *comparatively* constructive ways. Human beings make poor building blocks for utopia, the argument goes. They are inherently lustful for preeminence and power, and the market at least allows the bellicosity that formerly played out on the battlefield to express itself without carnage. We are, by nature, also insatiable in our desires, and the market at least manages to harness the greed and fundamental selfishness of the human animal for mostly constructive and productive purposes.

In evaluating our own social system, according to this view, it is dangerous to expect or seek perfection. Sound policy can be based only on realistic expectations. It would be foolish for us to go tinkering with our system only to end up with something much worse. What reason do we have for believing anything much better is *possible?* It is all well and good to decry the flaws of our market society. But the question arises, *compared to what?*

Two arguments, then, are made by conservative defenders of the status quo on the basis of the shortcomings of the unromanticized past: (1) if the past was worse then the present, there is no reason for thinking anything better than our current cultural approach is possible; and (2) if the past was worse than the present, those societies can offer no valid basis for critiquing the present.

Both of these arguments have flaws.

RESURRECTING OUR HUMANITY

One may grant the darkness of much of human history— one may feel that our times and our form of society are less benighted than much of our past—yet still believe the way is open for a future far more enlightened than our present.

There is more than one way to learn the wrong lessons from our history. If some utopians fall into the trap of romanticizing the past, the "realists" who defend the status quo make the mistake of inferring too much about human limitations from the shortcomings we have exhibited so far in history in the design and conduct of human societies. For *history is not human nature writ large.*

This is a fundamental implication of the parable of the tribes as a perspective on the evolution of civilization. The selection for the ways of power in social evolution has driven human societies, since the beginnings of civilization, to develop in directions that people did not choose but were powerless to avoid. Compelled to live in a world hostile to our natures, we human creatures have been suffering in a kind of exile. Our home has been of our creation but not of our design—as if we were slaves driven by the lash to construct a monument whose architecture was dictated by an invisible master. That master has been power. When we ask, therefore, "what kind of life are human beings capable of?" we cannot reliably point to the tyrannies and cruelties of past societies—or to the greed or selfishness of contemporary society—and say, This is what we are, this is what the human being does. We have not yet had a chance to discover what we are, or to build a world that stands as a monument to the flowering of our humanity.

Even if the past was worse than the present, that does not prove that the world of the future cannot be significantly better than—and in character quite dissimilar from—our world today. It was inevitable that civilization would emerge and develop in a destructive form. But it is not inevitable that we will remain ensnared in the trap of power.

In the world as it has been, these past ten millennia, our human energies have not been the impetus behind the turning of the evolutionary wheel but rather have been grist for the mill of civilization. The flow of causality has proceeded, predominantly, from the overarching intersocietal system. The anarchy and consequent struggle for power in that system has dictated the structure of the civilized societies within it, imposing somewhat narrow limits on how a society could organize human energies and still survive external threats to its existence. These power-oriented societies, in turn, have forced their human members to mold themselves to serve a system not governed by and thus not necessarily hospitable to human needs.*

---

*Are coherent social communities inevitably as intolerant of diversity as those we so often see in traditional societies? According to my understanding, articulated in some depth in *Out of Weakness*, the violence between ethnic groups is a not an inevitable by-product of there being differences between one cultural group and another. It is, rather, a result of the antago-

If we can realize the emerging possibility of ending the overarching anarchy of the international system, of creating a secure world order, then a very different direction of causal flow can shape a very different kind of civilization. At the core of the new world toward which we can be striving would be our humanity, these needs and creative potentialities we embody as products of the evolution of life on earth. In different communities, this humanity would flower forth in diverse cultural forms and be organized into societies whose function would be to nourish the humanity that lives within it. The global order, in turn, would be structured so as to make the world safe for these diverse and humane societies.

Toward such a world, it is not unrealistic for us to aspire and strive. Nor is it farfetched to imagine that in such a world we will find different paths, different approaches, different ways of organizing the elements of social life, than those we practice today.

In their struggle against each other, power and human choice have collaborated in creating a society like ours. Modern industrial democratic societies lie somewhere on a continuum defined by the two extremes described above. It would be a distortion to suggest that today's market societies are at the most enslaved end of the spectrum. But neither, I would suggest, is the particular combination of causal relations that shape our society nearly as benign as our commonsense image of our condition would have it. And it is the very constricted nature of this "common sense" that keeps us from envisioning the enormous potential that exists for progress in social evolution, for creating a society that more truly nourishes, and is more truly governed by, our humanity.

---

nism, *within each culture*, between the demands of the culture and the needs of the human being. This creates a split within the developing human personality that imbues the whole issue of "boundaries" with a hostile charge.

A cultural identity that grows organically with one's being is secure. But the identity shaped by a hostile culture sits precariously, like an ill-fitting mask; and the more insecure the identity, the more aggressively people will defend it, the more intolerant people will be of those whose differences suggest there are other ways to be.

A more benign culture, more truly in harmony with our humanity, could allow spiritually diverse and emotionally coherent cultural communities to embrace their differences rather than go to war over them.

THE GIRL WHO CAN'T DANCE

How sure can we be that the nostalgia for past worlds is wholly misguided? How equipped are we to evaluate the costs and benefits of the trade-offs in the choices among cultural possibilities? How much do we know about the inherent inclinations of human nature, or about how good human life can be?

The grim realities depicted by "realists" may not be as objective as they imagine. Perhaps the grimness is a reflection of the painful, grim reality within the realist—an inner reality that, unconsciously, he finds it less painful to discover instead in the world at large as an inescapable fact of life.

The historical process described by the parable of the tribes has wounded us. We have been compelled to adapt to a world that, in fundamental ways, is hostile to us. T. W. Adorno has written that "it is part of the mechanism of domination to forbid recognition of the suffering it produces."[5] The more we are afraid to acknowledge our suffering, to confront the ways that our wounds have disabled us, the more truncated will be our vision of human possibilities.

There is a Yiddish saying, "The girl who can't dance says the band can't play." Many of us who have been wounded by the particular structures of power that surround us become "realists" who, because we have been disabled from dancing, believe the music of life is devoid of the rhythmic invitations and enchanting melodies that "utopians" imagine they hear.*

If the utopians can romanticize the past, the grim realists can be tone deaf to some of the strains of our humanity that gained expression in past societies but have been muted in

---

*Here is why the generations so often disagree on what is possible in human life. The young are generally the idealists, full of aspirations. The older are the realists, grimly aware of the usual fate of high aspirations. The young have a vested interest in *possibility*, for to accept the notion that "this is all there is" is to forfeit cherished hopes. The old have a vested interest in *impossibility*, for, with much of their lives behind them, to accept the notion that "human life could be much more" would be to endure the painful realization that their lives may have been, in some perspective, wasted.

Who is right? The old are right, at least in the narrow sense of "this is all you're likely to get in the world as it has been." As for the larger question of the inherent possibilities of human life, there is an old Sufi saying that "Thirst is the surest proof of the existence of water."

our present world. The past, even if it is not superior in total to the present, can nonetheless serve as a reminder of values we are neglecting and parts of ourselves with which we have lost contact.

There is no reason to assume that everything we have lost is an inevitable cost of everything we have gained. Worlds await our invention—but first we need to know enough about our real needs to know the "specs" to which a system might be designed.

If we become but a truncated part of ourselves, our understanding of the "good life" will hardly measure up to our inborn aspiration for real meaning and vitality. The particular system of dominance in which we are embedded—the market system that, like a magnet, draws us to see the world in terms of the lines of force it radiates—leads us to a particular form of truncation: the overly materialistic vision of what we are, what we need, and the nature of the planet we live on. When the beer ad tells us, "It doesn't get any better than this!" we are being sold more than an intoxicating beverage.

Earlier in this work, I spoke of the "deadness" of the matter we have piled up around us, and the deadness of the ideas with which we generally apprehend our material apparatus. It becomes dead to us because we ourselves have lost contact with the vibrancy of our own human spirit, and with the spiritual dimensions of our relationship with the world. Norman O. Brown writes: "We no longer give the surplus to God [as past cultures did]; the process of producing an ever-expanding surplus is itself now our God."[6] We have become alienated from any sense of the Whole of which we are part.

We have become idolaters. The problem with idolatry is not that it is offensive to some jealous God, who will punish our disloyalty. It is, rather, that it represents aspiration gone astray. It is the human spirit on a dead end path. Losing our way in a spiritual cul-de-sac, we cannot even imagine where else we might go. Daniel Bell asks, "If there is no commitment to economic growth, what can [an industrial society like ours] hold out as a social goal for its people?"[7] Is that not an astonishing question! This incapacity to imagine social goals of a qualitatively different kind seems like the same kind of crippling of the imaginative vision represented by the recent

widely acclaimed treatise (by Francis Fukuyama) that sees our form of society as "The End of History." We have left our unfortunate history behind and arrived in the promised land.*
The guide who can't see says there is no place further to go.

BIGGER VISION

In the introduction to this work, I spoke of the choice I experience between seeing and not seeing. The problem with seeing—being aware of all that is being destroyed, both within and around us—is that it hurts. Thus we turn away from the recognition of our suffering not only because the "mechanism of domination" forbids it, as Adorno suggests, but because we are afraid to confront our pain.

One might speculate as to why the mainstream of our culture is so remarkably lacking in a vibrant vision for our future. It is not, I would argue, because we are already in the promised land. The answer lies not in our obvious wealth but in the hidden dimensions of our impoverishment.

The denial of ourselves and of our experience—the suffering that goes unrecognized, and all the aspects of one's being that are connected with that suffering—breeds a kind of depression. To the depressed spirit, the future has no life. Among the depressed, writes David Michael Levin in *Pathologies of the Modern Self*, "the future can hold forth no promise of relief because, in effect, it is denied any reality." In our culture at large, Levin submits, our relation to temporality exhibits "a pattern strikingly similar to the pattern played out in individual depressions."[8] No wonder we cannot envision a future much more full of life than the present.

This is not to deny the genuine blessings of present-day life in America. A "typical American family" today—perhaps living in a middle-class American home, attending reasonable schools and graduating with college degrees, working at white collar or professional jobs, vacationing in comfortable and sometimes exotic places, attending a friendly church, getting

---

*In a famous passage, Max Weber described his contemporaries and the advanced civilization they had developed: "specialists without spirit, sensualists without heart; and this nullity is caught in the delusion that it has achieved a level of development never before attained by mankind" (quoted in Berman, *All That's Solid*, p. 27).

together with family and friends for occasional backyard bar-
becues, watching whichever seems most appealing from the
many television shows available on cable and videos available
at the video store, with drinkable water available at the turn of
a knob and electric power at the flip of a switch, with access to
good medical care, free of obstacles to information on virtually
any subject and free also to voice their opinions about it—by
historical standards has a great deal to be thankful for.

But it is my conviction that we are profoundly mistaken if
we buy the idea that it doesn't get any better than this. The
blessings are real. But the costs are hidden in the fine print of
our experience, which we can read only to the extent that we
resurrect our humanity and own all that we are.

If human life contains possibilities that far transcend our
present concept of the good life, we will have to extricate ourselves from the confines of our present consciousness. The human experiment is still young. History is far from its end. How
would we, caught in the thicket of our own particular time,
molded by a society with its own amalgam of blessings and
curses, discern the full magnitude of human possibilities.

There is a story in Colin Turnbull's admirable book, *The
Forest People*, that may serve as a metaphor. After living with a
band of Pygmies in the Ituri Forest in Africa, the anthropologist Turnbull departed from the Pygmies' jungle domain, driving away by car. With him he took one of the Pygmies who had
become a special friend. After a time, Turnbull and his jungle
friend left the forest and came to a point where a great expanse
opened before them. Turnbull writes:

> Then he saw the buffalo, still grazing lazily several miles
> away, far down below. He turned to me and said, "What
> insects are those?"
>
> At first I hardly understood; then I realized that in
> the forest the range of vision is so limited . . . Out here in
> the plains, however, Kenge [Turnbull's Pygmy friend] was
> looking for the first time over apparently unending miles
> of unending grasslands, with not a tree worth the name to
> give him any basis for comparison. The same thing hap-
> pened later on when I pointed out a boat in the middle of
> the lake. It was a large fishing boat with a number of peo-
> ple in it but Kenge at first refused to believe this. He
> thought it was a floating piece of wood.

. . . Kenge still did not believe, but he strained his eyes to see more clearly and asked what kind of buffalo were so small. I told him they were sometimes nearly twice the size of forest buffalo . . . He began scraping the mud off his arms and legs, no longer interested in such fantasies.[9]

As we attempt to envision how rich human life might be, we are like the Pygmy. It is in a world of narrow vision that we have learned to see. When we look back into past worlds to assess the domains of value that have been lost or eroded in our evolving market society—the bonds of community, the immediacy of the sacred in people's experience, the primacy of character and virtue in human development, the sense of unity and harmony between human society and the natural world— these domains look to us, in the short-sighted vision fostered by our society, like insignificant specks. ("What insects are those?") It is difficult for us to gain an adequate perspective.

When we contemplate what kind of future we might choose, were we free to shape our own destiny, we are apt to imagine only more of the same. The parts of ourselves that are already being fed will get more, and the parts that are being starved we can barely see. The human spirit—what each of us naturally is—is also far larger than we know.

The Sufi overhears the ants discussing God. "He is not at all like us," says one ant to another. "We have only two feelers. But He has four!"

If we lack the capacity to envision the full magnitude of the good life to which we human beings might aspire, how can we proceed? If our present consciousness does not give us an adequate perspective, how can we move to realize the possibilities we are disabled from comprehending? Are we trapped by a catch-22 kind of paradox?

We are not trapped, for there is a place to start the process of liberation. The beginning place is to understand the structural forces that bind us and drive us to a destiny of their choosing and not of ours. In this work, we have explored the structural dynamics of the market system of our economy as well as, to a lesser extent, the political system of our democratic polity and the intersocietal system of sovereign societies. To move toward a future we freely choose, we do not need to know much about our destination. It is sufficient to commence with the removal of the obstacles to human freedom. Simply work to restructure our systems to neutralize their power over us, and, with the passage of time, the true nature of our options will naturally unfold before our eyes.

These transformations—the reform of our systems and the expansion of our awareness—will not happen overnight. But each small step makes the next step possible. Each step we take to bring our systems under genuine human control helps us create a world where people can realize more of their humanity. And the more of ourselves we can reclaim from the magnet of our power systems, the more clearly we will see how vital a task it is—for the sake of all we value—that we restructure our world to protect our capacity for genuine choice.

Notes

INTRODUCTION (pp. 1–30)

1. Francis, Fukuyama, "The End of History," *The National Interest*, No. 16, Summer, 1989.

2. Marx, *Capital*, 1. p. 46.

3. Marx and Engles, *The Communist Manifesto*, p. 22.

4. See the dissertation version of *The Parable of the Tribes*, pp. available from (Ann Arbor, Mich.: University Microfilms) 1189–1217. 1977.

5. Galbraith, *Affluent Society*, p. 130.

CHAPTER 1 (pp. 37–44)

1. Kaysen in Hook, *Human Values*, p. 209.

2. Friedman and Friedman, *Free to Choose*, p. 12.

3. Ibid., p. 61.

4. Quoted from Thomas Flanagan, "Hayek on Property," p. 339.

5. Friedman and Friedman, *Free to Choose*, p. 13.

CHAPTER 2 (pp. 45–59)

1. von Mises, *Human Action*, p. 2.

2. See the discussion of the free market ideologue, Raymond Moley, in Scott, *In Pursuit of Happiness*, p. 157.

3. von Mises, *Human Action*, p. 10.

4. See the section "Artificial Wholeness: Justice as the Antidote to Power," in Schmookler, *Parable of the Tribes*, pp. 238–44.

5. Macpherson, *Political Theory of Possessive Individualism*, p. 3.

6. Ibid.

7. John Stuart Mill, "On Liberty," in Edwin A. Burtt, ed., p. 956.

8. Novak, Michael, *The Spirit of Democratic Capitalism*, p. 112.

9. Friedman and Friedman, *Free to Choose*, p. 32.

10. Ibid., p. 217.

11. Morris, "10 Million Tons of Rock Salt," p. C8.

CHAPTER 3 (pp. 60–72)

1. Polanyi, *Great Transformation*, p. 163.

2. Quoted in James Fallows, *More Like Us*, p. 109.

3. Polanyi, *Great Transformation*, p. 163.

4. Ibid, p. 164.

5. Schmookler, *Parable of the Tribes*, p. 21.

6. ABC Television *World News Tonight*, December 13, 1989.

7. Berry, *Home Economics*, p. 183–84.

8. Ibid, p. 185.

9. Ibid.

10. Ibid.

11. Herndon, "Local Land Trusts Flex New Muscle.", p. 13.

12. Ibid.

13. Collett, Merrill, "Bolivia Blazes Trail . . . to Where?" *Christian Science Monitor*, July 10, 1989, p. 4.

14. Fallows, *More Like Us*, p. 209.

15. Marchand, *Advertising the American Dream*, p. 356.

16. Ibid, p. 357.

17. Polanyi, *Great Transformation*, p. 46.

18. Ibid, p. 57.

CHAPTER 4 (pp. 73–94)

1. Friedman and Friedman, *Free to Choose*, p. 26.

2. Ibid.

3. Scott, *In Pursuit of Happiness*, p. 149.

4. Smith, *Wealth of Nations*, p. 14.

5. Friedman and Friedman, *Free to Choose*, p. 3.

6. Novak, *Spirit of Democratic Capitalism*, p. 90.

7. Locke, *Civil Government*, in Edwin A. Burtt, ed., paragraph number 93.

8. Adam Smith, quoted in Friedman and Friedman, *Free to Choose*, pp. 28–29.

9. Fallows, *More Like Us*, Chapter 7.

10. Quoted in Friedman and Friedman, *Free to Choose*, pp. 196–97.

11. Brad Knickerbocker, "Fight for Federal Lands Spreads," *Christian Science Monitor*, March 14, 1990, p. 7.

12. Preston, *Great American Blow-Up*, p. 50.

13. Ibid, p. 56.

14. Gold, *Advertising, Politics, and American Culture*, pp. 132–33.

15. Saying originated with the late Jesse Unruh, Democratic politician from California.

16. Friedman and Friedman, *Free to Choose*, p. 216.

17. Marx, *Machine in the Garden*, p. 16.

18. Friedman and Friedman, *Free to Choose*, p. 209.

CHAPTER 5 (pp. 95–107)

1. Locke, "An Essay Concerning the True Original, Extent and End of Civil Government," in Burtt, *English Philosophers from Bacon to Mill*, p. 415.

2. Ibid., p. 416.

3. Ibid.

4. Novak, in Block, Brennan, and Elzinga, *Morality of the Market*, p. 576.

5. Scitovsky, "Two Concepts of External Economies," in Arrow and Scitovsky, *Readings in Welfare Economics*, p. 250.

6. Popper and Popper, "Saving the Plains," p. B3.

7. Berry, *Home Economics*, p. 128.

8. Ibid.

9. Repetto, "No Accounting for Pollution," p. B5.

10. Friedman and Friedman, *Free to Choose*, p. 218.

11. Novak in Block, Brennan, and Elzinga, *Morality of the Market*, p. 576.

12. This image was used in a kindred context by David Orr in the *Arkansas Gazette*, January 12, 1990.

CHAPTER 6 (pp. 108–120)

1. Stanley Diamond in Montagu, 1968 *Concept of the Primitive*, p. 127.

2. Berman, *All That Is Solid Melts Into Air*, p. 61.

3. Ibid., p. 78.

4. Mukerji, *From Graven Images*, p. 260.

5. Quoted in Montagu, *Touching*, pp. 124–25.

6. Williams, *Dream Worlds*, p. 98.

7. Belk, "Third World Consumer Culture," ms. p. 24.

8. William Ellis, personal communication.

9. Rostow, *Politics and the Stages of Growth*, p. 95.

10. David Kaplan, in Sahlins and Service, *Evolution and Culture*, p. 90.

11. Marlise Simons, "West Germans Get Ready to Scrub," p. A6.

12. Arnold Toynbee, in Urban, *Can We Survive Our Future: A Symposium*, p. 42.

CHAPTER 7 (pp. 127–132)

1. On these matters, Robert Bellah is a good source, both in his work *The Broken Covenant* and in the more recently coauthored work, *Habits of the Heart*.

2. Francis, David R. "As the economy goes, so goes the nation, this analyst indicates," *Christian Science Monitor*, February 16, 1988, p. 18.

3. Bellah, *Broken Covenant*, p. 65.

4. Shi, *Simple Life*, p. 23.

5. Ibid.

6. Ibid., p. 67.

7. Ibid.

8. Bell, *Cultural Contradictions of Capitalism*, p. 58.

9. Bellah, *Broken Covenant*, p. 72.

10. Schama, *Embarrassment of Riches*, p. 327.

11. Ibid., p. 331.

12. Ibid.

13. Ibid.

14. Williams, *Dream Worlds*, p. 66.

15. Ibid.

CHAPTER 8 (pp. 133–143)

1. Shi, *Simple Life*, p. 21.

2. Ibid., p. 35.

3. Rom. 7:19, 22–23.

4. Shi, *Simple Life*, p. 35.

5. Horowitz, *Morality of Spending*, p. 108.

6. Ibid., p. 5.

7. Slater, *Pursuit of Loneliness*, pp. 6–7.

8. Quoted in Shi, *Simple Life*, p. 102.

9. Quoted in ibid., p. 155.

10. Mukerji, *From Graven Images*, p. 261.

11. Bellah, *Broken Covenant*, p. 69 (italics added).

CHAPTER 9 (pp. 144–155)

1. Horowitz, *Morality of Spending*, p. xxii.

2. Lynn, *Dream of Success*, p. 7.

3. Cawelti, *Apostles of the Self-Made Man*, p. 195.

4. Ibid., p. 5.

5. Ibid., p. 182.

6. John Graham, quoted in Cawelti, *Apostles of the Self-Made Man*, p. 182.

7. Russell Conwell, quoted in ibid., p. 186.

8. Conwell, quoted in ibid., p. 188.

9. Cawelti, ibid., p. 177.

10. Lynn, *Dream of Success*, p. 7.

11. Heilbroner, *Quest for Wealth*, p. 88.

12. Bellah, *Broken Covenant*, p. 76.

13. Quoted in ibid.

14. Conwell, quoted in Cawelti, *Apostles of the Self-Made Man*, p. 186.

15. Charles Perkins, quoted in Cawelti, *Apostles of the Self-Made Man*, p. 187.

16. William Lawrence, quoted both in Heilbroner, *Quest for Wealth*, p. 200, and Bellah, *Broken Covenant*, p. 76.

17. Cawelti, *Apostles of the Self-Made Man*, p. 211.

18. Ibid.

19. Cf. Russell Belk, "Worldly Possessions," p. 7.

20. McKendrick, Brewer, and Plumb, *Birth of a Consumer Society*, p. 9.

21. Horowitz, *Morality of Spending*, p. xxvii.

22. Bell, *Cultural Contradictions of Capitalism*, p. 70.

23. Galbraith, *Affluent Society*, p. 171.

24. Fallows, *More Like Us*, p. 42.

25. Levy and Michel, "Why America Won't Save," p. C–1.

26. Samuel Butler quoted in Auden and Kronenberger, 1966, p. 367.

27. Ibid., p. C–2.

28. Schumacher, *Small is Beautiful*, p. 293.

29. Mukerji, *From Graven Images*, p. 33.

30. Ibid., p. 9.

31. Cawelti, *Apostles of the Self-Made Man*, p. 169.

32. Schumacher, *Small is Beautiful*, p. 293.

33. Heilbroner, *Quest for Wealth*, p. 200.

CHAPTER 10 (pp. 156–172)

1. Oscar Wilde, in Borges, Jorge Luis and Adolfo Bioy Casares, eds.

2. Fyodor Dostoyevski, *The Brothers Karamazov*, Part I, Book V, Chapter 5.

3. Shi, *Simple Life*, p. 34.

4. Ibid., p. 48.

5. Berman, *All That Is Solid*, p. 66.

6. Ibid., p. 67.

7. Johann Wolfgang von Goethe, *Faust*, lines 11239–52, quoted in Berman, *All That Is Solid*, p. 67.

8. Ibid.

9. Polanyi, *Great Transformation*, p. 172.

10. Ibid.

11. Will, "Real Game,", p. A19.

12. Quoted in Marchand, *Advertising the American Dream*, p. 31.

13. Will, "Bombarded by Ads," p. C7.

14. Marchand, *Advertising the American Dream*, p. xxi.

15. Rowe, "America Needs *Perestroika* for Ads," p. 13.

16. Ibid.

17. Schudson, *Advertising*, p. 235.

18. Schwartz, *Battle for Human Nature*, p. 257.

19. Ewen, and Ewen, *Channels of Desire*, p. 66.

20. Ibid.

21. Williamson, *Consuming Passions*, p. 11.

22. Ibid.

23. Goldberg, "Free Market Economics," , p. H1.

24. Ibid.

25. Jimmy Carter, quoted in David Shi, *Simple Life*, p. 271.

26. Ibid., p. 272.

PART III: INTRODUCTION (pp. 173–180)

1. Alex Inkeles, quoted in Berman, *All That Is Solid*, p. 26.

2. Ibid., p. 27.

3. Ibid., p. 165.

4. Ibid.

5. Ibid.

6. Ibid., p. 166.

7. Ibid.

8. This phenomenon of identification with the aggressor is discussed in two of my previous books: *Out of Weakness* and *Sowings and Reapings*.

CHAPTER 11 (pp. 181–209)

1. Berle and Means *Modern Corporation*, pp. 80–82 (italics in original).

2. Ibid., p. 82.

3. Ibid.

4. 1st Quarter Report, "Letter to Our Shareholders," March 31, 1990, Citizens Security Group, Inc.

5. Berle and Means, *Modern Corporation*, p. xxi.

6. *Corporate Examiner* 16, no. 8–9 (Spring 1987): p. 12.

CHAPTER 12 (pp. 210–237)

1. Mishan, *Economic Growth Debate*, p. 26.

2. Sahlins, *Culture and Practical Reason*, p. 221.

3. This is discussed in Daly *Steady-State Economics*, on, e.g., p. 102.

4. Galbraith, *Affluent Society*, p. 116

5. Daly, *Steady-State Economics*, p. 99.

6. Friedman and Friedman, *Free to Choose*, p. 191.

7. "Warring States Anecdote," in *Ancient Chinese Fables*, edited and trans. Yang Hsien-Yi and Gladys Yang (Peking; Foreign Language Press, 1957).

8. Abramowitz, "Economic Growth," , pp. 6–7.

9. Freedman, *Happy People,*, pp. 134–135.

10. Frank, *Choosing the Right Pond*, p. 12.

11. Adolf Lowe, quoted in Kassiola, *Death of Industrial Civilization*, p. 74

12. Ibid. (emphasis added), p. 12.

13. Statistics from the Bureau of Labor Statistics, by telephone. See also *The Statistical Abstract of the United States*, 1990, #695.

14. Frank, *Choosing the Right Pond*, p. 31.

15. E.g., Frank, *Choosing the Right Pond,*; Wachtel, *Poverty of Affluence*; Abramowitz, "Economic Growth".

16. Heilbroner, *Quest for Wealth*, p. 248.

17. Slater, *Wealth Addiction*, p. 95.

18. Festinger, Riecken, and Schachter, *When Prophecy Fails*, p. 27.

19. Ibid.

20. See especially Campbell.

21. Daly, *Steady-State Economics*, p. 17.

22. Ibid., p. 126.

23. Slater, *Wealth Addition*, p. 12.

24. Sahlins, *Stone Age Economics*, 1972, p. 1.

25. Joseph Hirschorn, quoted in Slater, *Wealth Addiction*, p. 95.

26. Ewen, *All Consuming Images*, p. 239.

27. Marchand, *Advertising the American Dream*, p. 162.

28. Ibid.

29. Howard Dickinson, of the George Patten Agency, quoted in Ibid.

30. Ibid., p. 244.

31. Quoted in ibid., p. 245.

32. Ralph Waldo Emerson, "Ode Inscribed to W. H. Channing"

33. Jeremy Bentram, quoted in Polanyi, *Great Transformation*, p. 117.

CHAPTER 13 (pp. 238–290)

1. Adam Smith, *The Wealth of Nations*, p. 12.

2. MacNeil/Lehrer News Hour, June 26, 1989.

3. Reuss, "U.S. Faces Challenge," p. 1.

4. Kennedy, p. xxiii.

5. Ibid.

6. Quoted by Paul Kennedy, in James Joll, p. *New York Review of Books*, ... , p. 38.

6.5. Darman, *Keeping America*, p. 7.

7. Fallows, *More Like Us*, p. 9.

8. Fallows, "America's Secret Weapon," p. D2.

9. Fallows, *More Like Us*, p. 11.

10. Mishan, *Economic Growth Debate*, p. 27.

11. Ibid., p. 27.

12. Lester Thurow, on *The Nightly Business Report*, June 1, 1989.

13. "World News Tonight," ABC News, February 22, 1989.

14. Morishima, *Why Has Japan 'Succeeded'?* p. 106.

15. H. D. Thoreau, *Walden*, pp. 109, 110.

16. "World News Tonight," ABC News, February 2, 1989.

17. Morishima, *Why Has Japan 'Succeeded'?* p. 183 (emphasis added).

18. Kennedy, *Rise and Fall*, p. 465.

19. Ibid.

20. Dalton, *Economic Systems*, p. 104.

21. Nevins, *Study in Power*, viii–ix.

22. Berman, *All That Is Solid*, p. 191.

23. Ibid.

24. Morishima, *Why Has Japan 'Succeeded'?*, p. 51.

25. Ibid., p. 16.

26. Ibid., p. 53.

27. Nicolai Shmelev, quoted in Kaiser, "Beyond the Summit," C1.

28. Kennedy, *Rise and Fall.*, p. xxii (emphasis in original).

29. Ibid., p. xvi (emphasis in original).

30. Ibid., p. 537.

31. Ibid.

32. Quoted in ibid., p. 465.

33. Fallows, *More Like Us*, p. 6.

34. Berlin, "Machiavelli," p. 26.

35. Lynn, "Anxiety and Economic Growth."

36. Mishan, *Economic Growth Debate*, p. 263.

37. Macpherson, *Political Theory of Possessive Individualism*, p. 59.

38. From personal conversation with officer in U.S. Department of Labor directly involved with such matters.

39. Slater, *Wealth Addiction*, p. 76.

40. John D. Rockefeller, quoted in ibid.

41. Ibid.

42. Henry Ford, quoted in Ibid.

CONCLUSION (pp. 291–306)

1. Fernand Braudel, quoted in McKendrick, Brewer, and Plumb, *Birth of a Consumer Society*, pp. 30–31.

2. Novak, *Spirit of Democratic Capitalism*, p. 24.

3. Moffett, "Israel Urges End to Nomadic Life," p. 4.

4. Ibid.

5. T. W. Adorno, quoted in Levin, *Pathologies of the Modern Self*, p. 19.

6. Brown, *Life Against Death*, p. 261.

7. Bell, *Cultural Contradictions of Capitalism*, p. 238.

8. Levin, *Pathologies of the Modern Self*, p. 493.

9. Turnbull, *Forest People*, pp. 252–53.

Bibliography

Abercrombie, Nicholas. *The Sovereign Individuals of Capitalism*. London: Allen and Unwin, 1986.

Abramowitz, Moses. "Economic Growth and Its Discontents." In *Economics and Human Welfare*. See Boskin 1979.

Andren, Gunnar, Larso O. Ericcson, Ragnar Ohlsson, and Torbjorn Tannsjo. *Rhetoric and Ideology in Advertising: A Content Analytical Study of American Advertising*. Stockholm: LiberForlag, 1978.

Appadurai, Arjun, *The Social Life of Things: Commodities in Cultural Perspective*. Cambridge: Cambridge University Press, 1986.

Arnold, Thurman W. *The Folklore of Capitalism*. New Haven: Yale University Press, 1937.

Arrow, Kenneth J., and Tibor Scitovsky, eds. *Readings in Welfare Economics*. Hollywood, Ill.: Richard D. Irwin, Inc., 1969.

Barber, Benjamin. "What Do 47-Year-Olds Know?" *New York Times*, December 26, 1987.

Barfield, Owen. *Saving the Appearances: A Study in Idolatry*. London: Faber and Faber, 1957.

Barol, Bill. "The Eighties Are Over." *Newsweek*, January 4, 1988.

321

Barrett, William. *The Illusion of Technique: A Search for Meaning in a Technological Civilization.* Garden City, N.Y.: Anchor Press, 1978.

Bateson, Gregory. *Steps to an Ecology of Mind.* New York: Ballantine Books, 1972.

Belk, Russell W. "Cultural and Historical Differences in Concepts of Self and their Effects on Attitudes Toward Having and Giving." MS.

————. "Materialism and Status Appeals in Japanese and US Print Advertising." *International Marketing Review*, Winter 1985.

————. "Materialism: Trait Aspects of Living in the Material World." *Journal of Consumer Research* 12 (December 1985).

————. "Possessions and the Extended Self." *Ms.*

————. "Third World Consumer Culture." *Research in Marketing* supp. 4 (1988).

————. "Worldly Possessions: Issues and Criticisms." MS.

Belk, Russell W., and Richard W. Pollay. "Images of Ourselves: The Good Life in Twentieth Century Advertising." *Journal of Consumer Research* 11 (March 1985).

Belk, Richard W., and Melanie Wallendorf. "The Sacred Meaning of Money." MS.

Bell, Daniel. *The Cultural Contradictions of Capitalism.* New York: Basic Books, 1976.

Bellah, Robert N. *The Broken Covenant.* MS.

Bellah, Robert N., Richard Madsen, William M. Sullivan, Ann Swidler, and Steven M. Tipton. *Habits of the Heart: Individualism and Commitment in American Life.* New York: Harper and Row, 1985.

Belsie, Laurent. "Water Quality Emerges as Key Issue." *Christian Science Monitor.* June 9, 1989.

Berle, Adolf A., and Gardiner C. Means. *The Modern Corporation and Private Property.* New York: Harcourt, Brace and World, 1968.

Berlin, Isaiah. "The Question of Machiavelli," *New York Review of Books,* November 4, 1972.

Berlow, Alan. "Ballots and Bullets." *The New Republic,* June 4, 1990.

Berman, Marshall. *All That Is Solid Melts Into Air: The Experience of Modernity.* New York: Simon and Schuster, 1982.

Berry, Wendell. *Home Economics.* San Francisco: North Point Press, 1987.

————. "The Profit in Work's Pleasure." *Harper's,* March 1988.

Block, Walter, Geoffrey Brennan, and Kenneth Elzinga, eds. *The Morality of the Market: Religious and Economic Perspectives.* The Fraser Institute, 1985.

Blum, Jeffrey D. *Living with Spirit in a Material World.* New York; Fawcett Columbine, 1988.

Borges, Jorge Luis and Adolfo Bioy Casares, eds. *Extraordinary Tales.* New York: Herder and Herder, 1971.

Bornemann, Ernest. *The Psychoanalysis of Money.* New York: Urizen Books, 1976.

Boskin, Michael J., ed. *Economics and Human Welfare.* New York: Academic Press, 1979.

Boulding, Kenneth. "Comment." In *Morality of the Market.* See Block 1985.

Braudel, Fernand. *Capitalism and Material Life, 1400–1800.* London; Fontana/Collins, 1974.

Brennan, Geoffrey. "Markets and Majorities, Morals and Madness." In *Morality of the Market.* See Block 1985.

Brooks, John. *Showing Off in America.* Boston: Little Brown, 1981.

Brown, Norman O. *Life Against Death.* Middletown, Ct.: Wesleyan University Press, 1985.

Brownstein, Ronald, and Nina J. Easton. "The New Status Seekers." *Los Angeles Times Magazine,* December 27, 1987.

Burtt, Edwin A. ed. *The English Philosophers From Bacon to Mill.* New York: Modern Library, 1939.

Butterfield, Stephen T. "Keeping A Short Bridge: Buddhist-Christian Dialogue." *The Sun,* (Chapel Hill, N.C.) October 1988.

Burlow, Alan. "Ballots and Bullets." *New Republic,* June 4, 1990.

Cabot, Robert, and Robert Fuller. "Empire's End, Russia's Rebirth." *Harvard Magazine,* May–June 1991.

Campbell, Colin. *The Romantic Ethic and the Spirit of Modern Consumerism.* New York: B. Blackwell, 1987.

Carnegie, Andrew. *The Gospel of Wealth*. Cambridge, Mass.: Harvard University Press, 1962.

Carpenter, Edmund. *Oh, What a Blow that Phantom Gave Me!*. New York: Holt, Rinehart and Winston, 1973.

Cavanaugh, John Francis. *Following Christ in a Consumer Society*. Maryknoll, N.Y.: Orbis Books, 1981.

Cawelti, John G. *Apostles of the Self-Made Man*. Chicago: University of Chicago Press, 1965.

Center for Science in the Public Interest. "Kids are as Aware of Booze as Presidents, Survey Finds." News Release, September 4, 1989.

Clark, Eric. *The Want Makers: The World of Advertising: How They Make you Buy*. New York: Viking, 1988.

Collett, Lily. "Step by step: A skeptic's encounter with the Twelve-Step program." *Utne Reader*, November–December, 1988.

Collett, Merrill. "Bolivia Blazes Trail. . . . to Where?" *Christian Science Monitor*, July 10, 1989.

Collins, Ronald K. L., and Michael F. Jacboson. "Commericalization Versus Culture." *Christian Science Monitor*, September 19, 1990.

The Corporate Examiner (The Interfaith Center on Corporate Responsibility, New York), 16, no. 8–9 (Spring 1987).

Czikszentmihalyi, Mihaly, and Eugene Rochberg-Halton. *The Meaning of Things: Domestic Symbols and the Self*. Cambridge: Cambridge University Press, 1981.

Dalton, George. *Economic Systems and Society: Capitalism, Communism and the Third World*. Middlesex, England: Penguin, 1974.

Daly, Herman E. "The Economic Growth Debate: What Some Economists Have Learned but Many Have Not." *Journal of Environmental Economics and Management* 14, (1987): 323–36.

——— . *Steady-State Economics: The Economics of Biophysical Equilibrium and Moral Growth*. San Francisco: W. H. Freeman, 1977.

Darman, Richard. *Keeping America First: American Romanticism and the Global Economy*. Washington, D.C.: Office of Management and Budget, 1990.

Doi, Ayako. " 'America-Bashing,' Japanese Style." *Washington Post*, July 6, 1989.

Dostoyevski, Fyodor *The Brothers Karamazov*, New York: Modern Library, 1973.

Douglas, Mary, and Baron Isherwood. *The World of Goods*. New York: Basic Books, 1979.

Easterlin, R. A. "Does Economic Growth Improve the Human Lot?" in P. A. David and M. W. Reder, eds. *Nations and Households in Economic Growth*. New York: Academic Press, 1974.

Elderkin, Phil. "Baseball Brew." *Christian Science Monitor*, July 27, 1988.

Elgin, Duane. *Voluntary Simplicity: An Ecological Lifestyle that Promises Personal and Social Renewal*. New York: Bantam Books, 1987.

Ellul, Jacques. *Money and Power*. Downers Grove, Ill.: Inter-Varsity Press, 1984.

Erasmus. *The Enchiridion*. translated and edited by Raymond Himelick, New York: Oxford University Press, 1981.

"Ethics and Corporate Goals." *Good Money: The Newsletter for Socially Concerned Investors*, May–June 1988.

Etzioni, Amitai. *The Moral Dimension: Toward a New Economics*. New York: Free Press, 1988.

Ewen, Stuart. *All Consuming Images: The Politics of Style in Contemporary Culture*. New York: Basic Books, 1988.

Ewen, Stuart, and Elizabeth Ewen. *Channels of Desire: Mass Images and the Shaping of American Consciousness*. New York: McGraw-Hill, 1982.

Faber, M. D. *Culture and Consciousness: The Social Meaning of Altered Awareness*. New York: Human Sciences Press, 1981.

Fallows, James. "America's Secret Weapon is America." *Washington Post*, March 26, 1989.

——— . "Japan: Playing by Different Rules." *The Atlantic*, September 1987.

——— . *More Like Us: Making America Great Again*. Boston: Houghton Mifflin, 1989.

Festinger, Leon, Henry W. Riecken, and Stanley Schachter. *When Prophecy Fails*. New York: Harper and Row, 1956.

Findhorn Community. *The Individual and the Collective.* Conference Newsletter, October 21, 1988.

Flanagan, T. E. "Hayek on Property." In *Theories of Property.* See Parel 1979.

Foster, Richard J. *Money, Sex and Power: The Challenge of the Disciplined Life.* San Francisco: Harper and Row, 1985.

Fowler, Jan. "Deep Ecology I: Relation to Image Finding." *Path Words,* Sevenoaks Pathwork Center, December, 1987.

Fox, Richard Wightman, and T. J. Jackson Lears, eds. *The Culture of Consumption: Critical Essays in American Histotry.* New York: Pantheon Books, 1983.

Francis, David R. "As the Economy Goes, So Goes the Nation, This Analyst Indicates." *Christian Science Monitor,* February 16, 1988.

Frank, Robert H. *Choosing the Right Pond: Human Behavior and the Quest for Status.* New York: Oxford University Press, 1985.

Freedman, Jonathan L. *Happy People.* New York: Harcourt Brace Jovanovich, 1978.

Friedman, Milton and Rose Friedman. *Free to Choose.* New York: Harcourt Brace Jovanovich, 1980.

Fukuyama, Francis. "The End of History." *The National Interest,* No. 16, Summer, 1989.

Galbraith, John Kenneth. *The Affluent Society.* Boston: Houghton Mifflin, 1971.

Gardner, Marilyn. "Rent-a-Family—The Latest Service Industry." *Christian Science Monitor,* May 16, 1989.

Gendlin, Eugene T. "A Philosophical Critique of the Concept of Narcissism: The Significance of the Awareness Movement." In *Technologies of the Modern Self.* See Levin 1987.

Gibbs, Nancy. "Workers are Weary, Parents Are Frantic, and Even Children Haven't a Minute to Spare." *Time,* April 24, 1989.

Gold, Philip. *Advertising, Politics, and American Culture: From Salesmanship to Therapy.* New York: Paragon House, 1987.

Goldberg, Jeffrey. "Free Market Economics, Old Testament Morality." *Washington Post,* October 23, 1988.

Goodman, Ellen. "Families Under Separate Roofs." *Washington Post*, September 8, 1990.

————. "Mortality is Not the Option of Choice." *Baltimore Sun*, April 29, 1988.

Grossman, Richard. *Earth Island Journal*, Spring 1987.

————. "Growth as Metaphor, Growth as Politics." *The Wrenching Debate Gazette*, July 1985.

Guenon, Rene. *The Reign of Quantity and the Signs of the Times*. London: Luzac, 1953.

Heilbroner, Robert L. *The Quest for Wealth*. New York: Simon and Schuster, 1956.

Hendin, Herbert. *The Age of Sensation*. New York: W. W. Norton, 1975.

Herndon, Nancy. "Local Land Trusts Flex New Muscle." *Christian Science Monitor*, June 7, 1989.

Hiatt, Fred, and Margaret Shapiro. "Japan's New Era: Sudden Riches Creating Conflict and Self-Doubt." *Washington Post*, February 11, 1990.

Hoffman, Eva. *Lost in Translation: A Life in a New Language*. New York: E. P. Dutton, 1989.

Hollis, Martin, and Edward J. Nell. *Rational Economic Man: A Philosophical Critique of Neo-Classical Economics*. London: Cambridge University Press, 1975.

Hollowell, Peter G. *Property and Social Relations*. London: Routlege and Kegan Paul, 1982.

Hook, Sidney, ed. *Human Values and Economic Policy: A Symposium*. New York: New York University Press, 1967.

Horney, Karen. *The Neurotic Personality of Our Time*. New York: W. W. Norton, 1937.

Horowitz, Daniel. *The Morality of Spending: Attitudes toward the Consumer Society in America, 1875–1940*. Baltimore: Johns Hopkins University Press, 1985.

Hostetler, John A. *Amish Society*. Baltimore: Johns Hopkins University Press, 1968.

Howe, Kenneth. "Wells Chairman Rated Top Calfornia Banker." *San Francisco Chronicle*, October 13, 1989.

Hughes, John. "Moscow's Consumer Revolution." *Christian Science Monitor*, September 15, 1989.

Johnson, Don Hanlon. "The Possibility of a Social Body" MS.

Joll, James. "The Cost of Bigness." *New York Review of Books*, February 4, 1988.

Kaiser, Robert G. "Beyond the Summit: The New Red Revolution." *Washington Post*, May 29, 1988.

————. "Red Intrigue: How Gorbachev Outfoxed his Kremlin Rivals." *Washington Post*, June 12, 1988.

Kassiola, Joel Jay. *The Death of Industrial Civilization: The Limits to Economic Growth and the Repoliticization of Advanced Industrial Society.* Albany: State University of New York Press, 1990.

Kendall, Willmoore. "Social Contract." *International Encyclopedia of Social Sciences.* New York: Macmillan, 1967.

Kennedy, Paul. *The Rise and Fall of the Great Powers: Economic Change and Military Conflict from 1500 to 2000.* New York: Vintage Books, 1987.

Klein, Melanie. *Envy and Gratitude.* New York: Delcore Press, 1975.

Klinkenborg, Verlyn. Review of *Killing Mr. Watson*, by Peter Matthiessen, *New Republic*, November 5, 1990.

Knickerbocker, Brad. "Fight for Federal Lands Spreads," *Christian Science Monitor*, March 14, 1990, p. 7.

Laszlo, Ervin. *The Inner Limits of Mankind: Heretical Reflections on Today's Values, Culture and Politics.* Oxford: Pergamon Press, 1978.

Lears, Thomas Jackson. *No Place of Grace: Antimodernism and the Transformation of American Culture 1880–1920.* New York: Pantheon Books, 1981.

Leiss, William. *The Limits to Satisfaction: An Essay on the Problem of Needs and Commodities.* Toronto: University of Toronto Press, 1976.

Levin, David Michael. *The Body's Recollection of Being.* London: Routledge and Kegan Paul, 1985.

————. "Clinical Stories: A Modern Self in the Fury of Being." In *Pathologies of the Modern Self*. See Levin 1987.

————. "Psychopathology in the Epoch of Nihilism." In *Pathologies of the Modern Self*. See Levin 1987.

————. ed. *Pathologies of the Modern Self: Postmodern Studies on Narcissism, Schizophrenia, and Depression*. New York: New York University Press, 1987.

Levy, Frank, and Richard C. Michel. "Why America Won't Save." *Washington Post*, February 4, 1990.

Liedloff, Jean. *The Continuum Concept: Allowing Human Nature to Work Successfully*. Reading, Mass.: Addison-Wesley, 1985.

Linden, Eugene. *Affluence and Discontent: The Anatomy of Consumer Societies*. New York: Viking Press, 1979.

Linder, Staffan Burenstam. *The Harried Leisure Class*. New York: Columbia University Press, 1970.

Lindgren, Henry Clay. *Great Expectations: The Psychology of Money*. Los Altos, Calif.: William Kaufmann, 1980.

Lowen, Alexander. *Depression and the Body*. New York: Coward, McCann and Geoghegan, 1973.

Lynn, Kenneth S. *The Dream of Success: A Study of the Modern American Imagination*. Boston: Atlantic Monthly Press, 1955.

Lynn, R. "Anxiety and Economic Growth," *Nature*, 219 (1968).

McCracken, Grant. *Culture and Consumption: New Approaches to the Symbolic Character of Consumer Goods and Activities*. Bloomington: Indiana University Press, 1988.

McKendrick, Neil, John Brewer, and J. H. Plumb. *The Birth of a Consumer Society: The Commericalization of Eighteenth-Century England*. Bloomington: Indiana University Press, 1985.

Macpherson, C. B.. *The Political Theory of Possessive Individualism: Hobbes to Locke*. Oxford: Clarendon Press, 1962.

————. "Property as Means or End." In *Theories of Property*. See Parel 1979.

"Madonna sells her soul for a song." *Boston Globe*, March 2, 1989.

Mandeville, Bernard. *The Fable of the Bees*. In Louis I. Bredvold, Alan D. McKillop, and Lois Whitney, eds., *Eighteenth Century Poetry and Prose*. 2d. ed. New York: Ronald Press, 1956.

Marcel, Gabriel, *Being and Having: An Existentialist Diary*, Harper and Row, New York, 1965.

Marchand, Roland. *Advertising the American Dream: Making Way for Modernity, 1920–1940.* Berkeley and Los Angeles: University of California Press, 1985.

Martin, David. "Comment." In *Morality of the Market.* See Block 1985.

Marx, Karl. *Capital: A Critique of Political Economy.* New York: Modern Library, 1906.

Marx, Leo. *The Machine in the Garden: Technology and the Pastoral Ideal in America.* New York: Oxford University Press, 1964.

Milbrath, Lester W. *Envisioning a Sustainable Society: Learning Our Way Out.* Albany: SUNY Press, 1989.

Miller, Alice. *The Drama of the Gifted Child.* New York: Basic Books, 1981.

————. *Thou Shalt Not Be Aware: Society's Betrayal of the Child.* New York: Farrar, Straus and Giroux, 1984.

Mises, Ludwig von. *The Anti-Capitalistic Mentality.* New York: Van Nostrand Reinhold, 1956.

———— *Human Action; A Treatise on Economics.* New Haven: Yale University Press, 1949.

Mishan, Ezra J. *The Economic Growth Debate.* London: George Allen and Unwin, 1977.

————. "Religion, Culture and Technology." In *Morality of the Market.* See Block 1985.

Moffett, George D. III. "Israel Urges End to Nomadic Life." *Christian Science Monitor,* October 31, 1989.

Montagu, Ashley. *The American Way of Life,* New York: G. P. Putnam's Sons, 1967.

————. *The Concept of the Primitive,* New York: Free Press, 1968.

————. *Touching: The Human Significance of the Skin.* New York: Harper and Row, 1978.

Montagu, Ashley, and Floyd Matson. *The Dehumanization of Man.* New York: McGraw-Hill, 1983.

Morishima, Michio. *Why Has Japan 'Succeeded'? Western Technology and the Japanese Ethos.* Cambridge: Cambridge University Press, 1982.

Morris, David. "Two Million Tons of Rock Salt." *Washington Post,* January 17, 1988.

Mukerji, Chandra. *From Graven Images: Patterns of Modern Materialism.* New York: Columbia University Press, 1983.

Nevins, Allen. *Study in Power: John D. Rockefeller, Industrialist and Philanthropist,* Vol. I, New York: Charles Scribner's Sons, 1953.

Norton, David L. *Personal Destinies: A Philosophy of Ethical Individualism.* Princeton, N.J.: Princeton University Press, 1976.

Novak, Michael. "Overview." In *Morality of the Market.* See Block 1985.

————. *The Spirit of Democratic Capitalism.* New York: Simon and Schuster, 1982.

Orr, David. "Pascal's Wager," *Arkansas Gazette,* January 12, 1990.

Parel, Anthony, and Thomas Flanagan, eds. *Theories of Property: Aristotle to the Present.* Waterloo, Ont.: Wilfrid Laurier University Press, 1979.

Percy, Walker. *The Message in the Bottle.* New York: Farrar, Straus and Giroux, 1975.

Perrin, Pat, and Wim Coleman. "Is Addiction Actually a Misguided Move toward Wholeness?" *Utne Reader,* November–December 1988.

Polanyi, Karl. *The Great Transformation.* New York: Farrar and Rinehart, 1944.

Popper, Frank J., and Deborah Epstein Popper, "Saving the Plains: The Bison Gambit." *Washington Post,* August 6, 1989.

Potter, David M. *People of Plenty: Economic Abundance and the American Character.* Chicago: University of Chicago Press, 1954.

Preston, Ivan L. *The Great American Blow-Up: Puffery in Advertising and Selling.* Madison: University of Wisconsin Press, 1975.

Reich, Robert B. "Who is Us?" *Harvard Business Review* Vol. 90, No. 1, January–February, 1990.

Repetto, Robert "No Accounting for Polution." *Washington Post,* May 28, 1989.

Rezzori, Gregor von. "A Stranger in Lolitaland." In *The Best American Essays.* See Talese 1987.

Reuss, Ronald. "U.S. Faces Challenge to Maintain Its Standard of Living." *Piper Market Digest* (Piper, Jaffray and Hopwood), March 1990.

Rostow, W. W. *Politics and the Stages of Growth.* Cambridge: Cambridge University Press, 1971.

Rowe, Jonathan. "Advertising and Children's TV." *Christian Science Monitor,* January 29, 1987.

———. "America Needs *Perestroika* for Ads." *Christian Science Monitor,* April 25, 1990.

———. "Gauging the Impact of Advertising." *Christian Science Monitor,* January 28, 1987.

Rudmin, Floyd W. "The Meaning and Morality of Voluntary Simplicity." manuscript.

Ryan, Alan. "Distrusting Economics." *The New York Review of Books,* May 18, 1989.

Sagoff, Mark. "Property Rights and Environmental Law." *Philosophy and Public Policy,* Vol. 8, No. 2, Spring, 1988.

Sahlins, Marshall. *Culture and Practical Reason.* Chicago: University of Chicago Press, 1976.

———. "Social Science, Or the Tragic Western Sense of Human Imperfection." manuscript.

Sahlins, Marshall. *Stone Age Economics.* Chicago: Aldine Atherton, 1972.

Sahlins, Marshall, and Elman R. Service, eds. *Evolution and Culture.* Ann Arbor: University of Michigan Press, 1960.

Sampson, Edward E. "The Challenge of Social Change for Psychology." *American Psychologist* Vol. 44, No. 6, June 1989.

Satin, Mark. "Breaking the Hold of Television Advertising." *New Options,* December 26, 1988.

Schaef, Anne Wilson. *When Society Becomes An Addict.* San Francisco: Harper and Row, 1987.

Schama, Simon. *The Embarassment of Riches: An Interpretation of Dutch Culture in the Golden Age.* New York: Alfred A. Knopf, 1987.

Schmookler, Andrew Bard. *Out of Weakness: Healing the Wounds that Drive Us to War.* New York: Bantam Books, 1988.

————. *The Parable of the Tribes: The Problem of Power in Social Evolution.* Berkeley, and Los Angeles: University of California Press, 1984.

————. *Sowings and Reapings: The Cycling of Good and Evil in the Human System.* Indianapolis: Knowledge Systems, 1989.

Schudson, Michael. *Advertising, the Uneasy Persuasion: Its Dubious Impact on American Society.* New York: Basic Books, 1984.

Schumacher, E. F. *Small Is Beautiful.* New York: Harper and Row, 1973.

Schwartz, Barry. *The Battle for Human Nature: Science, Morality and Modern Life.* New York: W. W. Norton, 1986.

Scitovsky, Tibor. *The Joyless Economy: An Inquiry into Human Satisfaction and Consumer Dissatisfaction.* New York: Oxford University Press, 1976.

Scott, William B. *In Pursuit of Happiness: American Conceptions of Property from the Seventeenth to the Twentieth Century.* Bloomington: Indiana University Press, 1977.

Shi, David E. *The Simple Life: Plain Living and High Thinking in American Culture.* New York: Oxford University Press, 1985.

Simons, Marlise. "West Germans Get Ready to Scrub the East's Tarnished Environment." *New York Times,* June 27, 1990.

Slater, Philip. *Earthwalk.* New York: Bantam Books, 1980.

————. *The Pursuit of Loneliness.* Boston: Beacon Press, 1970.

————. *Wealth Addiction.* New York: E. P. Dutton, 1980.

Smith, Adam. *The Wealth of Nations.* New York: The Modern Library, 1937.

Talese, Gay, ed, *The Best American Essays 1987.* New York: Ticknor and Fields, 1987.

Taylor, Paul. "For Disconnected Americans, Citizenship Fades." *Washington Post,* May 6, 1990.

Thevenin, Tine. *The Family Bed.* Wayne, N.J.: Avery Publishing Group, 1987.

Thoreau, Henry David. *Walden and Other Writings.* New York: Bantam Books, 1962.

Tocqueville, Alexis de. *Democracy in America.* New York: Random House, 1945.

Tournier, Paul. *The Meaning of Persons.* New York: Harper and Bros., 1957.

Trump, Donald, with Tony Schwartz. *Trump: The Art of the Deal.* New York: Random House, 1987.

Turnbull, Colin M. *The Forest People.* New York: Simon and Schuster, 1962.

Urban, G. R., ed. *Can We Survive Our Future?* New York: St. Martin's Press, 1971.

Veblen, Thorstein. *The Theory of the Leisure Class.* Boston: Houghton Mifflin, 1973.

"Voting with your wallet." *The Economist,* April 15, 1988.

Wachtel, Paul. *The Poverty of Affluence: A Psychological Portrait of the American Way of Life.* New York: Free Press, 1983.

Ward, Geoffrey C. "Tiger in the Road!" In *Best American Essays.* See Talese 1987.

Waterman, Alan S. *The Psychology of Individualism.* New York: Praeger, 1984.

Weber, Max. *The Protestant Ethic and the Spirit of Capitalism.* New York: Charles Scribner's Sons, 1958.

Weil, Andrew, tape of lecture on addiction and drugs, personal communication.

Wickse, John R. *About Possession: The Self as Private Property.* University Park, Pa.: Pennsylvania State University Press, 1976.

Will, George. "Bombarded by Ads." *Washington Post,* December 20, 1987.

———. "The Real Game: The Commercials." *Washington Post,* January 28, 1990.

Williams, Rosalind. "Corrupting the public imagination." *Christian Science Monitor,* March 20, 1981.

Williams, Rosalind H. *Dream Worlds: Mass Consumption in Late Nineteenth-Century France.* Berkeley and Los Angeles: University of California Press, 1982.

Williamson, Judith. *Consuming Passions: The Dynamics of Popular Culture.* London: Marion Boyars, 1986.

Wolfe, Alan. *America's Impasse: The Rise and Fall of the Politics of Growth.* New York: Pantheon Books, 1981.

Index